Lecture Notes in Computer Science   1995

Edited by G. Goos, J. Hartmanis and J. van Leeuwen

T0240092

Springer

Berlin
Heidelberg
New York
Barcelona
Hong Kong
London
Milan
Paris
Singapore
Tokyo

Morris Sloman   Jorge Lobo
Emil C. Lupu (Eds.)

Policies for Distributed Systems and Networks

International Workshop, POLICY 2001
Bristol, UK, January 29-31, 2001
Proceedings

 Springer

Series Editors

Gerhard Goos, Karlsruhe University, Germany
Juris Hartmanis, Cornell University, NY, USA
Jan van Leeuwen, Utrecht University, The Netherlands

Volume Editors

Morris Sloman
Emil C. Lupu
Imperial College, Department of Computing
180 Queen's Gate, London SW7 2BZ, UK
E-mail: {m.sloman/e.c.lupu}@doc.ic.ac.uk

Jorge Lobo
Bell Labs
600 Mountain Ave., Murray Hill, NJ 07974, USA
E-mail: jlobo@research.bell-labs.com

Cataloging-in-Publication Data applied for

Die Deutsche Bibliothek - CIP-Einheitsaufnahme

Policies for distributes systems and networks : international workshop ;
proceedings / POLICY 2001, Bristol, UK, January 29 - 31, 2001.
Morris Sloman ... (ed.). - Berlin ; Heidelberg ; New York ; Barcelona ;
Hong Kong ; London ; Milan ; Paris ; Singapore ; Tokyo : Springer, 2001
    (Lecture notes in computer science ; Vol. 1995)
    ISBN 3-540-41610-2

CR Subject Classification (1998): C.2, K.6, K.5, K.4, H.3.5, D.1.3, D.2

ISSN 0302-9743
ISBN 3-540-41610-2 Springer-Verlag Berlin Heidelberg New York

Springer-Verlag Berlin Heidelberg New York
a member of BertelsmannSpringer Science+Business Media GmbH
© Springer-Verlag Berlin Heidelberg 2001
Printed in Germany

Typesetting: Camera-ready by author, data conversion by Boller Mediendesign
Printed on acid-free paper   SPIN: 10782133   06/3142   5 4 3 2 1 0

Preface

Policy based systems are the subject of a wide range of activities in universities, standardisation bodies, and within industry. They have a wide spectrum of applications ranging from quality of service management within networks to security and enterprise modelling. This Lecture Notes volume collects the papers presented at the workshop on Policies for Distributed Systems and Networks held at the Hewlett-Packard Laboratories in Bristol, UK in January 2001. After a rigorous review process 16 papers were selected from 43 submissions.

Within the Internet community there is considerable interest in policy based networking. A number of companies have announced tools to support the specification and deployment of policies. Much of this work is focused on policies for quality of service management within networks and the Internet Engineering and Distributed Management Task Force (IETF/DMTF) is actively working on standards related to this area.

The security community has focused on the specification and analysis of access control policy which has evolved into the work on Role-Based Access Control (RBAC). There has been work over a number of years in the academic community on specification and analysis of policies for distributed systems mostly concentrating on authorisation policies. Although there are strong similarities in the concepts and techniques used by the different communities there is no commonly accepted terminology or notation for specifying policies.

Several research groups are looking at high-level aspects of policy related to enterprise modelling. An ISO Open Distributed Processing working group is defining policy and role concepts from the enterprise viewpoint. Enterprise goals or service level agreements can be considered as high-level abstract policies which must be progressively refined into implementable policies. The work on the specification and analysis of business rules is also relevant.

The common concept of policy, within all of the above communities, is that policies define a set of rules governing choices in the behaviour of the system. The motivation is to be able to modify a policy in order to change system behaviour without having to re-implement the system, or restructure the requirements specification.

The papers in this volume discuss topics from abstractions and notations for policy specifications to security, access control, implementations, applications, and management. They cover both practical experience and novel research concepts.

We are grateful for the financial and organisational support provided by Hewlett-Packard Laboratories in hosting the workshop.

January 2001

Morris Sloman
Jorge Lobo and Emil Lupu

Organisation

Workshop Chair:	Morris Sloman, Imperial College, UK
Programme Chairs:	Jorge Lobo, Bell Labs, USA
	Emil Lupu, Imperial College, UK
Local Organisation:	Jan Ward, HP Labs, Bristol, UK
Programme Committee:	David Black, EMC, USA
	Matt Blaze, AT&T, USA
	Naranker Dulay, Imperial College, UK
	Jan Chomicki, SUNY Buffalo, USA
	Ed Ellesson, Tivoli Systems, USA
	Kohei Iseda, Fujitsu, Japan
	Francisco Garcia,
	Agilent Laboratories, Scotland, UK
	Cheh Goh, HP Laboratories, UK
	Peter Linington, University of Kent, UK
	Hugh Mahon, HP, USA
	Ian Marshall, BT Labs, UK
	Zoran Milosevic, DSTC, Brisbane, Australia
	Naftaly Minksy, Rutgers University, USA
	Ken Moody, Cambridge University, UK
	Jonathan Moffett, University of York, UK
	Ravi Sandhu, George Mason University, USA
	Edgar Sibley, George Mason University, USA
	John Strassner, Cisco Systems, USA
	Vijay Varadharajan, University of Western Sydney, Australia
	Dinesh Verma, IBM, USA
	Andrea Westerinen, Cisco Systems, USA

Additional Referees

Ao, Xuhui	Hitchens, Michael	Raymond, Kerry
Bearden, Mark	Jaeger, Trent	Schoenwaelder, Juergen
Boutaba, Raouf	Minoura, Makoto	Steel, Jim
Cole, James	Montanari, Rebecca	Tran, Son C.
Fukuda, Kenichi	Murata, Takahiro	Ueno, Hitoshi
Garg, Sachin	Ogura, Takao	Radhakrishnan, T.
He, Ning	Polyrakis, Andreas	

Sponsoring Institution

Hewlett-Packard Laboratories, Bristol, UK

Table of Contents

Policy Specification and Analysis

RBAC and Security Policy

Network Policy Realization

Perspectives on Policy Architectures

Author Obliged to Submit Paper before 4 July: Policies in an Enterprise Specification

James Cole[1], John Derrick[2], Zoran Milosevic[1], Kerry Raymond[1&3]

1) Cooperative Research Centre for Distributed Systems Technology (DSTC),
University of Queensland, 4072, Australia
2) Computing Laboratory, University of Kent at Canterbury,
Kent, CT2 7NF, United Kingdom
3) CiTR Pty Ltd, PO Box 1643, Milton, Queensland 4064, Australia

colej@dstc.edu.au, j.derrick@ukc.ac.uk, zoran@dstc.edu.au, kerry@dstc.edu.au

Abstract. Specifying policies doesn't occur in splendid isolation but as part of refining an enterprise specification. The roles, the tasks, and the business processes of an ODP community provide the basic alphabet over which we write our policies. We illustrate this through exploring a conference programme committee case study. We discuss how we might formulate policies and show how policies are refined alongside the refinement of the overall system specification, developing notions of sufficiency and necessity. Policy delegation is also discussed and we categorise different forms of delegating an obligation.

Keywords: ODP enterprise viewpoint, enterprise policies, formalising and refining policies, delegation, case study.

1. Introduction

Enterprise distributed systems are increasingly requiring precise specification of policies that govern individual and collective behaviour of entities in the system. This is needed to support precise reasoning about the systems behaviour - in terms of constraints on their behaviour and also addressing the dynamic effects of changes in policies.

Precise enterprise specification is also needed to reflect the need for the separation of policy implementations from the implementation of the functional part of the system. The separation is required to allow for flexible changes of policies while preserving the main functionality of the system.

Our approach for specifying enterprise policies is based on the definition of policies and other related enterprise concepts as defined in the Open Distributed Processing (ODP) standards [1] [2].

M. Sloman, J. Lobo, and E. Lupu (Eds.): POLICY 2001, LNCS 1995, pp. 1-17, 2001.

The Reference Model for ODP (RM-ODP) defines an architecture for specifying and implementing distributed systems. Because the complete specification of any non-trivial distributed system involves a large amount of information, the RM-ODP uses multiple viewpoints to help structure the design and provide a basic separation of concerns.

In the enterprise viewpoint one can specify the purpose, scope and policies of a system and its environment separately from other aspects of its implementation.

In the RM-ODP, Foundations [1], a policy is defined as "a set of rules with a particular purpose" where "a rule can be expressed as an obligation, a permission or a prohibition". Further, permission is a prescription that a particular behaviour is allowed to occur. A prohibition is a prescription that a particular behaviour must not occur, and an obligation is a prescription that a particular behaviour is required.

These definitions of obligations, permissions and prohibitions are in style of the Standard Deontic Logic, in that they are impersonal (i.e. do not associate policy statements to the performers of actions) and that they are static (i.e. do not consider the temporal aspects for fulfilling obligations).

The new ODP Enterprise Language standard currently being standardised [3] provides an extension of the description of policies as stated in the RM-ODP to include personal statements, but has yet to address the temporal nature of obligations.

These extensions are introduced in the context of the RM-ODP community concept, as policies are created, changed and enforced by enterprise objects forming a community. The new ODP Enterprise Language standard also elaborates on the notions of policy assignment, including the concepts of delegation and authority. Some of the initial ideas of the new policy framework for ODP enterprise viewpoint can be found in [4].

The ODP Enterprise Language does not prescribe a particular template for the development of enterprise specifications, but rather identifies significant concepts and relationships that form the basis for structuring an enterprise language specification. Neither it does mandate a particular notation - this paper offers one such notation, which expresses policy concepts from the new ODP Enterprise Language standard.

For example, the concept of community is fundamental; it is the main structural element and reflects some grouping of people and resources in the real world. A grouping can be considered a community if it is formed to collectively achieve some objective. Communities are then specified in terms of:

- Roles (both within the community and in the environment of the community). Roles are an abstraction, enabling the community to be specified without regard to the particular entities (people, programs etc) which will fill those roles in some implementation of the specification. The roles within a community are those that are working towards the objective (i.e. the roles share community objective or are committed to some sub-objective), whereas the roles in the environment might not be committed to the community objective. For example, a business and its employees might be seeking to maximise the profit of the business, but the customers are not. Yet it would be impossible to specify the business without also specifying customers that form part of the environment of the business.

- Processes (a.k.a. business processes). Processes describe some commonly occurring sequence of tasks that contributes to the achievement of the objective (or a sub-objective). Processes are defined as a partial order of steps, each step comprising a task involving one or more of the roles. A task could be the customer placing an order with a salesman (an interaction of roles), or the warehouse delivering the goods. The ordering of steps in a process is generally determined by data flow (outputs must be produced before they can be input elsewhere) or by policies.
- Policies. Policies place additional expectations on the behaviour of roles within the community, and are perhaps the least well-understood aspect of ODP enterprise specifications.

In this paper we focus on the specification and nature of policies in the ODP enterprise viewpoint. We use a programme committee (PC) case study to analyse and refine policies and we are exploiting the policy notation proposed in [5][6] to express policies and their relationships. This notation (language) was developed for the specification of ODP enterprise policies. The notation is a combination of structured English and simple predicate logic, and was built on the top of the formal object oriented specification language Object-Z (to enable formal analysis of the policies to be carried out).

Note that the policies we specify in the enterprise viewpoint represent the policies in force in the enterprise under consideration. Whilst these policies clearly concern the implementation, they are not all necessarily directly representable or implementable in any system. The purpose of such policy specification is not necessarily to implement policies but to be explicit about the constraints within which the system will be constructed.

The purpose of the paper is twofold. Firstly we aim to develop a case study and show how the notation in [5][6] can be applied to a real example. Secondly, by developing the case study a number of issues arise which we subsequently discuss. These include the refinement of policies against a business plan and the notion of delegation.

The structure of the paper is as follows. In Section 2, we introduce our case study. Having establishing our framework for specifying policy in Section 3, we then develop the initial policies for our case study in Section 4. These policies are then further refined in Section 5. We document what we have learned about policies from our case study in Section 6, including a discussion on the ways in which obligation can be delegated. Finally we conclude in Section 7 with some open questions for future study.

2. Motivating Case Study

The case study we consider is that of the policies governing a conference programme committee (PC). This is an interesting example because most programme committees are very physically distributed and most of them use software and networking in some aspects of their work. Space limitations prohibit a complete presentation of the case study in this paper; only pertinent fragments are shown.

The starting point of the case study is the assumption that a programme committee is a community (formed within the larger context of a conference organising committee) with the objective of producing a papers programme and the conference proceedings. Typically, the organising committee will prescribe the general theme of the conference (e.g. DNA sequencing, policies in distributed systems), give some indication of the number of papers required (the PC is not free to develop a programme requiring more days than the venue is booked for etc), and usually set a deadline for providing the programme and the proceedings. For research conferences, there is the expectation that the papers in the programme will be the best available papers, where "best" combines a number of independent criteria: pertinent, original, significant, technically-sound, well-written, etc.

3. Framework for Specifying Policy

We begin by describing the basic set of premises that underlie the policies specified in this paper.

3.1. Policies Exist to Achieve an Objective

We observe that the objectives of a community can usually be expressed as a set of obligations with attendant permissions and prohibitions on how those objectives/ obligations can be achieved. If the community arises through refinement of some role/ entity in an existing enterprise specification, then its objectives will be the obligations that the initial role/entity were subject to. Such a community will also inherit any permissions and prohibitions to which the initial role/entity was subject to, and all of these policies (or their refinements) apply to the roles and processes of the new community.

This chain of refinement of policies parallels the refinement of an enterprise specification, ensuring that the atomic roles/entities of the system are bound by policies that collectively contribute to the overall objectives of the system. For example, the policy that a paper reviewer cannot review their own paper is a prohibition that contributes to the objective of a conference of high-quality papers.

3.2. Authority Derives from Community

In a lot of work on policies, the existence of a single global source of authority is often assumed. However, we view communities (as collections of objects cooperating towards an objective) as being the basis for all authority. By joining a community, an object undertakes to conform to the policies of that community, whether applied to the community as a whole or to its particular role within the community. Some communities may have specific roles with responsibility for the making and enforcing of policy, but the authority of such roles is delegated from the community itself. As an enterprise specification may include many communities (related to one another in a variety of ways), it follows that there are many authorities within the system and that individual roles/entities may only be subject to the communities of which they are a member.

Some communities are sub-communities of another community (e.g. the programme committee is a sub-community of the conference organising committee), and thus are subservient for policy purposes. However, other communities overlap in other ways, and their differing objectives may lead to policies on individual roles that are in conflict. For example, a paper reviewer may have conflicting obligations to review papers and do work for their employer. Also, the author of a paper seeks to achieve publication of their work, while the conference objective is to publish only high-quality papers.

Therefore every policy must include the community (or delegated authority within a community) from which policy is imposed. However, in most specifications, this community is obvious and not explicitly identified.

3.3. Scope of Policy Making

Turning to the policies we firstly note that it is easy to express any form of behaviour as a policy. However, it is not always useful to do so. There are a number of kinds of "non-policy" [4]:

- Imposing policies on roles outside the community. If they are outside the community, they are not committed to the objective of the community and hence are not motivated to conform to the policies of the community. For example, the policy that "Authors are obliged to submit their papers before the due date" is meaningless, as authors will obviously submit papers any time they like. Instead it is the programme committee that must be obligated to react correctly to the author's behaviour.
- Imposing policies on things that are subject to the laws of nature or mechanical operation. There is no point imposing a policy "The author is obliged to write the paper before it is reviewed" since clearly the paper could not have been reviewed

until after it was written. Policy-making only makes sense when the role subject to the policy possesses the potential for some free choice regarding the performance of the action discussed in the policy.

- Imposing policy that could equally well be expressed as rules in some other part of the specification. For example, the format prescribed for submitted papers (e.g. font, word processor etc) is better elaborated in an information specification than in a policy. It may be appropriate to make a policy enabling the PC to reject a paper that is improperly formatted, but it is not the purpose of policy to elaborate the meaning of properly-formatted.

4. Formalising the Policies

With this framework in mind, we begin to formalise our policy statements, which describe prohibitions, permissions and obligations in terms of actions of particular roles in our community (i.e. the PC). To simplify the presentation, we will introduce the actions as we proceed with the formalisation of the policies.

In this section we show how the policy language described in [5] [6] can, with some extensions, be used to formalise the policies in our case study. The formalisation also brings to light a number of issues that we discuss below.

We begin by identifying an action used in formulating the initial policy statements. This is the publish action, and is used with a parameter, allowing us to write "publish(programme)" and "publish(proceedings)", with the obvious intended meanings.

In addition #programme denotes the number of papers in the conference programme, and format(proceedings, Z) is a boolean condition which is true if and only if the proceedings are in a format acceptable to Z (which could be the publishers or the conference format).

Our initial policy statements can then be given as:

```
[[1]]   A PC is obliged to do publish(programme) before X where (30
        <= #programme <= 40)
```

```
[[2]]   A PC is obliged to do publish(proceedings) before Y where
        format(proceedings, IEEE)
```

Here X and Y are dates such that X < Y and represent the appropriate deadlines.

As we can see this syntax of our policy language is fairly simple (the reader is referred to [5][6] for full details). The general format is:

```
[[label]]A <role> is <modality> to do <action> ...
```

where the modality is one of "permitted", "prohibited" or "obliged".

All modalities may refer to the execution of an action. The action denotation consists of an action name followed by optional parameter specifications in brackets, e.g. proceedings is a parameter to the publish action in policy [[2]] above. There are a number of possible clauses after the action denotation, as described below.

We also observe that obligations are often associated with deadlines, either absolute or relative. Often these deadlines are implicit, but we recommend that they be made explicit wherever possible. If there is no deadline associated with an obligation, then it may be difficult to test whether the obligation has been violated ("I'll do it real soon now!").

Obligations thus have a before-clause, which contains a condition upon which the obligation should have been fulfilled, and both policies [[1]] and [[2]] above illustrate this form. Similarly prohibitions can be qualified by an until-clause and permissions by an after-clause.

Where-clauses (e.g. "where 30 <= #programme <= 40") are used to constrain the value of parameters of an action, and conditionality is captured in an obvious fashion by an if-clause.

5. Refinement of Policies

One observation that came about in considering the PC case study is that policy is expressed over some set of roles and some set of actions. Therefore, policy can only be refined/evolved as part of the overall refinement/evolution of the community; it is not something that can be developed independently, in spite of the roles and the actions that constitute the business processes. We observe that in real life, many policies are routinely ignored because of the perception that changing circumstances have made them redundant. For example, in Queensland until recently, cars had to be preceded by a man waving a red flag and ringing a bell to avoid frightening the horses, a law uniformly ignored by motorists and police alike.

In order to satisfy the policies [[1]] and [[2]] above, we refine them further. There are often many ways to refine a community into a set of roles, processes and policies to meet the objective. The choice of roles and processes made determines the exact structure of policies introduced. In the PC example, we have chosen to establish a process that issues a public Call for Papers (as opposed to soliciting papers from a closed set of individuals). Hence we must develop a set of policies based around the issuing of the Call for Papers. This set uses the following base actions:

- publishCFP(CFP, widely) - the call for papers is to be sent out to a wide audience.
- submit(paper) - submit a paper to the conference.
- receive(paper) - receive the paper
- refuse(paper) - refuse the paper (as distinct from reject the paper, see below), the opposite of submit
- notify(author, paper,outcome) - notify an author about whether the paper has been accepted.
- revise(paper) - revise the paper.
- reject(paper) - reject the paper from the conference.

The policies below introduce further deadlines $D1 < D2 < D3 < X$ and $D3 < D4 < Y$, where:

- D1 - last viable date for issuing a call for papers
- D2 - advertised deadline for submitting papers
- D3 - notification date of paper acceptance
- D4 - date that the proceedings goes to the printers
- X - date of publication of programme
- Y - date of publication of proceedings

The following [[a]] to [[g]] are imposed by the PC community (the authority), whereas the initial policies [[1]] and [[2]] were imposed by the conference organising committee.

[[a]] A PC is obliged to do publishCFP(CFP, widely) before D1

Notice how the subjective notion of advertising the CFP widely has been pushed into the action description to avoid the policy statements being subjective, e.g. writing it as "A PC is obliged to do publishCFP (CFP) widely before D1". That is, "widely" has been used as action parameter rather than a qualification on the policy. Indeed, as we see here, it is possible to refine some or all parts of a policy into the selection of specific actions (or processes), thus effectively "programming" the policy.

[[b]] A PC is obliged to do receive(paper) before D2 where format(paper,conf)

[[c]] A PC is permitted to do refuse(paper) after D2

It is interesting to note that [[c]] was not expressed as "A PC is prohibited from receive(paper) after D2". Refusal of a paper is a real action that occurs (e.g. an e-mail is sent to the author explaining the deadline has past) whereas the prohibition would simply ignore the author's attempt to submit the paper.

Similarly, [[c]] was not expressed as "A PC is obliged to refuse(paper) after D2" because the intention is to permit the PC to accept papers after D2 if they wish. This is expressed in the following policy:

[[d]] A PC is permitted to do receive(paper) after D2

Space prohibits the elaboration of the business processes of the PC but it should be noted that the actions of receive(paper) and refuse(paper) are alternative actions in response to a submit(paper). Remember that there are no policies directly on submitting, as the author is outside of the PC community.

However, no conference can continue to receive papers indefinitely. Given the business processes of the PC, it is not appropriate to receive a paper after notification has been sent to the authors:

[[e]]   A PC is prohibited to do receive(paper) after
        time(notify(author,paper,outcome))

where time returns the time at which a specified action occurs. As discussed further below, this illustrates how this policy language supports the specification of dynamic policies (see Section 6.2).

[[f]]   A PC is obliged to do notify(author, paper,outcome) before
        D3

In order to deal with violation of an obligation we introduce an otherwise clause. This clause details the policies applicable if the initial obligation is not met. Otherwise clauses can be nested, an example of which we will see below. First here is a simple example:

[[g]]   An AcceptedAuthor is obliged to do submit(revise(paper))
        before D4 otherwise a PC is permitted to do reject(paper)

Notice how the action of notifying an author that their paper has been accepted has a side-effect of introducing that author into the PC community as a new role within community called AcceptedAuthor, and hence subject to the policies of the community. (Note that the author's membership of the PC community does not imply that the author is a "PC member" which is a distinct role within the PC community.)

We can now talk about the relationship between the policy statements [[a-g]] and the original statements [[1]] and [[2]], and in particular whether the former are *necessary* or *sufficient* with respect to [[1]] and [[2]]. In fact we can only talk of necessity against a particular business plan, thus with respect to the plan of receiving and reviewing papers (i.e. the normal conference plan) the policies [[a-g]] are necessary. With the additions of actions to actually print proceedings these policies would also be sufficient, i.e. if [[a-g]] were met then so too would be [[1-2]].

The policies [[a]] through [[g]] above came about primarily through refinement of the community's objectives relative to its business process. Let us now consider policy refinements relative to the partitioning of the behaviour of a community into a set of roles. Let us look at the policy [[a]]. To refine this we consider roles PCChair and PCMember within the PC. In order to publish the CFP we need policies concerning the drafting and approval process. To do so we consider the following additional actions:

- draft(CFP) - the action to make an initial draft of the CFP
- approve(CFP) - the action to approve the CFP
- amend(CFP) - the action to amend the text of the CFP
- distribute(CFP) - the action to distribute the CFP, perhaps repeatedly,

and an additional condition:

- approve(PC, CFP) - a condition true if a majority of the PC have approves the CFP

and a new deadline:

- D0 - the deadline for drafting the CFP.

We then refine [[a]] as follows.

```
[[a1]] A PCChair is obliged to do draft(CFP) before D0
```

```
[[a2]] A PCChair is prohibited to do publishCFP(CFP) until
       approve(PC, CFP)
```

```
[[a3]] A PCMember is obliged to do approve(CFP) otherwise a
       PCMember is obliged to do amend(CFP) otherwise PCChair is
       permitted to do satisfy(approve(PC, CFP))
```

The action "satisfy" asserts the truth of a condition.

```
[[a4]] A PCChair is obliged to do publishCFP(CFP) before D1
```

```
[[a5]] A PCMember is obliged to do distribute(CFP) before D2
```

```
[[a6]] A PCMember is prohibited to do distribute(CFP) until a
       PCChair does a publishCFP(CFP)
```

6. Observations

In this section, we discuss some of our observations arising from our case study.

6.1. Default Policies

When one considers policies [[a5]] and [[a6]], it begs the question of whether a PCMember who is obliged to distribute the CFP actually has the permission to do so. Clearly, there are circumstances when this is a prohibited behaviour. Therefore, should the set of policies include "A PCMember is permitted to do distribute(CFP)" or similar? If we take this view, then we would also require permission for the PCChair to prepare a draft CFP, for PCMembers to approve the draft, etc. Clearly this would be tedious for both the reader and the writer of specifications. This suggests the need to establish some sensible default policy. There are a number of ways this could be done:

- When introducing the actions in the specification, indicate whether the default policy is permission or prohibition, based on the "sensitivity" of the specific action
- Through inheritance of default or explicit policies in outer communities
- Through the assumption that role-action pairs forming part in the business process are permitted
- Through the tagging of the community as being fundamentally permissive or restrictive

Further work is needed to clarify the best approach.

6.2. Dynamic Policies

Another observation that we found in the case study is that some policies seemed to alter other policies already in force. Consider policy [[e]]:

```
[[e]]  A PC is prohibited to do receive(paper) after
       time(notify(author,paper))
```

This policy illustrates how policies can come into force based on occurrence (or non-occurrence) of run-time events. Therefore, it may not be possible to determine in advance precisely which policies will be concurrently in force, and hence not be feasible to determine in advance if policies are in conflict.

There are other kinds of dynamic policies. For example, the programme committee is obliged to receive papers if submitted by the due date D2, permitted to receive papers if submitted after the due date, and prohibited from receiving papers after notification of the authors. However, the programme committee chair is permitted to postpone the due date D2 if insufficient papers have been received:

```
[[p]]  A PCChair is permitted to do extend(D2) if (#papers < 30
       and D2 < now[1] < D3)
```

Postponing the due date D2 impacts on all of the policies relating to the acceptance of papers relative to D2, changing the set of policies in force.

It also creates some interesting scenarios if some papers were not accepted under the policies embodying the original due date, but which must be accepted if assessed under the policies using the revised due date. In other scenarios, the reverse situation might apply; actions were permitted under the original policies that would be prohibited under the new policies. In either case, should there be some attempt to "roll back" the actions that have or have not occurred due to the old policies and then replay them under the new policies?

---

1. Notice how some policies are established within a time range, and to model this we use "now" which stands for the current time. It is typically used within an if-clause as this policy illustrates.

Or should all policy decisions be judged solely by the policies that applied at the time? Or should the roles involved in the policy be allowed to choose which policies (as a set or individually) apply to them "give them the benefit of the doubt". There is no hard-and-fast rule in real-life, and indeed, for resolution, one must look to the objectives from which the policies (original and revised) were refined for guidance. In the case of the PC, a paper which was initially refused due to its late submission would probably be included by applying the new rules (presumably with the knowledge and consent of the author) since the original objective was to select the best N papers, and so clearly more papers to chose from increases the overall likelihood of a high-quality conference.

There would seem to be scope for applying action-reversal or compensatory actions (where actions cannot be reversed) that are sometimes seen in transaction management systems.

6.3. Delegation of Obligation

Obligations are often delegated. In the PC example, a PCMember is obliged to review some papers.

[[q]] A PCMember is obliged to do review(paper) before D3.

However, the PCMember may wish to delegate this duty to a colleague. One way that this delegation might be formalised is to introduce the following 2 policies:

[[r]] A PCMember is permitted to do introduce (Reviewer, Colleague).

[[s]] A Reviewer is permitted to do review(paper) where not conflict-of-interest(Reviewer, paper).

The action introduce creates a new Reviewer (a role within the PC community), filled by the colleague. However this begs the questions:

- Is the Reviewer obliged to review the paper?
- Is the PCMember still obliged to review the paper?
- Does the PC need to consent to the delegation?

In exploring the nature of delegation of obligation, we found four different forms of delegations, which we named transfer, sharing, splitting and outsourcing. To understand the differences, we need to make explicit the authority imposing the policy. Figure 1 illustrates authority X obliging role Y to do action A (block arrow shows the 'direction' of this obligation, while the thin arrow depicts the role performing the action).

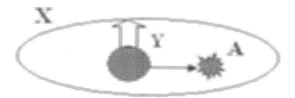

Figure 1. Original Obligation

6.3.1. Transfer of Obligation. A transfer of an obligation occurs if the original obligation is fulfilled by the creation of the new obligation. If original obligation is "X obliges Y to do A", then the transferred obligation is "X obliges Z to do A". Since X is the judge of the fulfilment of an obligation, it follows that X must consent to the transfer. Following the transfer, Y is no longer obligated. X will not regard Y as having failed if A does not occur. Figure 2 illustrates the consequences of transferring the obligation from Y to Z.

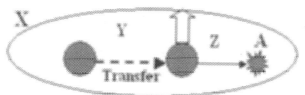

Figure 2. Transfer of Obligation

6.3.2. Shared Obligation. A shared obligation occurs when the obligation is extended to oblige an additional participant. That is, "X obliges Y to do A" becomes "X obliges Y and Z to do A". This implies that Y and Z collectively have the obligation to do A, the breakdown of responsibility between Y and Z is not specified. However, if A does not occur, X will consider that both Y and Z have failed (even if one of them carried out their allocated part of A). X's consent is required to share an obligation. Figure 3 illustrates sharing an obligation.

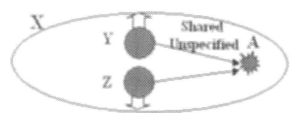

Figure 3. Sharing an Obligation

6.3.3. Split Obligation. A split obligation occurs when the action required is split into two (or more) parts. That is, "X obliges Y to do A" becomes "X obliges Y to do A1 and X obliges Z to do A2" (where A1 and A2 are some partitioning of A). If A1 occurs and A2 does not, then only Z is deemed to have failed by X (and vice versa). However, it should be noted that if A1 contains dependencies on A2, then Z's failure to complete to A2 may cause Y to fail to complete A2. Splitting requires the consent of X. Figure 4 illustrates splitting an obligation.

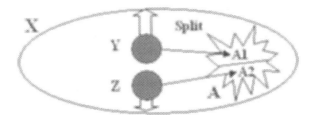

Figure 4. Splitting an Obligation

6.3.4. Outsourced Obligation. An outsourced obligation occurs when the obligee[2] obliges another to carry out all or part of the required behaviour. That is, "X obligates Y to do A" becomes "X obligates Y to do A and Y obligates Z to do part/all-of-A". If A does not occur, then X deems Y to have failed. If A did not occur because of Z's failure to carry out its actions, then Y may deem Z to have failed, but X will not make any judgement regarding Z, as X had no relationship with Z. As far as X is concerned, the full responsibility rested with Y. Outsourcing does not require X's consent. Indeed, outsourcing does not usually require the new obligee to be within the community. Figure 5 illustrates outsourcing of an obligation.

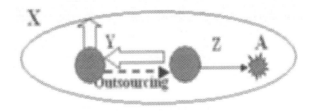

Figure 5. Outsourcing an Obligation

Note that the outsourcing of obligation is not meaningful if obligation on Y to do A implies that Y itself must do action A. In discussing outsourcing, we are making the assumption that the obligation to do A is in fact an obligation to ensure that A is done.

---

2. Yes, "obligee" *is* a real word; it means "one who is obliged".

In real life, the notion of obligation appears to include both interpretations, e.g. someone else may pay a traffic-offence fine for you, but may not go to jail for you - the fine can be outsourced, the jail term cannot.

6.4. Delegation of Permission and Prohibition

If obligations can be delegated, it invites the question of whether all policy can be delegated.

If the authority X is the only source of permissions to do A, then Y's permission to do A would appear to be distinct from Z's permission to do A. Also, there would appear to be little motivation for delegation, since, unlike obligation, permission is not personally onerous.

Similarly, there appears to be no meaningful interpretation of delegation of a prohibition. If X prohibits Y from doing A, then Z is free to decide to not do A without the involvement of X or Y.

In real life, permissions and prohibitions are often associated with obligations, often enabling (or preventing) specific sub-actions associated with the obligation. For example, the PC Chair is obliged to distribute the Call for Papers, and is permitted to use the Internet to do so but prohibited from printing paper brochures for that purpose. In such situations, the delegation of the obligation to another would seem to require that the permission and prohibition be similarly delegated.

6.5. Actions, Alternative Actions, and Inactions

As noted in Section 5, some actions are mutually-exclusive. When an author submits a paper, the PC may choose to receive it for reviewing or refuse it but not both! Therefore, the prohibition on one of these actions (in some circumstances) becomes an effective obligation to do the other. Similarly, an obligation to do one action is an effective prohibition on the other. Is it necessary to state both policies, or is it reasonable to allow one to be derived from the other? Or is this simply a matter of style?

The other alternative to an action may be inaction, and indeed, in real life, deliberate inaction is often used as a response to an awkward situation. Should inaction be the subject of policy-making too? Could the PC be permitted to do no-action in response to a paper submitted after the conference (say)? Arguably, "inaction" is effectively an action, since it involves someone performing the action of deciding to "do nothing" at some level of refinement.

6.6. One Action or Many Actions?

We also observe that cardinality of actions is an issue in policies. While prohibitions prescribe an absence of action, it is generally assumed that permission to do an action is a permission to do the action many times. With obligation, the expectation is that the action is done once, unless it is a standing obligation, in which the action is expected to be repeated continuously (possibly in response to some stimuli). For example, in policy [[a5]] we might wish that the 'distribute' action is repeatedly executed, whereas in policy [[a4]], we clearly want the 'publishCFP' action to occur just once. This is an issue that was not elaborated in our case study.

6.7. Policy on Actions or Policy on State?

The discussion of delegation of policy (see Sections 6.3 and 6.4) opens up the issue of whether policy should be made only about the performance of actions or whether policy should also be made about achieving a certain state of affairs, either through their own actions or the actions of others (equally their own inactions and the inactions of others). For example, obliging the PC to remain within budget is a significant constraint on their behaviour but not one that requires any specific kind of action to be performed.

6.8. Conflicts and Completeness

Policies are often in conflict. Although we do not have space to explore this issue here, one of the purposes of using a formal language for specifying policies is that it opens a way for conflict and consistency analysis to be applied. [5][6] discuss this issue briefly in the context of the translation of the policy language into the specification notation Object-Z.

Tools also have a role here, both in terms of conflict analysis and also in terms of change management in the presence of large scale policy specifications. The interested reader in this topic is referred to [7].

It is also difficult to judge whether a set of policy statements is complete, suggesting a need for policy simulation tools to be used for practical observation of a set of policies in action.

7. Conclusions and Open Questions

Specifying policies in a real-world case study turned out to be harder than we expected. Our experiences have lead us to a better understanding of the framework in which we write policies. Specifically, we have learned:

- that policies must be refined with respect to a business plan
- that using a policy notation is very useful in uncovering a number of subtleties in the policies themselves
- that default policies are necessary to avoid tedious and repetitious specifications
- that there are various forms of delegation of obligation

However, our real-world case study has left us with a number of open questions:

- how we should best specify default policies
- what linguistic support is needed to reflect the dynamic interaction of policies
- the interpretation of delegation of permissions and prohibitions

In many ways, our case study has asked more questions about policies in enterprise specifications than it has answered. However, it demonstrates the real need for extensive research into these issues by communities such as this workshop.

Acknowledgements

John Derrick gratefully acknowledges receipt of a University Of Queensland Visiting Scholars Travel Grant.

The work reported in this paper has been funded in part by the Co-operative Research Centre for Enterprise Distributed Systems Technology (DSTC) through the Federal Government's AusIndustry CRC Programme (Department of Industry, Science & Resources).

References

[1] ISO/IEC JTC1/SC21, "Basic reference model of open distributed processing, part 2: Descriptive model," ITU-T X.902 - ISO/IEC 10746-2, Aug. 1994.

[2] ISO/IEC JTC1/SC21, "Basic reference model of open distributed processing, part 3: Architecture," ITU-T X.903 - ISO/IEC 10746-3, 1995.

[3] ISO/IEC JTC1/SC7/WG17N0106, "Information Technology - Open Distributed Processing - Reference Model - Enterprise Language," ISO ISO/IEC 15414 | ITU-T Recommendation X.911, Jan. 2000.

[4] P. Linington, Z. Milosevic and K. Raymond, "Policies in Communities: Extending the ODP Enterprise Viewpoint". Proc. 2nd IEEE Enterprise Distributed Object Computing Workshop, San-Diego, Nov.1998.

[5] Formalising ODP Enterprise Policies. M.W.A. Steen and J. Derrick. In 3rd International Enterprise Distributed Object Computing Conference (EDOC '99), University of Mannheim, Germany, September 1999. IEEE Publishing.

[6] ODP Enterprise Viewpoint Specification, M.W.A. Steen and J. Derrick. In Computer Standards and Interfaces (to appear).

[7] E. Lupu and M. Sloman, "Conflicts in Policy-Based Distributed Systems Management". In IEEE Transactions on Software Engineering, 25(6): 852-869, Nov. 1999.

[8] E. Lupu, M. Sloman, N. Dulay, N. Daminaou, "Ponder: Realizing Enterprise Viewpoint Concepts", Proceedings, Fourth International Enterprise Distributed Object Computing Conference, Japan, 2000.

The Ponder Policy Specification Language

Nicodemos Damianou, Naranker Dulay, Emil Lupu, Morris Sloman

Department of Computing, Imperial College, 180 Queen's Gate, London SW7 2BZ
{n.damianou, n.dulay, e.c.lupu, m.sloman}@doc.ic.ac.uk

Abstract. The Ponder language provides a common means of specifying security policies that map onto various access control implementation mechanisms for firewalls, operating systems, databases and Java. It supports obligation policies that are event triggered condition-action rules for policy based management of networks and distributed systems. Ponder can also be used for security management activities such as registration of users or logging and auditing events for dealing with access to critical resources or security violations. Key concepts of the language include roles to group policies relating to a position in an organisation, relationships to define interactions between roles and management structures to define a configuration of roles and relationships pertaining to an organisational unit such as a department. These reusable composite policy specifications cater for the complexity of large enterprise information systems. Ponder is declarative, strongly-typed and object-oriented which makes the language flexible, extensible and adaptable to a wide range of management requirements.

1 Introduction

Large enterprise information infrastructures have to integrate inter-organisational networks and internet-based services, which makes the task of managing such systems very challenging. The development of mobile computing applications requires support from adaptive network architectures and customised services to the clients. Various techniques have emerged for programming network elements to support adaptive services, for example active networks, mobile agents and management by delegation. While all these approaches support the programming of new functionality into network elements and host devices, they increase the security concerns regarding access to network resources and services, and make the management task even more demanding.

Recent work on **policy based management** of networks and distributed systems (see www-dse.doc.ic.ac.uk/policies) provides promising solutions to these problems. In this work a *policy is a rule that defines a choice in the behaviour of a system*. Separating the policy from the implementation of a system permits the policy to be modified in order to dynamically change the strategy for managing the system and hence modify the behaviour of a system, without changing its underlying implementation [26].

M. Sloman, J. Lobo, and E. Lupu (Eds.): POLICY 2001, LNCS 1995, pp. 18-38, 2001.

There are a number of groups working on very different approaches to specifying policy. Network component manufacturers and the IETF/DMTF are concentrating on information models [6][20] and condition-action rules with the focus on the management of Quality of Service (QoS) in networks [7][9][11][17]. The security community have developed a number of models relating to specification of mandatory and discretionary access control policy [4]. This has evolved into work on **role based access control** (RBAC) [24] and role based management where a role may be considered as a group of related policies pertaining to a position in an organisation [15][16]. A lot of work within the greater scope of management has already resulted in architectures and technologies that provide the basic infrastructure required to implement policy-based management solutions [8][27].

Separate tools are emerging for policy-based management of systems and specifying security. What is lacking is a common language that will provide a unified approach to supporting the concepts of the policy models emerging from the various research communities. We identify the following requirements for a policy language:

- Support for security policies for access control, and delegation to cater for temporary transfer of access rights to agents acting on behalf of a client as well as policies to express management activity.
- Structuring techniques to facilitate the specification of policies relating to large systems with millions of objects. This implies the need for policies relating to collections of objects rather than individual ones.
- Composite policies which allow the basic security and management policies relating to roles, to organisational units and to specific applications to be grouped. Composite policies are essential to cater for the complexity of policy administration in large enterprise information systems.
- It must be possible to analyse policies for conflicts and inconsistencies in the specification. In addition it should be possible to determine which policies apply to an object or what objects a particular policy applies to. Declarative languages make such analysis easier.
- Extensibility is needed to cater for new types of policy that may arise in the future and this can be supported by inheritance in an object-oriented language.
- The language must be comprehensible and easy to use by policy users.

This paper describes Ponder [5], a declarative, object-oriented language for specifying security and management policy for distributed object systems. The language is flexible, expressive and extensible to cover the wide range of requirements implied by the current distributed systems paradigms identified above. Ponder is the result of experience gained in policy-based management at Imperial College over the past 10 years [15][16][14][18][26]. We present the language syntax through simple examples of its use; for the complete syntax of the language see [6].

Sections 2 and 3 present the basic policy types supported by Ponder. Constraints are described in section 4. The composite policy structures in Ponder are described in section 5. Section 6 discusses features that make the language both flexible and extensible. In section 7 we briefly compare Ponder with related work and section 8 presents conclusions and future work.

2   Access Control Policies

Access control is concerned with limiting the activity of legitimate users who have been successfully authenticated [1][23]. Our emphasis has been on non-discretionary access control (as defined in [1]), where administrators have the authority to specify security policies that are enforced by the access control system. Delegation and propagation of authority are permitted only within the scope defined by the security policy. However, this does not exclude the use of Ponder to specify discretionary or mandatory security policies. Ponder supports access control by providing **authorisation, delegation, information filtering** and **refrain** policies as described below.

We assume that all policies relate to objects with interfaces defined in terms of methods using an interface definition language. We use the term **subject** to refer to users, principals or automated manager components, which have management responsibility. A subject accesses **target** objects (resources or service providers), by invoking methods visible on the target's interface. The granularity of protection for access control in Ponder is thus an interface method. References to both subject and target objects are stored within domains maintained by a domain service. **Domains** provide a means of grouping objects to which policies apply and can be used to partition the objects in a large system according to geographical boundaries, object type, responsibility and authority or for the convenience of human managers [25]. This facilitates policy specification for large-scale systems with millions of objects. Domains are similar to directories and have been implemented using an LDAP service.

2.1 Authorisation Policies

Authorisation policies define what activities a member of the subject domain can perform on the set of objects in the target domain. These are essentially access control policies, to protect resources and services from unauthorized access. A positive authorisation policy defines the actions that subjects are permitted to perform on target objects. A negative authorisation policy specifies the actions that subjects are forbidden to perform on target objects. Authorisation policies are implemented on the target host by an access control component.

```
inst ( auth+ | auth- ) policyName      "{"
    subject  [<type>]    domain-Scope-Expression ;
    target   [<type>]    domain-Scope-Expression ;
    action               action-list ;
    [ when               constraint-Expression ; ]      "}"
```

Figure 1. Authorisation Policy Syntax

The syntax of an authorisation policy is shown in figure 1. Everything in **bold** is a language keyword in the figures presenting the syntax. Choices are enclosed in round brackets ( ) separated by |, optional elements are specified with square brackets [ ] and repetition is specified with braces { }. Constraints are optional in all types of policies and can be specified to limit the applicability of policies based on time or values of the attributes of the objects to which the policy refers. Constraints are discussed in detail in section 4. Elements of a policy can be specified in any order. Note that the subject and target elements can optionally include the interface specification reference within the specified domain-scope-expression on which the policy applies. This can be used to check that the objects do support the specified operations or to locate the interface specification. The name of a policy can be specified as a path, thus identifying the domain into which the policy must be stored.

Example 1 Positive and negative authorisation policies

```
inst auth+ switchPolicyOps   {
    subject           /NetworkAdmin;
    target <PolicyT> /Nregion/switches;
    action            load(), remove(), enable(), disable() ;
}
```

Members of the NetworkAdmin domain are authorised to load, remove, enable or disable objects of type PolicyT in the Nregion/switches domain. This indicates the use of an authorisation policy to control access to stored policies.

```
inst auth- /negativeAuth/testRouters   {
    subject           /testEngineers/trainee ;
    action            performance_test() ;
    target <routerT> /routers ;
}
```

Trainee test engineers are forbidden to perform performance tests on routers. The policy is stored within the /negativeAuth domain.

The above examples show direct declaration of policy instances using the keyword **inst**. The language provides reuse by supporting the definition of policy types to which any policy element can be passed as formal parameter. Multiple instances can then be created and tailored for the specific environment by passing actual parameters. Figure 2 shows the syntax for authorisation policy types and instantiations.

```
type ( auth+ | auth- ) policyType   "(" formalParameters ")"    "{"
    { authorisation-policy-parts } "}"

inst ( auth+ | auth- ) policyName = policyType "(" actualParameters ")" ;
```

Figure 2. Authorisation Types and Instantiations

The authorisation policy *switchPolicyOps* (from example 1) can be specified as a type with the subject and target given as parameters as shown in example 2.

Example 2 Declaring instances from types

```
type auth+ PolicyOpsT (subject s, target <PolicyT> t) {
    action load(), remove(), enable(), disable() ; }

inst auth+ switchPolicyOps=PolicyOpsT(/NetworkAdmins,/Nregion/switches);
inst auth+ routersPolicyOps=PolicyOpsT(/QoSAdmins, /Nregion/routers);
```

The two instances allow members of /NetworkAdmins and /QoSAdmins to execute the actions on policies within the /Nregion/switches and /Nregion/routers domains respectively.

It can be argued that the specification of negative authorisation policies complicates the enforcement of authorisation in a system. However, there are reasons to support the provision for negative authorisation policies. Administrators often express high-level access control in terms of both positive and negative policies; retaining the natural way people express policies is important and provides greater flexibility. Negative authorisation policies can also be used to temporarily remove access rights from subjects if the need arises. In addition, many systems support negative access rights (e.g., Windows NT/2000). The existence of negative authorisation policies in a system may result in conflicts with positive authorisation policies. These conflicts are modality conflicts and can thus be always detected through static analysis of the policy specification. Although this adds the need to analyse policies for conflict detection, this kind of conflicts may however indicate potentially unforeseen problems with the specification. For a discussion on conflicts between policies see [14].

2.2 Information Filtering Policies

Filtering policies are needed to transform the information input or output parameters in an action. For example, a location service might only permit access to detailed location information, such as a person is in a specific room, to users within the department. External users can only determine whether a person is at work or not. Some databases support similar concepts of 'views' onto selective information within records – for example a payroll clerk is only permitted to read personnel records of employees below a particular grade. Positive authorisation policies may include filters to transform input or output parameters associated with their actions, based on attributes of the subject or target or on system parameters (e.g., time). In many cases it is not practical to provide different operations as a means of selecting the information. Although these are a form of authorisation policy they differ from the normal ones in that it is not possible for an external authorisation agent to make an access control decision based on whether or not an operation, specified at the interface to the target object, is permitted. Essentially the operation has to be performed and then a decision made on whether to allow results to be returned to the subject or whether the results need to be transformed. Filters can only be applied to positive authorisation actions.

```
actionName { filter }
filter = [ if condition ]   "{" { ( in parameterName = expression ;  |
                                    out parameterName = expression ;  |
                                    result = expression ; ) } "}"
```

Figure 3. Filters on Positive Authorisation Actions

Every action can be associated with a number of filter expressions (see figure 3). Each filter contains an optional condition under which the filter is applied. If the condition evaluates to true, then the transformations (the assignment statements in the body of the filter) are executed. The **in/out** keywords are used to indicate input and output parameters of the action on which the filter is specified; **result** is used to transform the return value of the action.

Example 3 Information filter policy

```
inst auth+ filter1  {
    subject   /Agroup + /Bgroup ;
    target    USAStaff - NYgroup ;
    action    VideoConf(BW, Priority)
              { in BW=2 ; in Priority=3 ; }      // default filter
              if (time.after("1900")) {in BW=3; in Priority = 1; }
}
```

Members of Agroup plus Bgroup can set up a video conference with USA staff except the New York group. If the time is later than 7:00pm then the video conference takes parameters: bandwidth = 3 Mb/s, priority = 1. Otherwise the first filter restricts the parameters to bandwidth = 2 Mb/s, priority = 3.

2.3 Delegation Policies

Delegation is often used in access control systems to cater for the temporary transfer of access rights. However the ability of a user to delegate access rights to another must be tightly controlled by security policies. This requirement is critical in systems allowing cascaded delegation of access rights. A delegation policy permits subjects to grant privileges, which they possess (due to an existing authorisation policy), to grantees to perform an action on their behalf e.g., passing read rights to a printer spooler in order to print a file.

```
inst deleg+   "("associated-auth-policy  ")" policyName   "{"
    grantee     [<type>]   domain-Scope-Expression ;
  [ subject     [<type>]   domain-Scope-Expression ; ]
  [ target      [<type>]   domain-Scope-Expression ; ]
  [ action                 action-list ; ]
  [ when                   constraint-Expression ; ]
  [ valid                  constraint-Expression ; ]     "}"
```

Figure 4. Delegation Policy Syntax

A delegation policy is always associated with an authorisation policy, which specifies the access rights that can be delegated. Negative delegation policies forbid delegation. Note that delegation policies are not meant to be used for assignment of rights by security administrators.

Figure 4 shows the syntax of a positive delegation policy. Note that the only required part is the **grantee**. The rest of the parts (subject, target, action) must be subsets of those in the associated authorisation policy; if not specified they default to those of that policy. A positive delegation policy can specify delegation constraints to limit the validity of the delegated access rights, as part of the

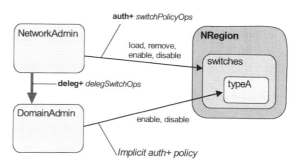

Figure 5. Delegation and Authorisation Policies

valid-clause. Such constraints can be time restrictions (duration, validity period) to specify the duration or the period over which the delegation should be valid before it is revoked. Note that negative delegation policies do not contain delegation constraints.

Example 4 Delegation policy

```
inst deleg+ (switchPolicyOps) delegSwitchOps  {
    grantee    /DomainAdmin ;
    target     /Nregion/switches/typeA ;
    action     enable(), disable();
    valid      time.duration(24) ;
}
```

The above delegation policy is associated with the switchPolicyOps auth+ policy from example 1. It states that the subject of that authorisation policy (NetworkAdmin), which is implicit in this policy, can delegate the enable and disable actions on policies from the domain /Nregion/switches/typeA to grantees in the domain /DomainAdmin. Note how the policy restricts the target to a subset of the switchPolicyOps policy target (See figure 5). The valid-clause, specifies that the delegation is only valid for 24 hours from the time of creation; after that it must be revoked.

A delegation policy specifies the authority to delegate, it does not control the actual delegation and revocation of access rights. It is implemented as an authorisation policy that authorises the subject (grantor) to execute the method *delegate* on the run-time system with the grantee as the parameter of the method. At run-time, when the subject executes the delegate method, a separate authorisation policy is created by trusted components of the access control system, with the grantee as the subject. Similarly the revoke method deletes or disables that second authorisation policy.

2.4 Refrain Policies

Refrain policies define the actions that subjects must refrain from performing (must not perform) on target objects even though they may actually be permitted to perform the action. Refrain policies act as restraints on the actions that subjects perform and are implemented by subjects. Refrain policies have a similar syntax to negative authorisation policies, but are enforced by subjects rather than target access controllers. They are used for situations where negative authorisation policies are inappropriate because the targets are not trusted to enforce the policies (e.g., they may not wish to be protected from the subject). The syntax of refrain policies is the same as that of negative authorisation policies (figure 1).

Example 5 Refrain Policy

```
inst refrain testingRes {
    subject s=/test-engineers ;
    target /analysts + /developers ;
    action  discloseTestResults() ;
    when    s.testing_sequence = "in-progress" ;
}
```

This refrain policy specifies that test engineers must not disclose test results to analysts or developers when the testing sequence being performed by that subject is still in progress, i.e., a constraint based on the state of subjects. Analysts and developers would probably not object to receiving the results and so this policy is not a good candidate for a negative authorisation.

3   Obligation Policies

Obligation policies specify the actions that must be performed by managers within the system when certain events occur and provide the ability to respond to changing circumstances. For example, security management policies specify what actions must be specified when security violations occur and who must execute those actions; what auditing and logging activities must be performed, when and by whom. Management policies could relate to management of QoS, storage systems, software configuration etc.

Obligation policies are event-triggered and define the activities subjects (human or automated manager components) must perform on objects in the target domain. Events can be simple, i.e. an internal timer event, or an external event notified by monitoring service components e.g. a temperature exceeding a threshold or a component failing. Composite events can be specified using event composition operators.

```
inst oblig policyName    "{"
  on                    event-specification ;
  subject     [<type>] domain-Scope-Expression ;
  [ target    [<type>] domain-Scope-Expression ; ]
  do                    obligation-action-list ;
  [ catch               exception-specification ; ]
  [ when                constraint-Expression ; ]    "}"
```

Figure 6. Obligation Policy Syntax

The syntax of obligation policies is shown in figure 6. Note the required event specification following the **on** keyword. The target element is optional as obligation actions may be internal to the subject, whereas authorisation actions always relate to a target object. If actions are to be invoked on a target, then they must be preceded by a prefix indicating the target set. Concurrency operators specifying whether actions should be executed sequentially or in parallel are used to separate the actions in an obligation policy. The optional **catch**-clause specifies an exception that is executed if the actions fail to execute for some reason.

Example 6 Obligation policy

```
inst oblig loginFailure {
  on              3*loginfail(userid) ;
  subject         s = /NRegion/SecAdmin ;
  target <userT>  t = /NRegion/users ^ {userid} ;
  do              t.disable() -> s.log(userid) ;
}
```

This policy is triggered by 3 consecutive loginfail events with the same userid. The NRegion security administrator (SecAdmin) disables the user with userid in the /NRegion/users domain and then logs the failed userid by means of a local operation performed in the SecAdmin object. The '->' operator is used to separate a sequence of actions in an obligation policy. Names are assigned to both the subject and the target. They can then be reused within the policy. In this example we use them to prefix the actions in order to indicate whether the action is on the interface of the target or local to the subject.

Types external to the policy specification can be specified assuming the corresponding specifications are accessible from a type repository.

Example 7 External types

```
type oblig printFail (string msg, QueueMan qMan)   {
    on          printfail(jobid, userid, filename);
    subject  s = printManager;
    target   ms = /servers/mailServer;
    do          ms.mailto(userid, filename+msg)   ||
                s.putInQueue(qMan, jobid);
}
```

The printFail obligation type accepts two parameters one of which is an external type called QueueMan. This is an interface specification of a printer queue manager object. The qman parameter is then used as a parameter in the call to putInQueue which is local to the printManager. The use of the || concurrency operator allows the actions to be performed in parallel.

4   Constraints

An important element of each policy is the set of conditions under which the policy is valid. This information must be explicit in the specification of the policy. The validity of a policy however, may depend on other policies existing or running in the system within the same scope or context. These conditions are usually impossible or impractical to specify as part of each policy and therefore need to be specified as part of a group of policies. Thus, it is useful to divide the constraints in two categories: constraints for single policies and constraints for groups of policies, which we call meta policies. A subset of the Object Constraint Language (OCL) [22] is used to specify constraints in Ponder. OCL is simple to understand and use and it is declarative – each OCL expression is conceptually atomic and so the state of the objects in the system cannot change during evaluation.

4.1 Basic Policy Constraints

Basic policy constraints limit the applicability of a basic policy and are expressed in terms of a predicate, which must evaluate to true for the policy to apply. Policy constraints can be considered as conjunctions of basic constraints, which can be either time or state based constraints. The analysis of a set of policies can then be substantially improved since time-based constraints can be compared for possible overlap and state based constraints can be either simultaneously satisfied or mutually exclusive if they relate to states of the same system component. We separate the different types of constraints based on:

- Subject/target state – the constraint is based on the object state as reflected in terms of attributes at the object interface.
- Action/event parameters – constraints can be based on event parameter values in obligations or action parameter values in authorisations or refrains.

- Time constraints specify the validity periods for the policy. A time library object is provided with Ponder to specify time constraints.

The policy compiler can resolve the different types of constraints at compile time and separate the constraints in order to aid in the analysability of policies.

Example 8 Use of attribute and time constraints

```
inst auth- testRouters {
   subject  s =/testEngineers;
   action   performance_test();
   target   /routers;
   when  s.role = "trainee";
}
```

TestEngineers cannot execute performance tests on routers if they are trainee testEngineers. This role attribute of the subject is used in the constraint.

```
inst auth+ filter1 {
   subject  /Agroup + /Bgroup;
   target   USAStaff - NYgroup
   action   VideoConf(BW, Priority);
   when     time.between("1600", "1800") ;
}
```

Members of Agroup plus Bgroup can set up a video conference with USA staff except the New York group. The time-based constraint limits the policy to apply between 4:00pm and 6:00pm.

4.2 Meta-policies

Meta-policies specify policies about the policies within a composite policy or some other scope, and are used to define application specific constraints. We specify meta policies for groups of policies, i.e. policies within a specific scope, to express constraints which limit the permitted policies in the system, or disallow the simultaneous execution of conflicting policies. A meta-policy is specified as a sequence of OCL expressions the last one of which must evaluate to true or false. The rest of the OCL expressions can be navigational expressions resulting in a collection. The **raises**-clause is followed by an action that is executed if the last OCL expression evaluates to true.

```
inst meta metaPolName raises exception [ "(" parameters ")" ] "{"
   { OCL-expression}
   boolean-OCL-expression "}"
```

Figure 7. Meta-Policy Syntax

The following examples indicate how meta-policies can be used to specify application dependent constraints on groups of policies.

Self-Management: *"There should be no policy authorising a manager to retract policies for which he is the subject"*, from [12]. This happens within a single authorisation policy with overlapping subjects and targets. This can be specified in Ponder as follows:

Example 9 Self-management meta-policy

```
inst meta selfManagement1 raises selfMngmntConflict (pol) {
  [pol] = this.authorisations -> select (p | p.action->exists (a |
      a.name = "retract" and a.parameter -> exists (p1 |
         p1.oclType.name = "policy" and p1.subject = p.subject))) ;
  pol->notEmpty ;
}
```

The body of the policy contains two OCL expressions. The first one operates on th eset of authorisations in the meta policy container (a composite policy), referred to by "this". It selects all policies (p) with the following characteristics: the action set of p contains an action named "retract", and whose parameters include a policy object with the same subject as the subject of policy p. The second OCL expression is a boolean expression; it returns true if the pol variable, which is returned from the first OCL, expression is not empty. If the result of this last expression is true, the exception specified in the raises-clause executes. It receives the pol set with the conflicting policies as a parameter

Example 10 Separation of duty

```
inst meta budgetDutyConflict raises conflictInBudget(z) {
  [z] = self.policies -> select (pa, pb |
      pa.subject -> intersection (pb.subject)->notEmpty     and
      pa.action -> exists (act | act.name = "submit")       and
      pb.action -> exists (act | act.name = "approve")      and
      pb.target -> intersection (pa.target)->oclIsKindOf (budget))
  z -> notEmpty ;
}
```

This metapolicy prevents a conflict of duty in which the same person both approves and submits a budget. It searches for policies with the same subject acting on a target budget in which there is an action submit and approve.

The above policy implements a static separation of duties in that it prevents the same person being authorised to perform conflicting actions. Dynamic separation of duties is a slightly different, in that all members of a group are authorised to perform potentially conflicting actions but after performing one action they cannot perform a conflicting one. This is implemented as constraints relating to attributes of the subject and target object rather than as a meta-policy.

Example 11 Dynamic separation of duty

```
inst auth+ sepDuty {
  subject  s = accountants ;
  action   approvePayment, issue ;
  target   t = cheques ;
  when     s.id <> t.issuerID ;
}
```

The same user from the accountants domain cannot both issue and approve payment of the same cheque. This assumes that the identity of the issuer/approver can be stored as an attribute of the cheque object.

5   Composing Policy Specifications

Ponder composite policies facilitate policy management in large, complex enterprises. They provide the ability to group policies and structure them to reflect organisational structure, preserve the natural way system administrators operate or simply provide reusability of common definitions. This simplifies the task of policy administrators.

5.1   Groups

This is a packaging construct to group related policies together for the purposes of policy organisation and reusability and is a common concept in most programming languages. There are many different potential criteria for grouping policies together – they may reference the same targets, relate to the same department or apply to the same application. Figure 8 shows the syntax for a group instance. It can contain zero or more basic policies, nested groups and/or meta-policies in any order. A meta-policy specifies constraints on the policies within the scope of the group.

```
inst group groupName     "{"
   { basic-policy-definition }
   { group-definition }
   { meta-policy-definition }  "}"
```

Figure 8. Group Syntax

Reusability can be achieved by specifying groups as types, parameterised with any policy element and then instantiating them multiple times. For instance, policies related to the login process can be grouped together since they must always be instantiated together (example 12).

Example 12 Group policy

```
inst group loginGroup {
    inst auth+ staffLoginAuth {
       subject /dept/users/staff ;
       target  /dept/computers/research;
       action  login; }

    inst oblig loginactions {
       subject s = /dept/computers/loginAgent ;
       on      loginevent (userid, computerid) ;
       target  t = computerid ^ {/dept/computers/}
       do      s.log (userid, computerid)  ->
               t.loadenvironment (userid); }

    inst oblig loginFailure { ... }  // see example 6
}
```

The login group policies authorises staff to access computers in the research domain, log login attempts, load the users environment on the computer and deal with login failures.

5.2   Roles

Roles provide a semantic grouping of policies with a common subject, generally pertaining to a position within an organisation such as department manager, project manager, analyst or ward-nurse. Specifying organizational policies for human managers in terms of manager positions rather than persons permits the assignment of a new person to the manager position without re-specifying the policies referring to the duties and authorizations of that position [16]. A role can also specify the policies that apply to an automated component acting as a subject in the system.

Organisational positions can be represented as domains and we consider a role to be the set of authorisation, obligation, refrain and delegation policies with the **subject domain** of the role as their subject. A role is thus a special case of a group, in which all the policies have the same subject.

```
inst role roleName    "{"
    { basic-policy-definition }
    { group-definition }
    { meta-policy-definition }   "}" [ @ subject-domain ]
```

Figure 9. Role Syntax

A role (figure 9) can include any number of basic-policies, groups or meta-policies. The subject domain of the role can be optionally specified following the @ sign. If it is not specified then a subject domain with the same name as the role is created by default.

Example 13 Role policy

```
type role ServiceEngineer (CallsDB callsDb)  {
    inst oblig serviceComplaint  {
        on       customerComplaint(mobileNo) ;
        do       t.checkSubscriberInfo(mobileNo, userid) ->
                 t.checkPhoneCallList(mobileNo) ->
                 investigate_complaint(userId);
        target   t = callsDb ;  // calls register   }

    inst oblig deactivateAccount { . . . }
    inst auth+ serviceActionsAuth {  . . .  }
    // other policies
}
```

The role type ServiceEngineer models a service engineer role in a mobile telecommunications service. A service engineer is responsible for responding to customer complaints and service requests. The role type is parameterised with the calls database, a database of subscribers in the system and their calls. The obligation policy serviceComplaint is triggered by a customerComplaint event with the mobile number of the customer given as an event attribute. On this event, the subject of the role must execute a sequence of actions on the calls-database in order check the information of the subscriber whose mobile-number was passed in through the complaint event, check the phone list and then investigate the complaint. Note that the obligation policy does not specify a subject as all policies within the role have the same implicit subject.

5.3 Type Specialisation and Role Hierarchies

Ponder allows specialisation of policy types, through the mechanism of inheritance. When a type extends another, it inherits all of its elements, add new elements and overrides elements with the same name.

```
type role roleTypeName "(" formalParameters ")"
    extends parentRoleType  "(" actualparameters ")"   "{"
  role-body  "}"
```

Figure 10. Inheritance Syntax

An example of the use of inheritance to extend a Role type is shown below. Similar syntax can be used to extend other types.

Example 14 Role inheritance

```
type role MSServEngineer (CallsDB vlr, SqlDB eqRegistry)
                                    extends ServiceEngineer(cdb)  {
    inst  oblig maintainProblems {
        on       MSfailure(equipmentId) ;   // MS = Mobile Station
        do       updateRecord(equipmentId) ;
        target   eqRegistry                  // Equipment identity registry
    }
}
```

The MSServEngineer (MobileStation Service Engineer) role extends the ServiceEngineer role specified in example 13. It inherits the policies of the parent role and adds an obligation policy that updates the equipment's record in the equipment identity registry (the target) when the mobile station signals a failure (the event).

Role and organisational hierarchies can be specified using specialisation. The role-hierarchy in figure 11 can be specified in Ponder by extending roles as shown in the following example.

Figure 11. A Role Hierarchy

Example 15 A role hierarchy

```
type role EmployeeT(...) { ... }
type role AdmStaffT(...)          extends Employee { ... }
type role ResearchStaffT(...)     extends Employee { ... }
type role SecretaryT(...)         extends AdmStaff { ... }
type role SoftDeveloperT(...)     extends ResearchStaff { ... }
type role ProjectManagerT(...)    extends ResearchStaff { ... }
```

5.4 Relationships

Managers acting in organisational positions (roles) interact with each other. A relationship groups the policies defining the rights and duties of roles towards each other. It can also include policies related to resources that are shared by the roles within the relationship. It thus provides an abstraction for defining policies that are not the roles themselves but are part of the interaction between the roles. The syntax of a relationship is very similar to that of a role but a relationship can include definitions of the roles participating in the relationship. However roles cannot have nested role definitions. Participating roles can also be defined as parameters within a relationship type definition as shown below.

Example 16 Relationship type

```
type rel ReportingT (ProjectManagerT pm, SecretaryT secr) {
    inst oblig reportWeekly {
        on        timer.day ("monday") ;
        subject   secr ;
        target    pm ;
        do        mailReport() ;
    }
    // . . . other policies
}
```

The ReportingT relationship type is specified between a ProjectManager role type and a Secretary role type. The obligation policy reportWeekly specifies that the subject of the SecretaryT role must mail a report to the subject of the ProjectManagerT role every Monday. The use of roles in place of subjects and targets implicitly refers to the subject of the corresponding role.

5.5 Management Structures

Many large organisations are structured into units such as branch offices, departments, and hospital wards, which have a similar configuration of roles and policies. Ponder supports the notion of management structures to define a configuration in terms of instances of roles, relationships and nested management structures relating to organisational units. For example a management structure *type* would be used to define a branch in a bank or a department in a university and then *instantiated* for particular branches or departments. A management structure is thus a composite policy containing the definition of roles, relationships and other nested management structures as well as instances of these composite policies.

Figure 12 shows a simple management structure for a software development company consisting of a project manager, software developers and a project contact secretary. Example 17 gives the definition of the structure.

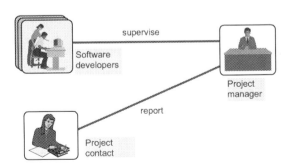

Figure 12. Simple Management Structure

Example 17 Software company management structure

```
type mstruct BranchT (...)   {
   inst  role  projectManager = ProjectManagerT(...);
         role  projectContact   = SecretaryT(...);
         role  softDeveloper = SoftDeveloperT(...);

   inst  rel   supervise = SupervisionT (projectManager, softDeveloper);
         rel   report = ReportingT (projectContact, projectManager);
}
inst  mstruct branchA = BranchT(...);
      mstruct branchB = BranchT(...);
```

This declares instances of the 3 roles shown in Figure 12. Two relationships govern the interactions between these roles. A supervise relationship between the softDeveloper and the projectManager, and a reporting relationship between the ProjectContact and the projectManager. Two instances of the BranchT type are created for branches within the organisation that exhibit the same role-relationship requirements.

6   Additional Features

6.1   Class Hierarchy

The class hierarchy of the language (figure 13), allows new policy classes that may be identified in the future to be defined as sub-classes of existing policy classes. The model also provides a convenient means of translating policies to structured representation languages such as XML. The XML representation can then be used for viewing policy information with standard browsers or as a means of exchanging policies between different managers or administrative domains.

Ponder is a strongly-typed language as every identifier and expression can be checked to be type consistent, and errors can be automatically detected if an operator or function is applied to the wrong type of data. Although most of the type checking occurs statically at compile time, Ponder also supports a form of dynamic type checking by accessing type

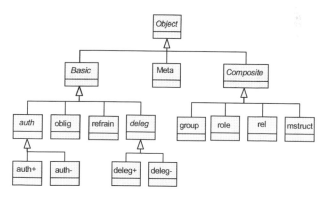

Figure 13. Ponder Object Meta Model

definitions in a type repository. Statically strongly typed is an important characteristic for a policy language. Note that Ponder does not allow casting, and thus avoids the loopholes created because of casting in typed languages. Policies might be used in situations where their validity is important (e.g. security policies). Since program testing is usually not going to be an option in a policy-based system, static type checking is important to capture type inconsistencies that might cause failure of a policy at run-time.

6.2 Scripting

An obligation action can be defined as a script using any suitable scripting language to specify a complex sequence of activities or procedures with conditional branching. Scripts are implemented as objects and stored in domains. Thus authorisation policies can be specified to control access to the scripts.

Scripts give the flexibility of including complex actions which cannot be expressed as single object method invocations and can contain conditional statements supported by the scripting language. For example a script could be defined to update software on all computers in a target domain as an atomic transaction which rolls back to the old version if any one of the updates fail.

If an interpreted language such as Java is used to program scripts, then the scripts could be updated using mobile code mechanisms to change the functionality of automated manager agents. Although this suffers from all the usual security vulnerabilities of mobile code [3], extending the functionality of manager agents is an operation on the agent's management interface and can be restricted by authorisation policies.

6.3 Imports

Import statements can be used to import definitions such as constants, constraints and events from external Ponder specifications stored in domains into the current specification. This allows reuse of common specifications in order to minimise errors that arise due to multiple definition. The following example shows how an event specification can be reused.

Example 18 Import statement

```
inst group /groups/groupA  {
   event e(userId) = 3*loginfail(userid) ;

   // other common specifications & basic-policies
}

inst group groupB {
   import /groups/groupA ;

   inst oblig FlexibleLoginFailure   {
       on           e(userId)|loginTimeOut(userId);
       subject      s = /NRegion/SecAdmin ;
       target       t = /NRegion/users ^ {userid} ; }
       do           s.log(userid);
}
```

GroupB imports the specification groupA from the /groups domain (where it is stored), and reuses the specification of the event e(userId) defined within loginFailure. The event of the new obligation policy is now 3 consecutive loginfail events or a loginTimeOut event, which is triggered when the user takes too long to enter the password after the prompt.

6.4 Self-Management

The Ponder framework is self-managed in that policies and other constructs such as roles and relationships are implemented as objects stored within domains. Ponder authorisation policies can therefore be used to specify who is permitted to add, delete, edit policies or any of the other entities. Furthermore, Ponder obligation policies can be used to specify what actions must be performed on policy objects when certain events occur. For example, obligation policies can be specified to enable new policies or disable existing ones in order to adapt to new circumstances such as failures, emergency conditions, etc.

7   Related Work

Most of the other work on policy language specification relates to security. None includes the range of policies covered in Ponder and most lack the flexibility and extensibility features of Ponder.

Formal logic-based approaches are generally not intuitive and do not easily map onto implementation mechanisms. They assume a strong mathematical background, which can make them difficult to use and understand. The ASL [12], is an example of a formal logic language for specifying access control policies. The language includes a form of meta-policies called integrity rules to specify application-dependent rules that limit the range of acceptable access control policies. Although it provides support for role-based access control, the language does not scale well to large systems because there is no way of grouping rules into structures for reusability. A separate rule must be specified for each action. There is no explicit specification of delegation and no way of specifying authorisation rules for groups of objects that are not related by type.

Ortalo [21] describes a language to express security policies in information systems based on the logic of permissions and obligations, a type of modal logic called deontic logic. Standard deontic logic centres on impersonal statements instead of personal; we see the specification of policies as a relationship between explicitly stated subjects and targets instead. In his approach he accepts the axiom $Pp = \neg O \neg p$ ("permitted p is equivalent to not p being not obliged") as a suitable definition of permission. This axiom is not suitable for the modelling of obligation and authorisation policies; the two need to be separated. Miller [19] discusses several paradoxes that exist in deontic logic. Since [21] contains only syntactical extensions to deontic logic, it also suffers from the same problems.

LaSCO [10] is a graphical approach for specifying security constraints on objects, in which a policy consists of two parts: the domain (assumptions about the system) and the requirement (what is allowed assuming the domain is satisfied). Policies defined in LaSCO have the appearance of conditional access control statements. The scope of this approach is very limited to satisfy the requirements of security management.

In [2], Chen and Sandhu introduce a language for specifying constraints in RBAC systems. It can be shown that their language is a subset of OCL and we can thus specify all of their constraints as meta-policies. Space limitations prevent further discussion of this issue.

The Policy Description Language (PDL) is an event-based language originating at the network computing research department of Bell-Labs [28][13]. Policies in PDL are similar to Ponder obligation policies. They use the event-condition-action rule paradigm of active databases to define a policy as a function that maps a series of events into a set of actions. The language has clearly defined semantics and an architecture has been specified for enforcing PDL policies. The language can be described as a real-time specialised production rule system to define policies. Events can be composite events similar to those of Ponder obligation policies. PDL does not support access control policies, nor does it support the composition of policy rules into roles, or other grouping structures.

8   Conclusion and Further Work

In this paper we have presented Ponder, a language for specifying policies for management and security of distributed systems. Ponder includes authorisation, filter, refrain and delegation policies for specifying access control and obligation policies to specify management actions. Ponder thus provides a uniform means of specifying policy relating to a wide range of management applications – network, storage, systems, application and service management. In addition, it supports a common means of specifying enterprise-wide security policy that can then be translated onto various security implementation mechanisms. We are currently implementing back-ends to the Ponder compiler for Firewall rules, Windows security templates and Java security policy.

The Ponder composite policies (groups, roles, relationships and management structures) allow structured, reusable specifications, which cater for complex, large-scale organisations. Ponder's object-oriented features allow user-defined types of policies to be specified and then instantiated multiple times with different parameters. This provides for flexibility and extensibility while maintaining a structured specification that can be, in large part, checked at compile time. Meta-policies in Ponder provide a very powerful tool in specifying application specific constraints on sets of policies. Ponder is declarative which aids in the analysis of policies [14].

The language specification leaves room for future additions in many areas. Relationships need to be extended with interaction protocols to specify the interaction between roles. We are also investigating sub-types of meta policies to cover concurrency constraints and user-role assignment constraints. Giving the language formal semantics will also be part of future work. A policy specification toolkit is under development for defining, compiling and analysing policies. The design and implementation of a generic runtime object-model for enforcement of Ponder policies on any object-based platform is also under development.

Acknowledgement

We gratefully acknowledge their support of EPSRC for research grants GR/L96103 (SecPol), GR/M86109 (Ponds) and GR/L76709 (Slurp).

References

For additional references see http://www-dse.doc.ic.ac.uk/policies.

1. Abrams, M.D. *Renewed Understanding of Access Control Policies*. In Proceedings of 16th National Computer Security Conference. 1993. Baltimore, Maryland, U.S.A.
2. Chen, F. and R.S. Sandhu. *Constraints for Role-Based Access Control*. In Proceedings of First ACM/NIST Role Based Access Control Workshop. 1995. Gaithersburg, Maryland, USA, ACM Press.
3. Chess, D.M., *Security Issues in Mobile Code Systems*, in Mobile Agents and Security, G. Vigna, Editor. 1998, Springer. p. 256.
4. Clark, D.D. and D.R. Wilson. *A Comparison of Commercial and Military Computer Security Policies*. In Proceedings of IEEE Symposium on Security and Privacy. 1987
5. Damianou, N., N. Dulay, E. Lupu, and M. Sloman. *Ponder: A Language for Specifying Security and Management Policies for Distributed Systems*. The Language Specification - Version 2.2. Research Report DoC 2000/1, Imperial College of Science Technology and Medicine, Department of Computing, London, 3 April, 2000.
6. Distributed Management Task Force, Inc. (DMTF), *Common Information Model (CIM) Specification*, version 2.2, available from http://www.dmtf.org/spec/cims.html, June 14, 1999.
7. Goh, G. *Policy Management Requirements*, System Management Department, HP Laboratories Bristol, April, 1998.
8. Hegering, H.-G., S. Abeck, and B. Neumair, *Integrated Management of Network Systems: Concepts, Architectures and Their Operational Application*, 1999: Morgan Kaufmann Publishers.
9. Hewlett-Packard Company, *A Primer on Policy-based Network Management*, OpenView Network Management Division, Hewlett-Packard Company, September 14, 1999.
10. Hoagland, J.A., R. Pandey, and K.N. Levitt. *Security Policy Specificaton Using a Graphical Approach*. Technical report CSE-98-3, UC Davis Computer Science Department, July 22, 1998.
11. Internet   Engineering   Task   Force,   *Policy   Working   Group* http://www.ietf.org/html.charters/policy-charter.html
12. Jajodia, S., P. Samarati, and V.S. Subrahmanian. *A Logical Language for Expressing Authorisations*. In Proceedings of IEEE Symposium on Security and Privacy. 1997, pp.31-42
13. Lobo, J., R. Bhatia, and S. Naqvi. *A Policy Description Language*. In Proc. of AAAI, July 1999. Orlando, Florida, USA
14. Lupu, E.C., and M. Sloman. *Conflicts in Policy-Based Distributed Systems Management*. IEEE Trans. on Software Engineering, 25(6): 852-869 Nov.1999.
15. Lupu, E.C. *A Role-Based Framework for Distributed Systems Management*. Ph.D. Thesis, Department of Computing, Imperial College, London, U. K.
16. Lupu, E.C. and M.S. Sloman, *Towards a Role Based Framework for Distributed Systems Management*. Journal of Network and Systems Management, 1997b. 5(1): p. 5-30.

17. Mahon, H. *Requirements for a Policy Management System*. IETF Internet draft work in progress, Available from http://www.ietf.org, 22 October 1999.
18. Marriott, D.A. *Policy Service for Distributed Systems*. Ph.D. Thesis, Department of Computing, Imperial College, London, U. K.
19. Miller, J., HELP! *How to specify policies?*, Unpublished paper, available electronically from http://enterprise.shl.com/policy/help.pdf
20. Moore, B., J. Strassner, and E. Ellesson, *Policy Core Information Model VI*, IETF Internet draft, Available from http://www.ietf.org, May 2000.
21. Ortalo, R. *A Flexible Method for Information System Security Policy Specification*. In Proceedings of 5th European Symposium on Research in Computer Security (ESORICS 98). 1998. Louvain-la-Neuve, Belgium, Springer-Verlag.
22. Rational Software Corporation, *Object Constraint Language Specification*, Version 1.1, Available at http://www.rational.com/uml/, September 1997.
23. Sandhu, R.S. and P. Samarati, *Authentication, Access Control, and Intrusion Detection*. Part of the paper appeared under the title "Access Control: Principles and Practice" in IEEE Communications, 1994. 32(9): p. 40-48.
24. Sandhu, R.S., E.J. Coyne, H.L. Feinstein, and C.E. Youman, *Role-Based Access Control Models*. IEEE Computer, 1996. 29(2): p. 38-47.
25. Sloman, M. and K. Twidle, *Domains: A Framework for Structuring Management Policy*. Chapter 16 in Network and Distributed Systems Management (Sloman, 1994ed), 1994a: p. 433-453.
26. Sloman, M.S., *Policy Driven Management for Distributed Systems*. Journal of Network and Systems Management, 1994b. 2(4): p. 333-360.
27. Sun Microsystems, Inc., *Java Management Extensions Instrumentation and Agent Specification*, v1.0, December 1999.
28. Virmani A., J. Lobo, M. Kohli. *Netmon: Network Management for the SARAS Softswitch*, IEEE/IFIP Network Operations and Management Symposium, (NOMS2000), ed. J. Hong, R., Weihmayer, Hawaii, May 2000, pp803-816.
29. Weis, R. Policy Definition and Classification: Aspects, Criteria and Examples. In Proceedings of IFIP/IEEE International Workshop on Distributed Systems: Operations & Management. 1994a. Toulouse, France.

IPSec/VPN Security Policy: Correctness, Conflict Detection, and Resolution[1]

Zhi Fu[1], S. Felix Wu[1], He Huang[2], Kung Loh[2],
Fengmin Gong[3], Ilia Baldine[3], and Chong Xu[3]

[1] Computer Science Department, North Carolina State University, USA
{zfu, wu}@eos.ncsu.edu
[2] Nortel Networks, NC, USA
{huanghe, kungloh}@nortelnetworks.com
[3] Advance Networking Research, MCNC, NC, USA
{gong, ibaldin, chong}@anr.mcnc.org

Abstract. IPSec (Internet Security Protocol Suite) functions will be executed correctly only if its policies are correctly specified and configured. Manual IPSec policy configuration is inefficient and error-prone. An erroneous policy could lead to communication blockade or serious security breach. In addition, even if policies are specified correctly in each domain, the diversified regional security policy enforcement can create significant problems for end-to-end communication because of interaction among policies in different domains. A policy management system is, therefore, demanded to systematically manage and verify various IPSec policies in order to ensure an end-to-end security service. This paper contributes to the development of an IPSec policy management system in two aspects. First, we defined a high-level security requirement, which not only is an essential component to automate the policy specification process of transforming from security requirements to specific IPSec policies but also can be used as criteria to detect conflicts among IPSec policies, i.e. policies are correct only if they satisfy all requirements. Second, we developed mechanisms to detect and resolve conflicts among IPSec policies in both intra-domain and inter-domain environment.

1 Introduction

IPSec [1] is receiving widespread deployment to restrict access or selectively enforce security operations for VPN implementation etc. IPSec is a typical policy-enabled networking service in that IPSec functions will be executed correctly only if policies are correctly specified and configured. IPSec policy database is manually configured in current practice. It is inefficient and error-prone for large distributed networking systems. Because of the growing number of secure Internet applications, IPSec policy deployment will be more and more complex in the near future. Therefore, a policy

---

[1] This Research is supported in part by the U.S. Department of Defense Advanced Research Projects Agency under contract DABT63-97-C-0045 and in part by Nortel Networks.
M. Sloman, J. Lobo, and E. Lupu (Eds.): POLICY 2001, LNCS 1995, pp. 39–56, 2001.

management system is clearly demanded to automatically and systematically configure and manage various IPSec policies.

Policy is to implement people or corporation's desired requirement. In a policy hierarchy [2], a requirement (high level policy) is an objective while implementation policies (low level policy) are specific plans to meet the objective. One requirement might be satisfied by different sets of implementation policies. Therefore, the policy specification process is the process to transform from requirement to specific implementation policies to realize the requirement. The current security policy proposals for IPSec [3,4,5] focus on policy rules that can be "deterministically" enforced by one or more network elements (i.e., PEP, Policy Enforcement Points). In other words, the security requirements of a policy domain have been manually transformed into LDAP Policy Framework rules. There is, therefore, a currently vague relationship between a desired security requirement and specific IPSec policies to realize the requirement. However, to manage policies for large distributed systems, it is desirable to separate requirement and policies because: 1) Policies are specific ways to implement requirements such that requirements are more static and policies are more dynamic. The separation allows requirement component to be reused while policies to be dynamically modified and improved without needs to alter the requirement component. 2) The separation permits automation of the process to transform from requirements to policies. 3) Explicitly specified requirements can be used as criteria to verify the correctness of low level policies.

At the first glance, it seems that requirement and IPSec policy may directly map to each other. We can use the following example to illustrate the difference between a security requirement and specific IPSec policies to fulfill the requirement.

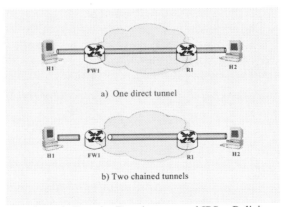

a) One direct tunnel

b) Two chained tunnels

Figure 1: Security Requirement and IPSec Policies

In figure 1, if a sensitive communication from a host machine H1 to another host machine H2 requires to be encrypted during transmission anywhere from H1 to H2 except the firewall FW1, which is trusted to review content, then both of configurations shown in the figure 1 satisfy the requirement. In configuration a), H1 directly builds an encryption tunnel with H2 to protect the sensitive traffic while in b), two IPSec tunnels are chained at FW1, which will decrypt the traffic from cipher text back to plain text, then re-encrypt again for the second encryption tunnel. Similarly, more different chained-tunnel configurations can satisfy the requirement if some other security gateways on the path are also trusted to review the content.

In a large distributed system or inter-domain environment, the diversified regional security policy enforcement can create significant problems for end-to-end communication. In the above example, suppose FW1 needs to examine traffic content for the purpose of intrusion detection and a policy is set up at FW1 to deny all encrypted traffic to enforce its content examination requirement. However, H1 and H2 build a direct tunnel without awareness of existence of the firewall and its policy rules. Therefore, all the traffic will be dropped by FW1. The scenario shows that each policy satisfies its corresponding requirement while all policies together can cause conflicts. In this case, if two chained tunnels are built as b) in figure 1, then both requirements are satisfied and the traffic will go through with appropriate protection. However, end users have no idea about topology or policy information to make right choice of policy configurations. A policy management system should be responsible to provide assurance of end-to-end protection and transmission.

The following shows another scenario that each policy may be satisfying individual requirement while all policies together cause violation:

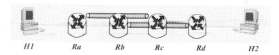

Figure 2: Overlapping tunnels

In this scenario, there are four routers Ra, Rb, Rc and Rd on the path from H1 to H2. Assume there are two requirements for the traffic from H1 to H2: one is integrity protection from Ra to Rc and the other is confidentiality protection from Rb to Rd. Two tunnels are built from Ra to Rc and from Rb to Rd accordingly. With the tunnels, the traffic will be encapsulated by Ra, then encapsulated again by Rb to send to Rd. When Rd decapsulates and finds the destination is Rc, Rd will send traffic back to Rc. Finally Rc will decapsulate and send traffic to its real destination. Although it is originally intended to encrypt traffic from Rc to Rd, the traffic is eventually sent in clear from Rc to Rd because of tunnel interaction.

Therefore, an IPSec policy management system will need to not only systematically specify policies to fulfill requirements but also tackle the topological interaction and conflicts among IPSec policies. This paper contributes to the development of an IPSec policy management system in two aspects: First we specified security requirements in a high level. Then, we developed mechanisms to detect and resolve conflicts among IPSec policies to ensure secure end-to-end communications.

The remaining paper is organized as follows. In section 2, we define security requirements and their satisfaction. Section 3 develops an algorithm to systematically verify the correctness of policies. Section 4 discusses the policy resolution problem and solutions. Then section 5 talks about deployment issues by introducing Celestial system that the conflict detection and resolution mechanisms can be deployed in to provide end-to-end security service. Finally, section 6 presents some related work and section 7 concludes the paper and outlines future work.

2 Security Requirements and Their Satisfaction

Requirement is high level objective while implementation policies are low level specific plans to meet the objective. One important task of IPSec policy management is to represent security requirements in a high level efficiently and unambiguously. We will first analyze the security requirements for IPSec policies. Since the requirements are implementation independent, the flow identities specified in requirements are of original flows regardless outer headers encapsulated for low-level policy enforcement.

2.1 Security Requirement Analysis

- **Access Control Requirement (ACR):** One fundamental function of security is to conduct access control that is to restrict access only to trusted traffic. A simple way to specify an ACR is: *flow id.* → *deny | allow*
- **Security Coverage Requirement (SCR):** Another important function is to apply security functions to prevent traffic from being compromised during transmission across certain area, which requires the security protection to protect the traffic from all links and nodes within the area. However, optionally, users can authorize certain nodes in the area to access content since some nodes on the path may need and be trusted to examine content. A simple way to specify a SCR to protect traffic from *"from"* to *"to"* by a security function with certain strength could be:
  flow id. → *enforce (sec-function, strength, from, to, trusted-nodes)*
- **Content Access Requirement (CAR):** Some nodes may need to access content of certain traffic, for example, a firewall with an intrusion detection system (IDS) may need to examine content to determine the characteristic of the traffic. However, one node is not able to view the content of traffic if an encryption tunnel is built across it. Similarly, there might be certain nodes that need to modify content for special processing but can not if authentication tunnels are built across them. We allow CAR to be explicitly specified to deny or allow certain security function to protect certain traffic from certain nodes. A simple way to specify a CAR could be: *flow id, sec-function, access-nodes* → *deny | allow*
- **Security Association Requirement (SAR):** Security Associations (SA) [1] need to be formed to perform encryption/authentication function. There might be needs to specify some nodes to desire/not desire to set up SA with some other nodes because of trust/distrust relationship or capability match/mismatch etc. A simple way to specify a SAR could be: *flow id, SA-peer1, SA-peer2* → *deny | allow*

The above four requirements expressed the needs of IPSec users with respect to not only the access control and protection of traffic but also impacts and attributes of security enforcement.

2.2 Definitions of Security Requirements and Implementation Policies

Definition 1: IPSec/VPN policy can be specified in two different levels: the requirement level security policies (or security requirements in short) and the implementation level security policies (or security implementation policies in short). Two level security policies are the same in basic form as defined below but different in attributes and semantics as will be defined respectively below. For example, the IPSec policies that are installed in security gateways to operate on the passing traffic are implementation policies.

Definition 2: A security policy P is a rule of the following form: If _condition_ C then _action_ A: $P = C \rightarrow A.$

Definition 3: The condition part of a security policy is composed of a set of sets $S_1, S_2, \ldots, S_N$, each of which is a finite set of values of a specific attribute, we call a selector, to associate certain traffic with a particular policy. The condition is met, or a packet is selected by a policy, if and only if each of the packet's value of a selector is an element of the corresponding set of the selector, which can be expressed by Cartesian product of the sets,

$$C = \mathop{\times}\limits_{i=1}^{N} S_i$$

For example, if selector attributes of a policy are source address and destination address, then the traffic from a to c will be selected by the policy with condition of source address $\{a,b\}$ and destination address $\{c,d\}$ because

$$a \in \{a,b\} \qquad c \in \{c,d\} \qquad thus \qquad (a,c) \in \{a,b\} \times \{c,d\}$$

Therefore, selectors are defined as the attributes used to match packets with policies. We will specify selectors and their values in detail for requirement level and implementation level security policies respectively below.

Definition 4: The action part of a security policy is of form $a(t_1, t_2, \ldots, t_M)$ where a is an action type with M parameters that specify attributes of the action. There is only one action type for each policy. We will define each action type and associated parameters in detail for requirement level and implementation level security policies respectively below. $A = a(t_1, t_2, \ldots, t_M)$

Definition 5: The requirement level security policies have the following selectors in the condition part:

> _flow identity_
> _[sec-function access-nodes][2]_
> _[SA-peer1 SA-peer2]_

and have the following action types and parameters in the action part:

> _deny_
> _allow_
> _enforce (sec-function strength [algorithm] from to [trusted-nodes])[3]_

---

[2] Attribute with [ ] is optional and can be specified to be empty.

In the condition part, each S_i is a finite set:

- *flow identity* is composed of 5~6 sub-selectors: *src-addr, dst-addr, src-port, dst-port, protocol, [user-id]* to identify the traffic flow;
- *sec-function access-nodes* is to specify the condition that certain security functions (e.g. authentication or encryption) are applied against particular nodes specified by the finite set *access-nodes*. This condition can be used in expressing the Content Access Requirement of certain nodes by denying certain security function(s) against them;
- *SA-peer1 SA-peer2* is to specify the condition that any node of the set of *SA-peer1* forms SA with any node in the set of *SA-peer2*. This condition can be used in expressing the Security Association Requirement by explicitly denying/allowing particular nodes to build association relationship.

In the action part, each t_j is a finite set:

- *sec-function* is to specify the security function(s) (e.g authentication or encryption) required for certain traffic;
- *strength* is to specify desired level of security protection such as ordinary, middle or high; optionally *algorithm* specifies the specific algorithms desired to use for the security protection;
- *from to* is to specify the areas outside the *from to* sets are to be protected against, for example, *from* (128.1.*.*) *to* (156.68.*.*) indicates the transmission going outside sub-domain 128.1.*.* before entering into sub-domain 156.68.*.* needs to be protected. Optionally, *trusted-nodes* is to specify the nodes that are allowed to access content rather than being protected from.

The above definition of requirement specification is capable of expressing four security requirements analyzed in section 2.1 and is extensible for new security requirements in the future.

Definition 6: The implementation level IPSec security policies check various header fields to select a packet. Therefore, the implementation level security policies have selectors of all possible header fields of an IP packet in the condition part as follows:

    src-addr, dst-addr, src-port, dst-port, proto, ah-hdr, esp-hdr, TOS, ah-next-hdr, etc.

and have the following action types and associated parameters in the action part:

    deny

    allow

    ipsec-action (sec-prot, algorithm[4], mode, from, to)

In the condition part, each S_i is a finite set used to match the header fields of a packet to the policy.

---

[3] Each attribute will be specified as a finite set, which can be specified as wildcard, list of values, ranges or optionally preceded by not to express all but some etc. e.g. ip addresses, ip address ranges, or dns names can be used to specify particular nodes.

[4] We use *algorithm* to also abstract other related attributes like *key-length* etc.

In the action part, each t_j is a single value except *algorithm:*

- *sec-prot* specifies either ah or esp;
- *algorithm* specifies all possible algorithms for ISAKMP to negotiate;
- *mode* specifies either transport or tunnel;
- *from to* specify two nodes to build an SA.

Implementation policies are to instruct certain security devices to set up specific SA and perform specific operations on the passing traffic. Therefore, in the definition, deterministic values will be assigned for the attributes of ipsec-action except *algorithm* of which multiple values can be specified for ISAKMP negotiation. Our definition is compliant with the specification language [3] proposed in IETF.

2.3 Security Requirement Satisfaction

2.3.1 Access Control Requirement Satisfaction
Notation:
➢ *path(x,f)*   : node x is on the path of flow f
➢ *drop(x,f)*   : node x drops flow f
➢ $R \leftarrow Q$: R is true if Q is true

Definition 7.1: *flow f → deny* is satisfied iff any node on the path of the flow f drops all packets of f.

$$R_{11} : flow f \rightarrow deny$$
$$R_{11} \leftarrow \exists x Path(x, f) \wedge Drop(x, f)$$

Definition 7.2: *flow f → allow* is satisfied iff none of node on the path of the flow f drops the flow.

$$R_{12} : flow f \rightarrow allow$$
$$R_{12} \leftarrow \neg \exists x Path(x, f) \wedge Drop(x, f)$$

2.3.2 Security Coverage Requirement Satisfaction
Notation:
➢ $sec-link(f, x, sfunc, strg)$: Traffic flow f is protected by a security function *sfunc* with strength *strg* on the link from node x to the next node on the path.
➢ $sec-node(f, x, sfunc, strg)$: Traffic flow f is protected by a security function *sfunc* with strength *strg* against the node x.

Definition 8: *flow f → enforce (sec-func, strength, from, to, trusted-nodes)* is satisfied iff
1) all the links within the protection area are secured against by all security functions specified in *sec-func* with strength equal or greater than the level specified in *strength*; and

2)   all the nodes within the protection area are also secured against with the security functions and strength except the nodes in the *trusted-nodes*.

R_2 : *flow f* → *enforce(sec-func, strength, from, to, trusted-nodes)*[5]

$R_2 \leftarrow sec\_links(f, sec-func, strength, fromA, toA)$

$\quad \& \; sec\_nodes(f, sec-func, strength, fromA, toA, trusted-nodes)$

$sec\_links(f, sec-func, strength, fromA, toA) \leftarrow$

$\forall x Path(x, f) \wedge (fromA \leq x < toA) \wedge$

$\forall_{sfunc \in sec-func} sec-link(f, x, sfunc, strg) \wedge (strg \geq strength)$

$sec\_nodes(f, sec-func, strength, fromA, toA, trusted-nodes) \leftarrow$

$\forall x Path(x, f) \wedge (fromA < x < toA) \wedge (x \notin trusted-nodes) \wedge$

$\forall_{sfunc \in sec-func} sec-node(f, x, sfunc, strg) \wedge (strg \geq strength)$

From the definition, we can see a SCR contains protection requirements for every link and node in the specified area. If one requirement has some element requirements such that the requirement is satisfied iff all its elements are satisfied, we call the elements the **sub-requirements** of the requirement. If one requirement has property that, the satisfaction of which will be determined as a single unit, we call it an **atomic requirement**. For example, a sub-requirement for a certain link or node with a certain security function is an atomic sub-requirement of a SCR, since it is either satisfied if the link or node is protected accordingly or violated otherwise and there is no partial satisfaction or violation. The verification of a non-atomic requirement can be accomplished by verifying if each of its atomic sub-requirements is satisfied.

2.3.3 Content Access Requirement Satisfaction

Definition 9: *flow f, sec-func access-nodes* → *deny* is satisfied iff all nodes in the *access-nodes* can access the traffic content that is not secured by any of the function in *sec-func*.

R_3 : *flow f*, *sec-func   access-nodes* → *deny*

$R_3 \leftarrow \forall x Path(x, f) \wedge (x \in access-nodes) \wedge \forall_{strg} \forall_{sfunc \in sec-func} \neg sec-node(f, x, sfunc, strg)$

It is composed of atomic sub-requirements of access requirement of each node in the *access-nodes*.

Although *flow f, sec-func access-nodes* → *allow* is satisfied unconditionally, it can be used in conjunction with *flow f, sec-func access-nodes* → *deny* to specify some CAR. For instance, a requirement that all nodes except *SG1* need to access content of flow *f* can be specified as:

flow f, encryption (access-nodes) SG1 → *allow*

flow f, encryption (access-nodes) * → *deny*

---

[5] *from to* might be specified as sets or sub-domains etc. *fromA toA* as denoted in definition 5 are two specific nodes to determine the protection area, which is between the two nodes. In addition, we did not explicitly list *algorithm* here since satisfaction of *algorithm* can be verified in a similar way.

2.3.4   Security Association Requirement Satisfaction

Notation:

➢ $peer(f, x_1, x_2)$:   node $x1$ and $x2$ form a SA peer for flow f.

Definition 10: *flow f, SA-peer1 SA-peer2 → deny* is satisfied iff none of node in *SA-peer1* set up SA with any of node in *SA-peer2* for flow f.

$$R_4 : flow f, SA-peer1 \quad SA-peer2 \rightarrow deny$$
$$R_4 \leftarrow \forall x \forall y (x \in SA - peer1) \wedge (y \in SA - peer2) \wedge \neg peer(f, x, y)$$

It is composed of atomic sub-requirements of peer requirement of each pair specified in *SA-peer1 SA-peer2* sets.

Although *flow f, SA-peer1 SA-peer2 → allow* is satisfied unconditionally, it can be used in conjunction with *flow f, SA-peer1 SA-peer2 → deny* to specify some SAR in a similar way as exemplified in the last subsection.

3   IPSec Policy Correctness and Conflict Detection

We call a set of implementation policies regarding a certain traffic flow *correct* iff the set of policies satisfies the set of requirements regarding the flow. We call a set of implementation policies regarding a certain traffic flow *conflicting* when the set of policies together does NOT satisfy all of the requirements regarding the flow, with the requirement satisfaction as defined below.

3.1 IPSec Policy Processing

The IPSec policies installed in security gateways will be consulted in processing either inbound or outbound traffic. As specified in [1], the IPSec policy will be processed at a particular node as follows:

- For inbound traffic, if the action in the policy for the traffic is *deny*, then the traffic is dropped; if *allow*, then forward the traffic. If it is the destination of the outer tunnel, then it needs to de-apply the security function. For tunnel mode, it also decapsulates to remove outer header before forward;
- For outbound traffic, if the policy is with action of *ipsec-action (sec-prot, alg, mode, from, to)*, then the node will apply the corresponding security function. For tunnel mode, it also encapsulates an outer header with new source and destination address to be addresses of tunnel entry and tunnel exit nodes. Finally it will forward the packets;
- All the forwarding is only based on destination address of outer header.

Traffic sometimes might be sent back and forth because of tunnel interaction as illustrated with figure 2 in the introduction part.

3.2 Policy Verification Algorithm

As we illustrated in the introduction, regionally enforced policies together might interact or cause conflicts. It is important for a policy management system to be able to
detect those conflicts. A *Policy Verification/ Conflict Detection Problem* can be
defined as follows: Given a set of security requirements for a particular traffic flow
$\{Req_1, Req_2, ..., Req_K\}$ and a set of implementation policies for the flow
$Imp_1, Imp_2, ...Imp_N$ that are installed in nodes along a linear path with N nodes
$Node_1, Node_2, ...Node_N$. Verify the correctness of the set of implementation polices.
From the correctness definition, we need to verify the satisfaction of the requirements
thus to verify satisfaction of all their atomic sub-requirements as defined in section
2.3.

Two points need to be emphasized before proceeds to the verification algorithm: 1)
Transmission at a link or a node is subject to protection of all the security functions
that are applied but not de-applied yet when the traffic travels to the link or node. 2)
Since traffic may travel to one link or node more than once, the security protections
are only the weakest one of all the trips to the link or node. To illustrate the two
points, we use an example as shown below.

Figure 3: Calculating Security Coverage

In this simple five nodes linear topology, traffic is to be sent from H1 to H2. First
traffic is tunneled to Rb with authentication. Then before it reaches tunnel exit Rb, it is
tunneled by Ra and send to Rc with encryption. Since authentication function is applied at node A and has not been de-applied yet at tunnel from Ra to Rc, the link Ra-
Rb and Rb-Rc are subject to protection of both authentication and encryption. Then
the encryption will be de-applied at node Rc and the traffic will be sent back to Rb
along Rb-Rc link with protection of authentication only. Then Rb will de-apply the
authentication function. At this moment, no any security function still applies such that
the third time the traffic travels the link Rb-Rc under no protection, which is the
weakest one of the three trips.

Based on the above analysis, we know a packet may be traveling in many different
ways rather than simply hop-by-hop ahead because of IPSec processing. However, the
processing at each node, which was described in section 3.1, is with fixed number of
operations and can be easily simulated. In the verification algorithm, we will simulate
IPSec policy processing to follow a packet's trip step-by-step from source to destination as well as record security protection and related information of each link and node
at every step that is necessary to prove the satisfaction of requirements. As described
in section 3.1, tunnel mode processing will encapsulate an outer header with addresses
of tunnel entry and tunnel exit as the new source and destination address. We will use

a stack to simulate the nested header such that new header will be pushed into the stack upon encapsulation and popped out upon decapsulation. In addition to header information, we also push security protection information associated with the tunnel into the stack when it is applied and pop it out when it is de-applied. Therefore, the security protection for a link or node is all those security functions on the stack at the moment that the traffic comes to it.

In the following, we will present an algorithm to follow the packets' trip and collect protection information based on actions of policies along the path.

There are N nodes on the path. $Imp[n]$ is the policy of the corresponding node n. We need to use action information of each policy to calculate required information while action part can be represented by:

$$Imp[n].action = deny \mid allow \mid ipsec \to (sec\text{-}prot, alg, mode, from, to)$$

in which $ipsec$ point to a link list of one or more ipsec actions. There is only one action type in one policy though we allow multiple actions with the same type and different parameters in one policy.

We also need the following data structures in the algorithm:

- $sec\_link[N]$ is an array of link list, each of which is to mark what security protection covers link from $Node_n$ to $Node_{n+1}$. One link might be subject to multiple protections, e.g. $sec\_link[n] = esp\ cast \to ah\ hmac5$.
- $sec\_node[N]$ is an array of link list, similar to the above, each of which is to mark what security protections are against the corresponding node.
- $SA\_peer[M][2]$ is used to record all SA peers in the policies.
- A stack S is used to store series of $(sec\text{-}prot, alg, from, to)$ and simulate encapsulation/ decapsulation, security function application/ de-application. $top = 0$ initially and the destination address of encapsulated outer header will always be destination address to on the top of the stack S.

Algorithm: Policy Processing Along The Path

```
top = 0; m = 0; n =0;    //stack is empty, from the first node
sec_link[N] = sec_node[N] = null  // no travel yet

while  ( n < N)   // at node n
{  // inbound processing
     if (Imp[n].action == deny)
            report and exit
   // calculate what the node n is secured against
     if ( top == 0)
            sec_node[n] = 0  // no protection
     else
     {        //decapsulates first if tunnel exit
          while ( S[top].to == Node[n])
          {        pop (S)
                   top - -
          }
//protection are all those in the stack and the real one
//is always the weaker one of this trip and previous trips.
```

```
            If (stack is weaker than sec_node[n])
                update sec_node[n] to be those in the stack
      }

   // Outbound processing
   // encapsulate and record SA information for ipsec
      if ( Imp[n].action == ipsec)
      {    push (sec-prot, alg, from, to) into the stack
           record all pairs ( from, to) in SA_peer
      }
      // send packet out; record protection for link
      if (top == 0)
      {      sec_link[n] = 0 // no protection
             n ++              // forward
      }
      else ( S[top].to > Node[n])          // forward
      {  if (stack is weaker than in sec_link[n])
             update sec-link[n] with those in stack
             n ++
      }
      else    // backward and travel the link n to n-1
      {if (stack is weaker than in sec_link[n-1])
             update sec-link[n-1] with those in stack
        n - -
      }
   }
```

The algorithm can be run in polynomial time[6]. With the security protection and attribute information collected using the algorithm, we can verify the satisfaction of all requirements as defined in Section 2.3.

4   IPSec Policy Conflict Resolution

Once we found conflicts, next step is to find ways to resolve them. Ideally, we want to satisfy all the security requirements. However, there may be circumstances that in no way can all requirements be simultaneously satisfied. Violation of any requirement will cause some damage. If there has to be some damage, then our goal is to find a set of policies that minimize the possible damage. We will first discuss the mapping from the requirements to implementation policies.

There are *trusted-nodes* in SCR such that the nodes in *trusted-nodes* are not necessarily protected from. In an example shown below, a SCR requires to protect certain traffic from H1 to H2. Between H1 and H2, there are Ra and Rb that are in the *trusted-nodes*. Then all the following configurations satisfy the SCR (we assume every tunnel is with appropriate security function and strength):

---

[6] Because of space limitation, the detail complexity analysis is omitted here.

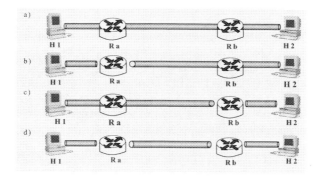

Figure 4: Four different configurations that satisfy one SCR

Sometimes it is advantageous to build several chained tunnels to implement one SCR rather than one direct tunnel for the preference of other requirements. For instance, in the above figure, if Rb is required to examine the content, then Rb has to be a connecting node of tunnels to be able to access the content. In another example, Rb also requires to examine content. Additionally, H1 and Rb is not suitable to set up SA as specified in one SAR, while H1 and Ra, Ra and Rb are allowed to build SA, then we can use Ra, Rb as connecting nodes to build three SAs rather than one for the SCR.

In addition to satisfaction of CAR and SAR, another reason to use several tunnels instead of one is to resolve overlapping as illustrated below.

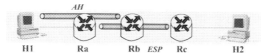

a)   Overlapping causes SCR violation

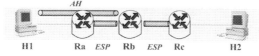

b)   Breaking the lower tunnel up eliminates the overlap

Figure 5: Breakup to resolve overlapping

In the example shown in the figure 5, as we explained and calculated in section 3.3, the configuration will make traffic to be sent back from Rc to Rb, then sent in clear from Rb ahead which may violate the SCR for the link Rb-Rc. If the lower tunnel is broken up as shown in b), then the traffic will not be sent back and the link Rb-Rc will be protected by the tunnel from Rb to Rc. The reason that we do NOT build additional tunnel from Rb to Rc to resolve lack of security coverage caused by overlapping is that the additional tunnel does not compensate the security coverage. In the above example, even though we can build additional ESP tunnel from Rb to Rc, the traffic sent back from Rc to Rb is still not encrypted.

The problem is then to evaluate the tradeoff and find one configuration that results in minimal total damage. Since each tunnel can be implemented by an IPSec policy with ipsec-action, the policy resolution problem becomes that, from all set of policies of alternative chained tunnel configurations, choose one that minimizes damage caused by violation of requirements. We quantify the damage associated with any requirement violation as a non-negative value called *penalty*. If one requirement is not atomic, there might be different penalties associated with violation of each of its atomic sub-requirement. For example, a CAR may specify that Ra, Rb need to examine content while the penalty that Ra is not able to access content might be much greater than that of Rb.

If there is K_1 SCRs and the members of each subset can be selected from a set with J nodes, then the total number of possible configurations are $2^J \times 2^J \times ... \times 2^J = 2^{J \times K_1}$. The solution space can be expressed as $(x_1, x_2, ..., x_{J \times K_1})$ where $x_i = 1 | 0$, value 1 represents chaining at a certain node while 0 represents not. However, most time we do not need to break one tunnel up if the tunnel already satisfies the requirement. We only test different breakup configurations when violation occurs. Therefore, we can start from building one tunnel for each SCR first. If one tunnel plan cause no conflict, then we are done. Otherwise we will try different breakup plans for those problematic tunnels to search for optimal configurations. To find those tunnels that need to be resolved, we can first define the following tunnel relationship types. There are two tunnels with end points (from$_i$, to$_i$) and (from$_j$, to$_j$). We say tunnel i **contains** tunnel j iff from$_i$ < from$_j$ < to$_j$ < to$_i$. Tunnel i **overlaps** with tunnel j iff from$_i$ < from$_j$ < to$_i$ < to$_j$; Tunnel i and tunnel j are **disjoint** iff from$_i$ < to$_i$ <= from$_j$ < to$_j$; Tunnel i and tunnel j **nests** with each other if they are not disjoint (either containing, contained or overlapping); Tunnels are **a group of nesting tunnels** iff every tunnel nests with at least on other tunnel in the group.

Nested tunnels need to be considered as a whole in seeking optimal breakup plans because breaking one up may cause additional overlapping among nested tunnels. Those disjoint groups can be considered separately because any kind of breakup for one group will not have any effect on the other group. Having these in mind, we can group those tunnels with corresponding requirements and resolve each group separately. We only try different breakup plans for those groups that caused violations and leave others as they are. Resolution for some groups might be very easy. For instance, if one group is only with one tunnel that only violated one CAR of one node Ra, then the only work to do is to compare and make a decision whether or not break the single tunnel up at the node Ra. However, at the worst case, given a group of tunnels, we may need to test all possible configurations before an optimal one can be found.

Among those optimization problems with solution as a n-tuple $(x_1, x_2, ..., x_n)$, **backtracking** [7] is a commonly used algorithm. The basic idea of the *backtracking* algorithm is to continuously build and test partial vector $(x_1, x_2, ..., x_i)$ to see if it can possibly lead to an optimal solution. If not, then all possible values of latter part of vector $(x_{i+1}, x_{i+2}, ..., x_n)$ can be ignored entirely. The process can be also illustrated by constructing a solution tree. A bounding function is used to test whether a branch has any chance to lead to an optimal solution and a node is killed immediately without generating any of its children when it is found to be with no chance to success. Then it will go back to an upper layer node to construct other branches of the solution tree.

When we search for optimal configurations for nested tunnels, with *backtracking* algorithm, we can calculate the penalty with partial configuration to help to kill non-optimal breakup plans at its earliest stage. The verification algorithm developed in section 3 can be easily modified to calculate the total penalty for a set of policies. The idea of using *backtracking* here is that if some portion of a configuration already cause penalty greater than a so-far-minimal penalty, then we will not investigate any other portion of this configuration further, which may greatly reduce the number of configurations that are really calculated.

The complexity of backtracking algorithm mainly depends on two factors: 1) the time to calculate the penalty; 2) the number of branches that not being killed. We may greatly improve efficiency if we initially have a known configuration with a small penalty that can help to kill more branches earlier. Combining heuristic and random mechanisms, we may first choose an initial configuration with a small although not smallest penalty. We can first sort the set of requirement penalties and find those largest penalties. Then we randomly choose dozens of configurations that avoided the large penalty violation. For example, if one largest penalty caused by violation of a SAR, then we select initial value only from the configurations that do not build the undesirable SA. Then from the randomly selected dozens of configurations, we use penalty calculation algorithm to find out the one with smallest penalty to be as our initial penalty.

Although *backtracking* can vary greatly in time complexity for different problem instances, for a lot instances in large scale, backtracking indeed can find out solution in very short time. Monte Carlo [7] method can be used to estimate the efficiency of the backtracking algorithm for a specific instance. Besides *backtracking* algorithm, other algorithms like **branch and bound** [7], *genetic algorithm* [8] etc. can also be used for policy optimization problem. *Genetic algorithm* normally could get a good solution very fast but can not guarantee the optimality of the solution.

5   Celestial – An Inter-domain Security Management System

In our conflict detection and resolution algorithms, we need information about requirements and implementation policies as well as the route path for the flow. For intra-domain policy management, the required information might be obtained from a central policy server of the domain. For inter-domain communication, an inter-domain security management system like Celestial system [9] is needed to collect and manage the information.

Celestial system aims to provide reliable and scalable end-to-end security services using multiple distributed security mechanisms. In Celestial system, Security Management Agent (SMA) is to sit in management plane of any SMA-enabled node (switch, router, security gateway etc.) and is responsible for coordinating all security-related activities on a network system. Inter-Domain SMA Coordination Protocol (ISCP) [10] provides the transport function for security service negotiation and reservation in order for the Celestial system to gather relevant information and manage security services end-to-end. In Celestial, security context establishment is done in two phases. In the discovery phase, the application's service requirements are distributed along the communication path and the service capabilities/policies of the nodes along the path are collected. Then the SMA who is authoritative to the receiver will determine an optimal configuration plan using certain policy resolution algorithm based on the collected information, and then invokes the reservation phase that distributes assignments to the nodes selected for providing the security services. Refreshing messages are periodically sent to collect updated policy and path information and distribute new reservation/ assignment information, which helps the system dynamically adapt to changes and maintain adequate security service for users.

6   Related Work

Another research on end-to-end IPSec policy management is Policy Based Security Management (PBSM) system [11,12] developed in BBN. PBSM is a distributed systems with Policy Servers (PS) that can manage IPSec security policies for multiple domains. The system answers end-to-end security service query by merging policies among Policy Servers (PS). Along with PBSM, they developed Security Policy Specification Language (SPSL) [3]. However, the potential conflicts and topological interactions have not been analyzed in their work. In addition, without distinguishing the requirement level and implementation level security policies, SPSL itself can not ensure the correctness of policy specification.

The needs of separating high-level requirements and low-level policies were addressed in [2,6]. Our work applied the concepts to a specific policy service by defining IPSec security requirements in a high level. Some recent work [13,14] analyzed two types of conflicts: one is co-existence of both positive and negative policies, which can be detected by checking syntax; the other one is application specific conflicts. In this research, we analyzed IPSec specific conflicts caused by topological interaction etc. The developed algorithm can detect all possible conflicts among IPSec policies in a distributed environment. The consistency analysis of security policies in [15] focuses on access control policy while our work focuses on topologically interacted IPSec policies.

7   Conclusion and Future Work

It is critical for IPSec/VPN security policies to be specified correctly in order to enforce access control and traffic protection appropriately. Although security policy specification and configuration received a lot of attention, one important problem has not been carefully studied: How to ensure policy's correctness? In this research, we studied and analyzed potential conflicts caused by various interactions among policies, which are hard to resolve in one level. We clearly defined security policies in two levels: requirement level security policy and implementation level security policy. The correctness of implementation level security policies can be verified by checking satisfaction of requirement level security policies, which can be automatically done using our conflict detection algorithm. When conflicts are detected, a resolution is demanded. We developed an optimization model to abstract this problem, in which we find a policy set to optimize the overall satisfaction.

In this research, we focus on conceptually centralized conflict detection and resolution in which we resolve policies when all relevant information is collected. We will further work on a decentralized collaboration model in which conflicts can be detected in a distributed manner.

References

1.   Kent, S., Atkinson, R.: Security Architecture for the Internet Protocol. RFC-2401, IETF, Nov. 1998.
2.   Moffett, J. D., Sloman, M. S.: Policy Hierarchies for Distributed Systems Management. IEEE Journal on Selected Areas in Communication, vol. 11, pp. 1404-1414, 1993
3.   Condell, M., Lynn, C., Zao, J.: Security Policy Specification Language. Internet Draft, <draft-ietf-ipsp-spsl-00.txt>, March, 2000
4.   Jason, J.: IPsec Configuration Policy Model. Internet Draft <draft-ietf-ipsp-config-policy-model-00.txt>, March, 2000
5.   Pereira, R., Bhattacharya, P., IPSec Policy Data Model. Internet Draft <draft-ietf-ipsec-policy-model-00.txt>, Feb. 1998
6.   Moffett, J. D.: Requirements and Policies. Position paper for Policy Workshop 1999
7.   Horowitz, E., Sahni, S.: Fundamentals of Computer Algorithms. Computer Science Press Inc.,1978.
8.   Gen, M.,   Cheng, R.: Genetic Algorithms & Engineering Optimization. Wiley-Interscience, 2000
9.   Xu, C., Gong, F., Baldine, I., Sargor, C., Jou, F., Wu, S. F., Fu, Z., Huang, H.: Celestial Security Management System. DARPA Information Survivability Conference and Exposition, 2000. DISCEX '00. Proceedings, Volume: 1, 1999, Page(s): 162 -172 vol.1
10. Fu, Z., Huang, H., Wu, T., Wu, S.F., Gong, F., Xu, C., Baldine, I: ISCP: Design and Implementation of An Inter-Domain Security Management Agent (SMA) Coordination Protocol. Proceedings, NOMS 2000, Pages 565-578.
11. Sanchez, L.A., Condell, M.N: Security Policy System. Internet Draft, <draft-ietf-ipsec-sps-00.txt>, Nov. 1998
12. Zao, J., Sanchez, L., Condell, M. Lyn, C., Fredette, M., Helinek, P., Krishnan, P., Jackson, A., Mankins, D., Shepard, M., Kent, S.: Domain Based Internet Security Policy

Management. DARPA Information Survivability Conference and Exposition, 2000. DIS-CEX '00. Proceedings ,1999, Pages: 41 -53 vol.1

13. Lupu, E.C., Sloman, M: Conflict Analysis for Management Polcies. Proc. 5th IFIP/IEEE International Symposium on Integrated Network Management, pages 430-443, 1997

14. Lupu E.C., Sloman, M: Conflicts in Policy-Based Distributed Systems Management. IEEE Transaction on Software Engineering. Vol. 25, No. 6, pages 852-869, Nov./Dec. 1999

15. Cholvy L. and Cuppens, F.: Analyzing Consistency of Security Policies. IEEE Symposium on Security and Privacy, 1997, Proceedings

Monitors for History-Based Policies

Jan Chomicki[1] and Jorge Lobo[2]

[1] Dept. of Computer Science and Engineering
University at Buffalo
Buffalo, NY 14260-2000
chomicki@cse.buffalo.edu
[2] Network Computing Research Dept.
Bell Labs
Murray Hill, NJ 07974
jlobo@research.bell-labs.com

Abstract. We investigate the issue of conflict detection and resolution for policies formulated as sets of event-condition-action rules. We focus on the temporal dimension of policies. In particular, we consider sequence events in rules, conflict resolution through cancellation or delay, and temporal action constraints. We formally define monitors – procedures for resolving conflicts. We present algorithms for the computation of optimal monitors.

1 Introduction

Policies are common in many software application areas: electronic commerce, network management, telecommunications, security etc. Recently, there has been a significant growth of interest in languages for formulating policies and mechanisms for their implementation.

In [14] a declarative policy language $\mathcal{PDL}$ was proposed. $\mathcal{PDL}$ programs are sets of ECA (Event-Condition-Action) rules. A paramount issue for such programs is how to detect and resolve action conflicts [7,9,11]. We characterized action conflicts as violations of *action constraints* in [7] and [9], in the context of a subset of $\mathcal{PDL}$ containing rules for which the event part of the rule consisted of primitive events and boolean operators. The actions produced by such rules depend only on the current set of input events; past events are irrelevant. Thus policies specified by such rules may be termed *stateless*. (They can be formally defined as mappings from event sets to action sets.) We proposed the *cancellation* of conflicting actions as a basic technique for resolving conflicts. We also showed how to implement cancellation monitors–the procedures for detecting and resolving conflicts.

However, the flow of time is important for policies. Not only concurrent but also sequential occurrence of events is meaningful. There are rules with *sequence events* in the full $\mathcal{PDL}$. The actions produced by such rules depend not only on the current set of input events but also on the history of past events. Time adds also another dimension to conflict resolution. Conflicting actions can be *delayed*

M. Sloman, J. Lobo, and E. Lupu (Eds.): POLICY 2001, LNCS 1995, pp. 57–72, 2001.

until they can be executed without conflict. This observation leads to another class of monitors, namely *delay* monitors. To illustrate the difference between cancellation and delay monitors, consider the following example.

Example 1. Suppose we want to restrict concurrent access to a resource, so if there are two or more concurrent conflicting requests for the resource, only one can be granted. A cancellation monitor will ignore all but one of such requests. A delay monitor will delay the ignored requests instead, until they can be executed without conflict.

The criteria to select the appropriate monitor in the context of a specific application must consider the properties of conflicting actions in more detail. If a conflicting action is unlikely to be repeated and makes sense even when it is delayed, then it is better to use a delay monitor. Otherwise, a cancellation monitor is more appropriate.

Actions should not be cancelled (or delayed) arbitrarily. Clearly, a monitor should be as close to the policy as possible. This can be interpreted in two ways. If we focus on canceling (or delaying) a minimal set of conflicting actions, we get *action* monitors. On the other hand, if we choose to apply the original policy to a maximal consistent reduction of the original input, we get *event* monitors.

To appreciate the need for event monitors, consider the following observation. Sometimes a group of actions is always executed in tandem and if one of them is cancelled, all of them must be cancelled. This is similar to a database transaction. For example, suppose a piece of merchandise ordered by a customer arrived at the stock location. After this event happens two actions are executed: the piece of merchandise is shipped to the customer and the customer credit card is charged. If the shipment is stopped by a conflict with another action (such as a recall of the product due to a manufacturing defect), the charge should not be made. This dependency is captured by event monitors. In action monitors, two actions caused by the same event (or events) can be cancelled or delayed independently.

The last dimension of time addressed in the present paper deals with *temporal* action constraints. Such constraints make it possible to restrict not only concurrent but also sequential execution of actions.

To sum up, we extend in this paper the approach to conflict resolution proposed in [7] and [9] to wider classes of policies and monitors. We show how to define monitors for policies with rules that refer to *sequence events*. We also show how to specify *delay monitors*. Finally, we address the issue of more general action constraints formulated in *Past Temporal Logic*. All the above extensions are founded on a more general notion of policy: a mapping from sequences of event sets to sequences of action sets. In fact, the monitors defined in this paper are applicable not only to $\mathcal{PDL}$ but also to any other policy language with the formal semantics of the same kind.

The plan of the paper is as follows. In Section 2, we provide the basic definitions. We introduce the syntax of $\mathcal{PDL}$ and define action constraints. In Section 3, we define monitors, introduce several basic classes of monitors and show how such monitors may be computed. In Section 4, we introduce temporal action constraints and show how to accommodate such constraints in the monitors. Section

5 describes our current implementation of a $\mathcal{PDL}$ policy server. In Section 6, we briefly survey related work. We conclude the paper in Section 7.

2   Definitions

In [14], Lobo, Bhatia and Naqvi introduced the language $\mathcal{PDL}$, a policy description language that is being used as a programming language of a policy-based network management system [16]. We consider here a subset of $\mathcal{PDL}$.

2.1   Policies

A policy can be described as a reactive system that observes events happening in the environment and reacts to them by trying to affect the environment through the execution of actions (procedure calls). The reaction could be caused by the occurrence of a single event or a number of events.

To write programs that implement policies we assume that both the events observed by a policy and the actions that the policy generates have the structure of terms. We fix two disjoint set of function symbols: *primitive event* symbols and *action* symbols. These symbols are system-dependent and are given to the user that defines the policies. There is also a set of standard ordered types such as integers, floats, character strings, etc. Action and primitive event symbols may be of any nonnegative arity. We refer to the arguments of a primitive event as its *attributes* and to the arguments of an action as its *parameters*. Every attribute and parameter has an associated type.

Definition 1. *A* policy *is a finite collection of well-typed policy rules of the form*

$$event \textbf{ causes } action \textbf{ if } condition, \tag{1}$$

where the event, action *and* condition *parts of a rule are defined below.*

Definition 2. *The* event *part of a policy rule is either an expression of the form:*

1. $e_1 \& \ldots \& e_n$ *where each* e_i *is an event term (defined below) and* $\&$ *is interpreted as a* conjunction *of events; or an expression of the form*
2. $e_1, \ldots, e_n$ *where each* e_i *is a conjunction of event terms and* ",", *is interpreted as a* sequence *of events; or an expression of the form*
3. $[e_1, \ldots, e_n]$ *where each* e_i *is a conjunction of event terms and the sequence is interpreted as a* relax-sequence *of events.*

An event term *is a typed term of the form* $e(t_1, \ldots, t_n)$, *where* e *is a primitive event symbol of* n *arguments and each* t_i *is a constant or a variable. An* event instance *is a ground event term (i.e., an event term without variables).*

Definition 3. *The* action *part of a policy rule is a typed* action term *of the form* $a(t_1, \ldots, t_n)$*, where* a *is an action symbol of* n *arguments and each* t_i *is either (1) a variable that appears in the event part of the rule, (2) a constant, or (3) a well-formed expression of variables, constants and operations from the standard types. An* action *is a ground action term.*

Definition 4. *The condition part of a policy rule is an expression of the form* $p_1, \ldots, p_n$*, where each* p_i *is a predicate of the form* $t_1 \theta t_2$*,* θ *is a relation operator from the set* $\{=, \neq, <, \leq, >, \geq\}$ *and each* t_i *is either (1) a variable that appears in the event part of the rule, (2) a constant, or (3) a well-formed expression of variables, constants and operations from the standard types. The condition represents the conjunction of the predicates.*

In general, several events can occur simultaneously in the environment. We refer to the collection of event instances that are considered to occur simultaneously as an *epoch*. From the policy point of view, the epoch defines simultaneity. The implementation of the concept though is domain-dependent. In some cases the right epoch granularity is an hour, in other a day, or even an arbitrarily defined period of time. An implementation of epochs is described in Section 5. To a policy the environment is presented as a finite sequence of epochs to which the policy responds by generating actions.

Definition 5. *A finite set of event instances is an* epoch*. A finite set of actions is an* action set*. A finite sequence of epochs is called an* E-history*, and a finite sequence of action sets an* A-history*.*

Definition 6. *A substitution is a function that maps typed variables to constants of the appropriate type. The application of a substitution* σ *to a term* t*, denoted by* $t\sigma$*, is the simultaneous replacement of the variables in* t *that are in the domain of* σ *by the constants assigned to the variables by* σ*.*

Note: Our notion of substitution corresponds to that of the *ground* substitution in logic programming.

We say that:

- an event e *occurs* in an epoch if an instance of the event term $e(X_1, \ldots, X_n)$ is member of the epoch[1];
- a conjunction $e_1 \& \ldots \& e_m$ of event instances occurs in an epoch if each e_i, $1 \leq i \leq m$, occurs in the epoch.

Definition 7. *Given an E-history* $\mathcal{H}_E = (E_1, \ldots, E_n, E_{n+1})$*, we say that*

1. *the conjunction of event instances* $e_1 \& \ldots \& e_m$ *occurs in* $\mathcal{H}_E$ *if it occurs in* E_{n+1}*,*

---

[1] In the term the X_i's are distinct variables of the appropriate type.

2. *the sequence of conjunctions of event instances $e_1, \ldots, e_m$ occurs in $\mathcal{H}_E$ if every e_i, $1 \leq i \leq m$, occurs in $E_{n+1-(m-i)}$,*
3. *the relax-sequence of conjunctions of event instances $[e_1, \ldots, e_m]$ occurs in $\mathcal{H}_E$ if there is a sequence of epochs $E_{j_1}, \ldots, E_{j_m}$ such that (1) $1 \leq j_1 < \cdots < j_m = n + 1$, (2) for all i, $1 \leq i \leq m$, e_i occurs in E_{j_i}, and (3) for all i, $1 \leq i \leq m - 1$, e_{i+1} does not occur in any epoch between E_{j_i} and $E_{j_{i+1}}$.*

The difference between sequence and relax-sequence of events is that in the latter the events do not have to appear in *consecutive* epochs.

Definition 8. *The semantics of a policy P is recursively defined as the following function T_P from E-histories to A-histories:*

1. *For an E-history $\mathcal{H}_E = (E_1)$, of length 1, $T_P(\mathcal{H}_E) = (A_1)$ iff for every $a \in A_1$, there is a policy rule "E causes A if C" in P and a substitution σ such that $E\sigma$ occurs in $\mathcal{H}_E$, $C\sigma$ is satisfied and $A\sigma = a$.*
2. *For an E-history $\mathcal{H}_E = (E_1, \ldots, E_{n+1})$, of length $n + 1$, $T_P(\mathcal{H}_E) = (A_1, \ldots, A_n, A_{n+1})$ iff for every $a \in A_{n+1}$, there is a policy rule "E causes A if C" in P and a substitution σ such that $E\sigma$ occurs in $\mathcal{H}_E$, $C\sigma$ is satisfied, $A\sigma = a$, and $T_P((E_1, \ldots, E_n)) = (A_1, \ldots, A_n)$.*

Note that by definition policies are prefix-closed. That is, for any E-history

$$\mathcal{H}_E = (E_1, \ldots, E_n, E_{n+1}),$$

if

$$T_P(\mathcal{H}_E) = (A_1, \ldots, A_n, A_{n+1})$$

then

$$T_P((E_1, \ldots, E_n)) = (A_1, \ldots, A_n).$$

This is essential for policies to be evaluable incrementally. The output of a policy on a given E-history never changes when the history is extended with further epochs.

Example 2. A CD club service wants to implement its customer policy using $\mathcal{PDL}$. The club gives bonuses to clients that place orders in two consecutive months if the total cost of the orders in those months is above a certain threshold c. A client can close an account in any month, and orders are shipped as soon as they are received. This policy can be written with three $\mathcal{PDL}$ rules:

$$order(Cust, Cost, Itm) \textbf{ causes } ship(Cust, Itm).$$
$$order(Cust, Cost_1, Itm_1), order(Cust, Cost_2, Itm_2) \textbf{ causes } bonus(Cust)$$
$$\textbf{if } Cost_1 + Cost_2 > c.$$
$$close(Cust) \textbf{ causes } closeAcc(Cust).$$

2.2 Action Constraints

Independently of the policies there might be some restrictions imposed on the kind of A-histories that are considered possible or correct in the system. For example, there might be restrictions, identified by the policy administrators, that do not let two particular actions appear in the same action set in the history (i.e., the actions cannot be executed simultaneously). The restrictions on A-histories are called *action constraints*. Thus, action conflicts are captured as violations of action constraints.

Definition 9. *An* action constraint *is an expression of the form*

$$\textbf{never}\quad a_1 \wedge \ldots \wedge a_m \ \textbf{if}\ C.$$

Each a_i in the expression is an action term and C a condition like in (1). Variables in C must also appear as parameters of the action terms. The informal reading of the constraint is: "never allow the simultaneous execution of the actions $a_1, \ldots, a_m$ if the condition C holds." The constraint formally represents the formula $\forall \neg(a_1 \wedge \ldots \wedge a_n \wedge C)$.

Example 3. Returning to our CD club example we can specify the restriction that we cannot simultaneously close an account and process a shipment associated with the same account using the constraint:

$$\textbf{never}\quad ship(Cust, Item) \wedge closeAcc(Cust).$$

Example 4. We extend the CD club example with several rules about enrollment. Assume that a customer receives an initial offer upon enrollment but can enroll only once. Subsequent attempts to enroll by the same customer result in a declination. This can be expressed in $\mathcal{PDL}$ as:

$$enroll(Cust) \ \textbf{causes}\ offer(Cust).$$
$$[enroll(Cust), enroll(Cust)] \ \textbf{causes}\ decline(Cust).$$

and the constraint

$$\textbf{never}\quad offer(Cust) \wedge decline(Cust).$$

To complete this example, we need to indicate that if both *offer* and *decline* are generated in an epoch, *decline* should have priority (being more specific). We will show how to do it in the next section.

Definition 10. *Let a be an action, $ac \equiv$ "**never** $a_1 \wedge \ldots \wedge a_m$ **if** C" an action constraint, and A an action set. Using the standard logical notation, we write $A \models \alpha$ to denote that A is a model of α. Specifically:*

1. $A \models a$ iff $a \in A$;
2. $A \models ac$ if for every substitution δ, $C\delta$ is false or there is an i, $1 \leq i \leq m$, $A \not\models a_i\delta$.

An A-history $\mathcal{H}_A = (A_1, \ldots, A_n)$ satisfies ac (resp. AC) if $A_n \models ac$ (resp. $A_n \models AC$). $\mathcal{H}_A$ is prefix-consistent with AC if for every $m \leq n$, $(A_1, \ldots, A_m)$ satisfies AC.

This definition generalizes to sets of constraints in an obvious way.

3   Monitors

A monitor of a set of action constraints generates only outputs without conflicts (without constraint violations).

Definition 11. *Given a set of action constraints AC, an AC-monitor ω_{AC} is a mapping from E-histories to A-histories of the same length such that for every E-history $\mathcal{H}_E$, $\omega_{AC}(\mathcal{H}_E)$ is prefix-closed and prefix-consistent with AC. (If the set of constraints AC is clear from the context, we will use the term "monitor" instead of "AC-monitor".)*

Notice that every monitor is prefix-closed, and thus – like a policy – can be evaluated incrementally. Our goal is to take policies together with action constraints and automatically generate monitors. We have identified two basic ways in which a monitor can handle conflicts. One is for the monitor to cancel some of the actions that generate the conflict. Such a monitor will be called a *cancellation monitor*. The other is to delay some conflicting actions until their execution does not cause conflicts. Such a monitor will be called a *delay monitor*. Within the classes of cancellation and delay monitors we introduce further subdivisions into *action* and *event monitors*. Intuitively, action monitors decide which actions to delay or cancel looking exclusively at the output of a policy (a set of actions). Event monitors, on the other hand, take also the input events into account.

Example 5. Consider again Example 2. Assume an *order* event and a *close* event occur in a single epoch. Therefore, because of the conflict between *ship* and *closeAcc*, one of those actions needs to be cancelled (or delayed). Assume *ship* is cancelled (delaying it does not make much sense). Assume also that another *order* event occurred in the preceding epoch and the condition for the *bonus* action to be executed is satisfied. The *bonus* action can be executed without conflict but it does not seem natural to do that since the order supporting the bonus was cancelled. An event-cancellation monitor avoids this problem by ignoring the event *order* and therefore also indirectly cancelling both actions it causes. Such a monitor selects a consistent reduction of the input epoch, in that case the reduction contains only the *close* event. Therefore, both *ship* and *bonus* are effectively cancelled.

In some cases ignoring all the actions caused by an event is not necessarily desirable.

Example 6. Consider Example 4 in the case when an enrollment event of a customer is followed by another enrollment event of the same customer. In this case the second event causes two actions: *offer* and *decline*, which result in a conflict. An event monitor cancels or delays that event, and consequently neither of the actions is output. Intuitively, this is not a correct behavior: we expect exactly one of them to be output in this situation.

A comprehensive policy management system should provide both action and event monitors, as well as their combinations. Consequently, we will have four basic classes of monitors: action-cancellation, event-cancellation, action-delay, and event-delay. The monitors will be defined through algorithms that construct them. Each algorithm is nondeterministic and thus defines a family of monitors. Each of those will, however, enjoy suitable maximality properties, as elaborated in the next section.

3.1   Action Monitors

Notation: $tail((A_1, \ldots, A_n)) = A_n$.

The following algorithm computes

$$M_{ac}^P(E_1, \ldots, E_n) = (A_1, \ldots, A_n)$$

for some action-cancellation AC-monitor M_{ac}^P of P:

Action Cancellation Monitor **for** $i := 1$ **to** n **do**
$\quad A_i := \emptyset$
$\quad U := tail(T_P((E_1, \ldots, E_i)))$
$\quad$**while** true **do**
$\quad\quad$select $a \in U - A_i$ such that $A_i \cup \{a\} \models AC$
$\quad\quad$**if** select successful **then** $A_i := A_i \cup \{a\}$
$\quad\quad$**else** break
$\quad$**end**
end

The following algorithm computes

$$M_{ad}^P(E_1, \ldots, E_n) = (A_1, \ldots, A_n)$$

for some action-delay AC-monitor M_{ad}^P of P:

Action Delay Monitor $D := \emptyset$
  for $i := 1$ **to** n **do**
    $A_i := \emptyset$
    $U := D \cup tail(T_P((E_1, \ldots, E_i)))$
    while true **do**
      select $a \in U - A_i$ such that $A_i \cup \{a\} \models AC$
      if select successful **then** $A_i := A_i \cup \{a\}$
      else break
    end
    $D := U - A_i$
  end

In some cases it is natural to define a priority ordering between actions. For example, if an action represents an exception, it should have priority over the more general action. In Example 4, we remarked that *decline*, being more specific, should have priority over *offer*. Action priorities can be easily added to the above algorithms: the action selection inside the **while** loop should be selected according to the priorities.

3.2 Event Monitors

In this case, the set of actions is computed in two steps. First, a reduction of the input E-history is computed and then the policy is applied to this reduced E-history to obtain a set of actions without conflicts.

The following algorithm computes

$$M_{ec}^P(E_1, \ldots, E_n) = (A_1, \ldots, A_n)$$

for some event-cancellation AC-monitor M_{ec}^P of P:

Event Cancellation Monitor **for** $i := 1$ **to** n **do**
  $E' := \emptyset$
  while true **do**
    select $e \in E_i - E'$
    such that $tail(T_P(E_1, \ldots, E_{i-1}, E' \cup \{e\})) \models AC$
    if select successful **then** $E' := E' \cup \{e\}$
    else break
  end
  $A_i := tail(T_P(E_1, \ldots, E_{i-1}, E'))$
end

The following algorithm computes

$$M_{ed}^P(E_1, \ldots, E_n) = (A_1, \ldots, A_n)$$

for some event-delay AC-monitor M_{ed}^P of P:

Event Delay Monitor $D := \emptyset$
  for $i := 1$ **to** n **do**
    $E' := \emptyset$
  while true **do**
    select $e \in D \cup E_i - E'$
    such that $tail(T_P(E_1, \ldots, E_{i-1}, E' \cup \{e\})) \models AC$
    if select successful **then** $E' := E' \cup \{e\}$
    else break
  end
  $A_i := tail(T_P(E_1, \ldots, E_{i-1}, E'))$
  $D := D \cup E_i - E'$
  end

Similar to action monitors, priorities of events can be incorporated into the event selection inside the **while** loops. There are also situations in which events cannot be ignored or delayed, for example time events always occur. persistent events can also be incorporated by never selecting them in algorithms. However, having persistent events may caused a policy to have no event cancellation monitors.

3.3   Computational Complexity

It is easy to see that all the above monitors can be computed in time polynomial in the number of events in the input E-history. In [9] we showed that the simulation problem for event-cancellation monitors of stateless $\mathcal{PDL}$ policies is NP-complete. That result does not contradict the above observation: The simulation problem requires the monitor to produce a given set of actions and thus is possibly more difficult than the problem of computing an arbitrary (maximal) monitor.

3.4   General Properties of Monitors

Note that according to the definitions, a monitor that cancels all the actions for any input is an AC-monitor for any policy P and set of constraints AC. It is even an action delay and an event delay monitor since the effect of such a monitor can be characterized as delaying the actions or the events for ever. However, it does not make sense to cancel (or delay) an action or an event if it is not involved in a conflict. If we could order the monitors in such a way that the higher the monitor in the order the closer its behavior is to the original policy, we would certainly like monitors that are maximal in this order. Such monitors would cancel or delay the minimum number of actions or events needed to eliminate conflicts. Furthermore, in the case of delay monitors, actions and events should be delayed as little as possible.

We have developed formal characterizations of the orders suitable for comparing monitors in all the classes discussed in this paper: action cancellation/delay and event cancellation/delay. We have proved that the monitors defined by Algorithms 1-4 are maximal in these orders. Details of the definitions and proofs can be found in [8].

4 Temporal Action Constraints

In many applications, it is natural to impose constraints not only on concurrent but also on sequential execution of actions. For example, some actions should (or shouldn't) appear in a specific order. This kind of constraint cannot be directly captured within the framework described so far. However, the appropriate extension is rather easy.

We add *temporal connectives* to the language of action constraints. We choose the past connectives of linear-time temporal logic [6]. The language of action constraints allows now not only action terms but also *action expressions*. An action expression is:

1. an action term,
2. **previous** a where a is an action expression (meaning "a was executed in the previous epoch"), or
3. a_1 **since** a_2 where a_1 and a_2 are action expressions (meaning "a_1 has been executed in every epoch since a_2 was executed").

Formally, we define satisfaction for temporal action constraints by extending Definition 10.

Definition 12. *Let a be an action expression, $ac \equiv$ "**never** $a_1 \wedge \ldots \wedge a_m$ **if** C"*
a temporal action constraint, and $\mathcal{H}_A = (A_1, \ldots, A_n)$ an A-history. Now

1. *$\mathcal{H}_A \models a$ iff:*
   (a) a is an action term and $A_n \models a$, or
   *(b) $a \equiv$ **previous** a' and $n > 1$ and $(A_1, \ldots, A_{n-1}) \models a'$, or*
   *(c) $a \equiv a'$ **since** a'' iff for some i, $1 \le i < n$, $(A_1, \ldots, A_i) \models a''$ and for all*
   j, $i < j \le n$, $(A_1, \ldots, A_j) \models a'$.
2. *$\mathcal{H}_A \models ac$ iff for every substitution δ, $C\delta$ is false or there is an i, $1 \le i \le m$,*
   $\mathcal{H}_A \not\models a_i\delta$.

Using this language, one can formulate constraints such as an action B shouldn't be executed before A as follows:

$$\textbf{never} \ \ A \wedge (true \ \textbf{since} \ B)$$

where *true* is an action executed in every epoch (there are several ways to define such an action).

The monitors defined in Section 3 should be appropriately generalized. Now action constraints need to be evaluated not only in the last state in a history but in the entire history. The techniques that automatically derive what kind of auxiliary historical information needs to be kept in every state to avoid looking at the entire history are well known [6].

5   System Implementation

In this section we present an algorithm for evaluating policies specified using $\mathcal{PDL}$. The algorithm is implemented as the Policy Engine of a Policy Server embedded in the "softswitch", a next generation switch for circuit and packet telephony networks, and has been used to implement policies for detecting alarm conditions, fail-overs, device configuration and provisioning, service class configuration, congestion control etc., [16]. This implementation covers the full version of $\mathcal{PDL}$, which is more general than the language we consider in the paper. The softswitch manages an unbounded number of policy servers that are able to run policies written in $\mathcal{PDL}$.[2] When a policy is loaded into a policy server the server creates a policy evaluator for the input policy, contacts the devices (i.e., routers, hubs, computers, etc.) that can potentially generate instances of the events of interest to the policy, and registers the interest with the devices. The registration happens at policy enabling points (PEPs) that wrap around the devices to act as interfaces between the devices and the policy servers. Events generated by a device are intercepted by its assigned PEP, translated into event terms and sent to the appropriate policy server. When an event arrives at a policy server, the server gives copies of the event to each policy evaluator that is running a policy that mentions the event. Each evaluator accumulates the events in a buffer and using a time constant T given to the evaluator during initialization, the evaluator groups events from the buffer into epochs based on the following criterion:

> An event e arriving at a buffer at time T_1 belongs to the same epoch than the previous event in the buffer if the difference between the time of the beginning of the previous event epoch and T_1 is less than or equal to T. Otherwise, the arriving event belongs to a new epoch and the beginning time of this new epoch is set to T_1. For the special case in which e is the first event sent to the evaluator, the first epoch is started with the beginning time also set to T_1.

Each policy evaluator runs with the appropriate epoch as input. The evaluator works by simulating the finite automata encoded in the *event* part of a policy rules. The transitions of the automata are labeled by set of primitive event symbols. Sequences are translated directly: there is a transition and a state per each conjunction of events in the sequence plus the initial state. For relax-sequences there is also a transition and a state per each conjunction of events, but in addition there is a self-loop transition coming out from each state that skips irrelevant events until the next conjunction of events in the relax-sequence appears.

We present the algorithm for a single policy rule since rules can be evaluated independently of one another. At any epoch t the algorithm maintains for the policy rule, the set $R(t)$ of all its possible distinct partial evaluations in the event history that may lead to the triggering of an action in a rule in some future epoch. We refer to these distinct partial evaluations as *active threads* and they are built

---

[2] It is bounded only by the capacity of the computers used.

as follows. Let a "sub-epoch" of an epoch refer to a subset of the primitive events in the epoch. Note that a "sub-epoch" is by definition an epoch. Given an E-history $\mathcal{E} = (E_1, \ldots, E_n)$, a sequence of "sub-epochs" $\mathcal{E}' = (E_1', \ldots, E_n')$ is a sub-history of $\mathcal{E}$ if and only if $E_i' \subseteq E_i$ for $1 \leq i \leq n$.

An active thread $A(t)$ at epoch t is maintained as a tuple $(A_1(t), A_2(t))$ where $A_1(t)$ is a path in the automaton for the event E of the policy rule and $A_2(t)$ is a sub-history (called the partial trace) of a suffix of the history at epoch t. The path $A_1(t)$ starts from an initial state of the automaton and is the path taken when the automaton is simulated on input $A_2(t)$. An active thread also carries with it the attribute values of the different events that come from the partial trace $A_2(t)$ and are necessary to evaluate the condition and the action of the policy rule. Note that an active thread may have, in a future epoch, enough information to fully evaluate the policy rule. The algorithm ensures that every active thread leads to a distinct evaluation of the policy rule. Each time an epoch is evaluated new threads are started and active threads are moved or killed according to their location in the automata. Details of the algorithm and complexity results on policy evaluation can be found in [3]. Following the policy evaluations, each policy evaluator returns a set of actions. The server takes these actions and sends them to the appropriate PEPs which translate them into device-specific operations. The architecture of the server is depicted in Figure 1. The system is completely written in Java except for some parts of the PEPs which are device-dependent.

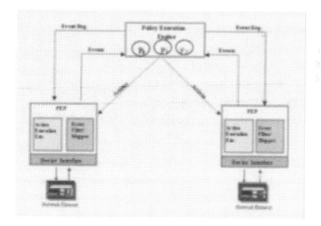

Fig. 1. System Architecture

Given that monitors, like policies, are prefix-closed, we can compute the A-history output by the monitor incrementally: when a new epoch is input only the new action set of the corresponding expanded A-history is computed.

To implement an action cancellation monitor we only need to intercept the set of actions generated by a policy evaluator each time an epoch is evaluated.

Then, we run the **while** loop in Algorithm 3.1 setting U to be the set of actions returned by the evaluator and $i = n$. The actual action set sent to the PEPs is the resulting set A_n.

To implement an event cancellation monitor, following Algorithm 3.2, E_i is set to the current epoch, and $T_P((E_1, \ldots, E_{i-1}, E' \cup \{e\}))$ is replaced by a simulation of the policy evaluation with $E' \cup \{e\}$ as the input epoch. The simulation is done to trap the actions triggered by the epoch and check whether the set of action constraints AC is violated. If the AC set is violated, the selection fails and a new event has to be selected. After all the events from E_i have been covered and E' has been completed, an actual execution (not a simulation) of the policy evaluation is done with E'. The set of actions generated by the execution is sent to the PEPs.

The implementation of delay monitors is a little bit trickier since the information that events or actions are being delayed must be passed from the current epoch to the next epoch. This effect is achieved by introducing "fake" events and new rules triggered by these events into the policy. In the case of action delay we introduce a new event symbol e_a for every action symbol a with the same arity as a. Also, we extend the original policy P to an extended policy P' that contains all the rules of P plus a rule of the from "$e_a(X_1 \ldots, X_n)$ **causes** $a(X_1 \ldots, X_n)$" for each action symbol a. If an action $a(t_1, \ldots, t_n)$ is ignored, the corresponding event $e_a(t_1, \ldots, t_n)$ will be added to the next epoch by the policy evaluator.

Similarly, for event delay, we introduce a new event symbol e' for every original event e. Also, we extend the original policy P to an extended policy P' that contains all the rules of P plus the copies of the rules in P in which every event e is replaced by e'. When an event is ignored, the event e' is added to the incoming epoch. If the event e' is ignored again, the same e' is added to the next epoch.

6   Related Work

Conflict resolution for production rules in AI and databases has been addressed in [1,4,12]. Results about the complexity of testing consistency of production rules can be found in [5]. However, in contrast to our view, those works assume interpreted actions (variable assignments or database updates) and mostly ignore the event part of the rules. Also, conflicts are typically between rules, not actions. The work in [13] deals with a model that is closer to ours, although the conflicts studied are still between rules, not actions, and the events are not taken into account.

The notion of *action constraints* was independently introduced in [7] and [11]. Conflict resolution is only one of the many issues addressed in [11] and the authors limit themselves to proposing a construct equivalent to maximal action cancellation monitors for stateless policies. Event cancellation, sequence events, conflict resolution through delay, or temporal action constraints are not considered.

7 Conclusions

In this paper we have studied conflict resolution for history-based policies. We have defined monitors (procedures for resolving action conflicts) and identified several dimensions of monitors: action vs. event-based (introduced in [9] in the context of stateless policies), cancellation vs. delay-based (new). We have provided polynomial algorithms for computing maximal monitors in each class.

The techniques presented in this paper can be generalized to more general policies. For instance, handling negated events in history-based policies can be done along the same lines as in stateless policies [9]. The solution proposed there is based on making ignored events undefined, as opposed to making their negations true.

We envision several directions for future research. It should be worthwhile to study further classes of monitors, in particular *hybrid* monitors that allow cancellation of some events and delay of others. Another direction is static analysis of policies. Perhaps some policies never lead to conflicts – for them monitors represent an unnecessary overhead. This question becomes interesting in the presence of negated events or additional information about events. Work on detecting statically potential conflicts is reported in [15]. This work might be useful to generate the action constraints we need as input for the monitors. Still another direction consists of studying the expressive power of different subsets of $\mathcal{PDL}$.

References

1. R. Agrawal, R. Cochrane, and B. G. Lindsay. On maintaining priorities in a production rule system. In *VLDB*, pages 479–487, 1991.
2. C. Baral, J. Lobo, and G. Trajcevski. Formal characterizations of active databases: II. In *Proc. of the International Conference on Deductive and Object Oriented Databases*, Lecture Notes in Computer Science. Springer, Switzerland, December 1997.
3. R. Bhatia, J. Lobo, and M. Kohli: Policy Evaluation for Network Management. In *Proc. of the 19th Conference on Computer Communication*, INFOCOM 2000. Israel, March 2000.
4. L. Brownston, R. Farell, E. Kant, and N. Martin. *Programming Expert Systems in OPS5: An Introduction to Rule-Based Programming.* Addison-Wesley, 1985.
5. H. Kleine Büning, U. Löwen, and S. Schmitgen. Inconsistency of production systems. *Journal of Data and Knowledge Engineering*, 3:245–260, 1988/89.
6. J. Chomicki. Efficient Checking of Temporal Integrity Constraints Using Bounded History Encoding. *ACM Transactions on Database Systems*, 20(2):149–186, June 1995.
7. J. Chomicki, J. Lobo, and S. Naqvi. Axiomatic conflict resolution in policy management. Technical Report ITD-99-36448R, Bell Labs, February 1999.
8. J. Chomicki and J. Lobo. Monitors for History-Based Policies. Technical report, Lucent Bell Labs, 2000.
9. J. Chomicki, J. Lobo, and S. Naqvi. A Logic Programming Approach to Conflict Resolution in Policy Management. In *International Conference on Principles of Knowledge Representation and Reasoning*, Breckenridge, Colorado, April 2000.

10. T. Eiter and V.S. Subrahmanian. Heterogeneous active agents, II: Algorithms and complexity. *Artificial Intelligence*, 108:257–307, March 1999.
11. T. Eiter, V.S. Subrahmanian, and G. Pick. Heterogeneous active agents, I: Semantics. *Artificial Intelligence*, 108:179–255, March 1999.
12. Y. E. Ioannidis and T. K. Sellis. Supporting inconsistent rules in database systems. *Journal of Intelligent Information Systems*, 1(3/4), 1992.
13. H. V. Jagadish, A. O. Mendelzon, and I. S. Mumick. Managing conflicts between rules. In *Proc. 15th ACM SIGACT/SIGMOD Symposium on Principles of Database Systems*, pages 192–201, 1996.
14. J. Lobo, R. Bhatia, and S. Naqvi. A policy description language. In *Proc. of AAAI*, Orlando, FL, July 1999.
15. E. C. Lupu and M. Sloman. Conflict analysis for management policies. In R. Stadler A. Lazar, R. Saraco, editor, *Proc. 5th IFIP/IEEE International Symposium on Integrated Network Management*, pages 430–443, 1997.
16. A. Virmani, J. Lobo, and M. Kohli. NETMON: Network management for the SARAS softswitch. In *Proc. of the IEEE/IFIP Network Operations and Management Symposium*, April 2000.

A Type/Domain Security Policy for Internet Transmission, Sharing, and Archiving of Medical and Biological Data

Roberto Viviani

Abteilung Psychiatrie III, Universitätsklinik Ulm, Leimgrubenweg 12, D-89075 Ulm,
Germany
roberto.viviani@medizin.uni-ulm.de
http://www.psychiatrie.uni-ulm.de

Abstract. We present a security model to regulate the exchange and pooling of medical information over a wide-area distributed system. The policy is an abstraction of the principles that guided the implementation of such a system at the University of Ulm. The entities introduced to express the policy are defined by the ethical and legal constraints imposed on a medical informatics system. This policy regulates bulk data interactions between cooperating organizations. As such, it is designed to supplement other security policies regulating access to information at a finer granularity within each of the organizations taking part in the exchange. As an example of such integration, we compare it with the guidelines of the British Medical Association.

1 Background

This security policy grew from the experience gained from designing and implementing a system for the on-line exchange of clinical data between psychiatric departments. The system, developed at the Department of Psychiatry of the University of Ulm, was designed to address a number of functional and legal requirements:

- The system was designed to support quality management, where information on the medical progress of patients from different medical institutions must be pooled and compared.
- Similarly, scientific research with the collaboration of several organizations was another goal that required pooling of clinical data.
- Clinicians on the wards needed real time access to relevant data.
- Much of the data was produced by direct input, with the patients themselves logging on to the system.
- The security model of the system was primarily determined by the necessity to comply with the Directive of the European Union [1], the guidelines of the Council of Europe on medical data [2], and the German Federal State on data privacy [3].

At first, the system was designed by trying to comply with all the stated requirements in an *ad hoc* fashion. It was soon realised, however, that adding an abstract level of indirection between requirements and implementation, namely a security policy, would lead to a cleaner design. For example, it helped to distinguish

M. Sloman, J. Lobo, and E. Lupu (Eds.): POLICY 2001, LNCS 1995, pp. 73–87, 2001.

the decisions that had to be taken because of legal requirements from those which instead followed only from implementation convenience.

More importantly, the policy is an instrument of communication at a high level. The adoption of a system such as the one described must be approved by the relevant authorities in each of the cooperating organizations. Given the legal responsibilities associated with such a decision, the designer must be able to explain to management what the system will do as clearly, succinctly and unambiguously as possible. This can be done much more effectively through a policy rather than through a less structured and more verbose description of the system's functionality. It also becomes easier to split the responsibilities: the managers must ensure that the stated policy is acceptable to their organizations given the existing ethical, legal and efficiency constraints; the designers and implementers must ensure that the system they build respects the agreed policy.

Organizations taking part in data exchange are likely to have their own internal security policy. However, such security policies, or the effect of considering them collectively, will not usually specify the security settings of the exchange of data between organizations. Medical establishments protect themselves with firewalls that prevent inbound and especially outbound flows of information. To exchange information over the Internet, dedicated trusted applications must be written to handle the information flow. Each new application, or any change to an existing application, must be certified separately as to its compliance with existing regulations. Where the controlling authorities of the involved exchange sites differ, the certification process must in principle be repeated (in Germany, each *Land* has its own authority). What is needed is a high-level common policy to regulate information flow among administratively independent organizations. Each organization should be able to agree to the terms of the policy independently, thus opening the way for interconnection and interoperability.

The security policy model we present here was formulated with this goal. It was originally developed as an abstraction of the software system; several stepwise refinements in one influenced the other and vice versa, and we still consider the present version a work in progress. We present it here with the intent of stimulating debate and soliciting the critical scrutiny of the scientific community.

2 Legislative Framework

The protection of sensitive data is currently regulated by the national laws of several European countries. However, the development of on-line services constitutes a challenge to a nationally based regulatory system. The broad diffusion of such services, the rapid pace of change, and the nature of the Internet all tend to disregard territorial boundaries. Fortunately, at least in Europe, most legislation is inspired by the same core set of principles as set out in a small number of international documents such as the Council of Europe's Convention No. 108 [4], OECD's privacy guidelines [5], and the Recommendation of the European Council on Medical Data [2]. Furthermore, the European Union is actively engaged in a process of harmonization of national legislation, and has already issued specific directives to this end (Directive 95/46/EC of the European Parliament [1] – hereinafter „Directive"). These documents constitute a consistent regulatory framework towards which national legislation is expected to converge [6]. One of the main goals of a security policy for the transmission and sharing of medical and biological data over the Internet is to formulate security constraints in ways that highlight their relationship to the relevant regulatory issues. Three critical issues in European data protection law affect the way in which sharing and transmission of data should be constrained.

- The first issue concerns the obligations and responsibilities for the treatment of personal information. The crucial requirement is that personal information should be collected for specific and legitimate purposes, and that any further use of such information should be compatible with those purposes ([1], Art. 6.1.a and Art. 6.1.b; [4], Art. 5). An important exception to this principle is the subsequent use of data for scientific research ([1], Paragraph 29 of the Introduction, Art. 6.1.b., and Art. 6.1.e. Exemptions applicable to scientific research are also considered in [4], Art. 9.3). The Directive mandates the regulation of use of data for research purposes to national legislation. In general, it is safe to assume that only anonymous data may be used for scientific research unless explicit consent was given by the subject to this further use ([1] Art. 6.1.e; [5], Art. 12). The German law on data privacy [3], for example, requires that data used for scientific purposes be made anonymous as soon as practically possible. Because of the legal and practical importance of anonymization, our security policy contains a specific mechanism for the anonymization of data.

- The second issue is the need for special protection of sensitive data, a category that includes medical information ([4], Art. 6). The Directive prohibits the processing of medical data unless it is part of prevention, diagnosis, treatment, or the management of health-care services by professionals bound by professional secrecy ([1], Art. 8.3). The Recommendation No.R (97) 5 of the European Council explicitly limits the use of genetic data to medical or scientific research purposes ([2], Art. 4.7-4.9). The British Medical Association's Guidelines for clinical security emphasise that special precautions must be taken with respect of psychiatric information, HIV status, and contraceptive status [7]. However, the special protection accorded to medical data does not invalidate the provisions for its further use in scientific research.

- The third issue is the requirement for personal information to be processed transparently. Art. 10 of the Directive demands the notification of the collection of personal information to the individual concerned. Similarly, the guidelines adopted by the British Medical Association [8, 9] state that the individual should be notified of each change in the list of principals that have access to her data. Furthermore, several articles of the Directive demand the institution of controlling authorities. Hence, it is desirable that the operations on any personal database system be open and understandable to such authorities.

The first fundamental concept of the security policy we propose is the notion of *domain*. In its intended use, a domain will be an organization or part of an organization with a clearly defined professional or statutory role. For example, individual hospitals, private firms offering administrative or quality control services to hospitals, analysis laboratories, are all candidate domains in an interconnected system. Because of their clearly defined role, the legitimacy of the collection and use of data within each domain should be easily established.

By being expressed at the level of domains, security requirements are specified at a very coarse level of granularity. This has two consequences. Firstly, it enhances transparency because it makes data access decisions explicit at a level where the degree of complexity is low. Secondly, since the security policy does not specify security constraints within individual domains, it needs to be complemented with other security models. Hence, to be effective, the policy and its implementations should be orthogonal to any additional security system that is in operation within each domain. We shall refer to such infra-domain security policies as 'partner security policies', meaning that each partner domain in the global inter-domain network may have implemented its own internal security model. We envisage our security policy imposing constraints that add to any other existing security constraint in the partner security policies and that enable inspection of the appropriateness of inter-domain data exchange. We will discuss the orthogonality of our security policy to the lattice security model [10] in section 5. To further illustrate this point, we will examine the integration of our security policy with the Interim Guidelines of the British Medical Association [7].

The second concept we introduce is that of *type*. Because of their different roles, organizations will be entitled to access different types of data. This is relevant to the legitimacy of data exchange, as all regulatory frameworks and ethical considerations authorize the diffusion and use of sensitive data only for a specific purpose. Furthermore, different types of data may call for different security requirements. The appropriateness of data exchange between organizations can be monitored because data access decisions are taken for each type separately, so that the legitimacy of the exchange can be judged with respect of the purposes of the organizations belonging to each domain.

The notion of type is also useful to address the problem of anonymization. Personal information such as name, surname and date of birth will be classified into a specific type. By suitably restricting access to information of this type, an anonymized view of the underlying data is obtained. This type of anonymization is sufficient for the purposes of most collaborative research projects.

Finally, in the policy we include an auditing mechanism, which provides the basic tool with which a notification mechanism may be built.

3 Specification

The security policy we describe is similar to the Domain and Type Enforcement (DTE) policy proposed by Badger and coll. [11, 12]. Like DTE, our policy is aimed at formulating uniform security restrictions for entire sets of data and user groups, and is meant to be integrated with an existing security policy with as little impact on the user as possible. Our policy, however, differs from DTE in that we formalize the role of the domains where information originated as the administrators of the access rights to that information. There are as many nodes in which access rights are defined as there are domains where data are generated. In contrast, DTE centralizes access rights definition within a single, global table. Furthermore, the goal of our policy is to formulate the minimal set of requirements that express the constraints contained in the legislation, while DTE constitutes a general-purpose security model.

The definitions used to specify the type/domain security policy are summarized in Table 1 at the end of this section.

3.1 Basic Definitions

All information that is subject to the policy shall be classified as belonging to one, and at most one, *security type* (there is no practical limit to the number of security types the system supports). Let T be the set of all security types. If I is the set of all atoms of information, then T partitions I. Examples of I might be text, digitized images, persisted recordsets, tagged elements of an XLM document, etc. Examples of T might be „clinical data", „identity data", „administrative data", etc.

At all times, each element of I is contained in one or more of a number of *domains* (again, there is not practical limit to the number of available domains). Let D be the set of all domains. Each element of D therefore defines a subset of I (the atoms of information contained in each domain). Domains are introduced to model organizations or parts of organizations with a definite purpose in the collection and processing of data. Examples of domains might be „St. John's Hospital", „the accounting offices of St. Mary's Hospice", „The Hill Road General Practice", „Quality Control Partners Ltd.".

At all times, each atom of information shall belong to one, and at most one, *security group*. We define the set G of all possible security groups as follows. For each element d of D there exists a subset of I that we shall indicate as c(d), containing the items of I that were created in domain d. The set C of all c(d) is a partition of I. Each security group g is obtained as the intersection of an item of C and an item of T. It trivially follows that the set G of all security groups is a set of subsets of I, and a partition of I. Conceptually, we are modeling as security groups such sets as „the information atoms of type identity data created at St. John's Hospital", „the information atoms of type quality control data created by Quality Control Partners", etc. If types and domains are configured appropriately, a security group captures the security requirements of information in terms of the place and the purposes of its collection. As we shall see, a security group is the smallest entity for which we can define distinct access rights. We will refer to the domain of a security group as the *administrator domain* of elements of I belonging to that security group.

3.2 Access Rights

Let M be the set of all information access modalities. The members of M are {read, write}. Let R be the set of all subsets of M. R defines all *access rights*.

For each domain, access rights for each security group shall be specified. There shall be an *access function* from G x D to R, whose value r for any given tuple (g, d) will determine the access rights r for domain d with respect to data in group g. We will refer to the domain who is trying to access data in a group as the *receiving domain*. As an example, assume that g is „clinical data created at St. John's Hospital" and d is „St. John's Hospital's Outpatient Clinic". Then r(g, d) may return {read}, allowing the outpatient clinic to follow up patients discharged from the wards. In another example, data traveling through the Internet are implicitly placed within a domain that has no access rights for all elements of G.

The set of access modalities returned by the access function shall be decided only by the administrator domain of the security group. Administrators or users of the receiving domain shall not change the value returned by the access function so as to enlarge the access rights of the receiving domains. For example, an implementation shall ensure that viewing an atom of information as if it belonged to a type or an administrator domain for which the receiving domain has access will not result in unwarranted access to the atom. Hence in a large, distributed system involving several organizations, administrators of each organization do not have to be trusted to refrain from attempting to gain access to information to which the organization is not entitled.

3.3 Anonymization

We refer to security types that contain identification data such as surname, name, date of birth, etc. as *identification types*.

An administrator domain may specify that for a given security group no read access will ever be returned by the access function. When applied to the identity type, this specification corresponds to the notion of irreversible anonymization.

In certain cases, the information contained in an identification type may be useful even no access is granted to it. For example, a research site may set up a database where the primary key of the patients table is the identification type. If the research site has no read access to the type, the database is said to be anonymized.

3.4 Reclassification

If the receiving domain has read access to a security group of a first type and is the administrator domain of a second security group, then information of the first security group may be *reclassified* into the second security group.

3.5 Auditing

The system shall provide an auditing facility to monitor access operations.

4 Implementation

Our implementation is based on the idea of building a set of trusted components that administered a set of cryptographic keys. Information to be retrieved from an archive or the Internet has to go through these components, which ensure that information remains in encrypted form unless the key for its decryption is known. Likewise, the components will permit archiving or sending information to the Internet only if it can be encrypted, an operation for which the encryption key is needed. Access to information is controlled by encoding information with different security requirements with different keys, and controlling the distribution of the keys among the connected nodes.

Table 1. Entities defined in the type/domain security policy specification

Security type	An attribute of each atom of information classifying it in terms of security requirements, including those regulated by the law. Each atom belongs to one and only one security type
Identification type	The security type classifying personal information data, which by the law are subject to special regulations
Domain	An attribute of the location of atoms of information, such as the objects of the partner security policy, an archival medium, the Internet. When attributes of the objects of a partner security policy, domains classify locations belonging to the same organization or part of an organization with a definite purpose in the collection and use of data. Atoms must at all times be located in a domain
Administrator domain	The domain where an atom of information was created, and which owns the atom's security group
Receiving domain	The domain where an atom of information is located
Security group	An attribute of each atom of information composed of the atom's security type and the domain in which the atom was created
Access function	A function defined for each domain and security group specifying the access rights to atoms of information. The function is invoked with the receiving domain and the security group of the atom to be accessed
Reclassification	The operation by which the security type of an atom of information is changed

4.1 Basic Issues, Creation of Information

Information is kept in encrypted form until it is accessed. Thus, the implementation does not need to control how information flows, as it cannot be accessed unless the encryption keys are known.

Each atom of information is tagged by the system to mark its security group. The tag consists of the security type to which the atom belongs and the name of the administrator domain.

Each administrator domain creates and maintains a set of keys for each type of information that is created in the domain. Atoms of information are never kept in their native, unencrypted form, but are encrypted using an asymmetric encryption algorithm as soon as possible after creation. After encryption, each atom of information is tagged. Once encrypted, the atom of information cannot be accessed unless the encryption keys are known.

The regular user in the domain has no access to the encryption keys. Administration of the encryption keys is reserved to the administrators of the domains, and to a selected group of users in charge with the verification of the system. Instead, the regular user implicitly selects the encryption key by generating or accessing information of a specific type.

For creation of information as well as for any other access operation, the system relies on a partner security policy in the selection of authorized users. Similarly, the appropriate configuration of the firewall isolating the components that implement the policy in internet-enabled applications must be verified independently.

4.2 Access Rights

Each receiving domain maintains a table of administrator domains and types. The system provides a facility through which the private (read) and public (write) keys of the encryption algorithm used by each administrator domain for each type can be written (or deleted) in the table. There are several ways in which this could happen. In one scenario, the administrators of the domain are simply told the keys. In a more complicated scenario, the keys themselves will be encrypted; the system may then be initialized with the appropriate keys by the administrators, who would however ignore the value of the keys.

The system also provides a facility through which administrators or special users entrusted with control roles may verify what security groups can be accessed in the receiving domain.

Whenever an atom of information must be accessed, the system reads the tag of the atom to determine its security group, then looks up the appropriate encryption key in the table. If the private key is found, then the atom of information is decrypted, and read access is granted. If the public key is found, the encryption algorithm may be applied to the atom of information, and write access is granted.

Because access to an atom of information depends on using the right encryption key, changing the security tag of the atom of information will not result in unwarranted access.

The implementation ensures that information will at all times be contained within a domain by implicitly considering the space outside domains as a domain with no keys.

4.3 Anonymization

When irreversible anonymization is desired, a one-way algorithm is used instead of asymmetric encryption. There is only one key, the write key, which is concatenated with the in-clear content of the atom of information before being given to the one-way function. The value returned by the function might also be used in a database application as the primary key of patient records, irrespective of the access rights of the domain where the database is held.

4.4 Reclassification

Reclassification is not an additional feature of the system requiring special implementation mechanisms. Instead, its mention in the specification alerts to an unavoidable consequence of distributing reading rights to receiving domains. This consequence must be taken into consideration when reviewing the appropriateness of the distribution of access rights among organizations.

4.5 Auditing

Since the system must fetch the values of encryption keys on behalf of the user to access information, key requests may be hooked to provide auditing facilities. A requirement of electronic medical records in [9] is that the patient be notified of who has accessed her information; auditing is the basic tool to implement this requirement.

4.6 Integrity

To protect the integrity of the data transmitted through the Internet, we implemented the SKID3 protocol for authentication of the TCP/IP connections [13]. Each atom of information is also hashed with a key and the value of a message counter; the hash is transmitted with the atom to ensure data were not modified under way.

5 Orthogonality with Partner Security Policies

In this section we will informally discuss the issue of integration with partner security policies. This is an important issue as the type/domain policy only addresses the security concerns related to the transmission of data through the Internet. Hence, in practical applications it is crucial to understand the division of tasks between policies.

For our purposes, a partner security policy is characterized by the degree of detail with which access is specified, in contrast to the coarse level in which access is specified in the type/domain security policy. Furthermore, because our implementation sets no requirements in information flow, the partner security policy has a free hand to control it. The role of the partner security policy is that of ensuring that information does not fall in the wrong hands within an organization comprising one or more domains.

Since the type/domain security policy regulates the exchange of information between domains, the names of types and domains are shared across the whole network of interconnected organizations, while the names given to security entities in the partner security policy will presumably be valid only within each organization. Hence, it is desirable that the security groups of the type/domain security policy are represented in the partner security policy so as to allow administrators to easily integrate the information flowing through the firewall with permission rules within the local area network. For example, if a security type includes clinical information, we will want to allow only users belonging to the clinicians group to have access to it.

By contrast, it is not necessary that the security entities of the partner security policy be represented in the type/domain policy, as usually such entities will be specific to each local area network.

For the purposes of our discussion, we will assume that the partner security policy can be represented by a generic access control mechanism as summarized in the lattice model studied by Denning [10]. In the lattice model, *processes* (the active agents responsible for information flow) and *objects* containing information are associated to *security classes*. A Boolean *flow relation* function is defined on pairs of security classes to specify if information is permitted to flow from the first to the second argument. In an access control system, the security class of each process establishes the lowest security class of the object to which the process can write, and the highest security class of the object from which it can read. A *class-combining operator* is defined for the case of a process accessing more than one object at the same time for a read or a write operation. For example, when process p attempts to read from object a and b, the class combining operator is applied to the security classes of a and b, returning a security class that can be used with the flow relation function to determine if the operation should be permitted. In what follows, we will use Denning's terminology consistently to refer to the lattice model to avoid confusing its conceptual entities from those belonging to the type/domain model.

Two conditions must be satisfied to ensure the orthogonality of the two policies. The first condition requires that each process of the lattice model be confined to a single domain. Typically, this condition is ensured by protecting the networks of each organization with a firewall, as it was the case in our implementation. The second condition requires that each atom of information of the type/domain security policy be contained in an object. Containment of information in a secure object is generally guaranteed by the implementation of the partner security policy. If these two conditions are satisfied, then the access rights are determined by the security classes of the process, the domain in which the process runs, the object being accessed, and the security group(s) of the type(s) of information contained in the object. Access will be permitted according to the most restrictive subset of the access rights determined by the flow relation function in the partner security policy and the access function in the type/domain policy. In our implementation, most restrictive access is guaranteed by the fact that irrespective of the security class of a process or object, information cannot be encrypted or decrypted unless the respective keys are known.

Our implementation additionally allows the partner security policy to associate a security class to the security groups themselves. This enables the security groups of the type/domain security policy to be represented in the partner security policy. Administrators can assign access rights in the partner security policy at the level of security types. Conceptually, the class-combining operator of the lattice model is applied to the security class of the security type and to the security class of the object containing the information. In our implementation, access control lists are bound to the encryption keys and to the processes that access the encryption keys on behalf of the user.

As an illustration of how we envisage our security policy being integrated with a partner security policy, we will here consider the model proposed by Anderson [8, 9], to which we will refer as the 'medical model'. In the medical model, the smallest entity for which access rights are defined is the single field, or a group of fields, of a single record containing data about a patient. This entity is called 'clinical record' although it is logically equivalent to a subset of the whole record; hence, the whole record of a patient will consist of one or more clinical records. Splitting the whole record is a key aspect of the medical model, because access control lists can then be set separately for each clinical record. For example, data about a patient might be split into three clinical records: a generic one open to all clinicians in the practice; a highly sensitive record containing psychiatric details that is only open to the patient's GP; a record of heart disease open to clinicians and casualty staff.

The medical model specifies a series of rules to establish which users should be on the control list of the clinical records. This aspect of the policy must strike a balance between keeping the list as short as possible and providing for the considerable turnover of clinicians and staff, especially during on call duties, that is typical of large hospitals [14]. One of the clinicians is charged with the responsibility of adding and removing users from the control lists of the clinical records of a specific patient. A rule is also specified to constrain information flow between clinical records. These rules are a good example of what should be handled by the partner security policy because of the level of granularity at which they are specified (the single medical record).

By contrast, the sets of fields making up the clinical records (generic clinical data, details on psychiatric treatment, data relevant to emergency treatment) are good candidate security types, and the described organizational entities (the general practice, an individual GP, casualty) are good candidate domains. In addition, the type/domain security policy would isolate personal data in a type of its own. Auditors and researchers may have read access rights to clinical information as appropriate, but not to information belonging to the identity type.

Our policy helps where the medical model registers the existence of a problem without offering a definitive solution. The medical model requires the institution of effective measures to prevent the aggregation of personal health information. There is an important logical difference, however, between deciding which doctors should have access to the record of an individual patient and deciding that psychiatric information in general should not be available to all departments. Using the same mechanisms that implement control on individual records to regulate aggregation places a double burden on the clinician responsible for the access lists. In addition, the decisions of each clinician would not necessarily be mutually consistent. As a remedy, in the medical model aggregation is controlled *a posteriori* through the inspection of an auditing trail. The type/domain security policy centralizes aggregation permissions so as to prevent invalid aggregation operations and to facilitate independent review.

Another source of concern mentioned by Anderson is the effective anonymity of clinical databases from which personal information has been removed, as malicious queries on such databases may succeed in inferring the identity of certain subjects. These concerns can be in part addressed by creating a specific security type for the clinical information that is prone to the inference problem. Appropriately different access restrictions can then be set for such information.

6 A Case Study

We briefly present here a case study illustrating how the security policy may be applied. The case study consists of a system for quality management being developed at the Department of Psychiatry of the University of Ulm.

Quality management is a field where computerized, internet-enabled systems offer great prospects of innovation but also present great challenges to data privacy. Quality management consists of the review of the effectiveness of the care administered in individual medical institutions. To be carried out effectively, quality management must collect data from health professionals as well as from patients. These data must be collected across institutions, as data are analyzed comparing hospitals, not patients. Data related to quality management need not be personal and constitute an identifiable type in our security model.

Because of a certain aura of boredom surrounding quality management, we have attempted to integrate the data collection system with clinical activities. This means that the data collected from patients about their treatment are immediately made available to clinicians who can use them to monitor and if necessary adjust their treatment. Our goal was to increase motivation and commitment of both patients and staff to the quality review process. However, to be useful on the wards, such quality control data do need to be coupled with personal information identifying the patients from which they stem. Thus, we decided to include data belonging to the identification type in our collection process.

A domain was set up to contain the database of quality management information. Information is exchanged between this database and each institution participating in the quality management program. This domain was initialized with the read access permission for the quality data type. Two domains were set up in each clinic that decided to make use of the system. The first domain was given read and write permission for the identification type, as well as read permissions for the quality data type. This first domain is used by clinicians on the wards to monitor data generated by patients. The second domain includes terminals freely accessible on the wards on which patients can log on to answer questions on the efficacy of their treatment. This domain was initialized only with write permissions for both data types.

As soon as they are generated, quality control data are shipped to the central domain maintaining the database. Identity data are read automatically from the German insurance card that patients insert in a chip card reader to initiate the session and sent to both the central database domain and the domain of the clinicians. In the central database domain, identity data are just binary values indexing the records of patients. In the domain of the clinicians identity data are available in both clear and encrypted form. Whenever a clinician wants to look up the data on a patient, the application generates a query selecting the record indexed by the encrypted identity data from the central database. The record is shipped to the workstation on the clinic and displayed.

Because distinct domains are allocated to each clinic, patients moving from one to another clinic maintain separate identities. This follows from the fact that the write keys of the identity type differ between the domains of each clinic. However, if a clinic is constituted by separate physical parts, such as buildings placed in different parts of town (as it is often the case with outpatient services), all these parts can be configured to belong to the same domain. In this case, data relating to a patient automatically follow the patient in her movements between the parts. As soon as the patient logs on in the new building, workstations in the clinical domain will generate a query on the identity data that will retrieve all quality control data generated in the domain.

7 Final Comments

In considering the utility of this security policy, it is important to bear in mind the necessity of its integration with its partner security policy, such as one based on access control lists. This necessity determines the area of application of this security policy, the type of security concerns it is supposed to address, and by converse the threats that it cannot effectively contain. In practical applications it is crucial to understand the division of tasks between policies.

An important matter of concern in this respect is the uncontrollable extension of rights from users or administrators within organizations through the indiscriminate use of reclassification mechanisms. We should point out that, while this possibility is real, it stems from problems originating within a domain, rather than in the exchange of data between domains. In many practical contexts, it is the transmission of data via Internet, and not the integrity of individual medical organizations, that is the source of much anxiety. In our case study, the partner security policy ensured that only users belonging to the clinicians group could initiate the query operation by controlling access to the identity type keys and the files containing identity data.

Several limitations of our security policy emerge in the comparison with DTE. The type/domain policy limits access rights and interactions between domains to read and write permissions. DTE, by contrast, contains provisions for a more extensive set of rights such as execute, signal, destroy, etc. The limitations of our policy mirror the more restricted use for which it is envisaged. While DTE is designed to run on a UNIX system, potentially permeating each operation, our policy prevalently addresses the security needs of interacting applications sitting on the respective firewalls.

On the positive side, these same limitations also carry some benefits. Our policy has a more limited impact on an existing system than DTE, supporting the cooperation of organizations with potentially different operating systems and partner security policy configurations. Furthermore, information that is not being accessed is automatically placed in an implicit domain with no access permissions. This greatly reduces the assumptions that have to be made about the security requirements of the environment in which information is located. Finally, our policy is flexible with respect of the scheme with which new types are created. In a network of three interconnected organizations, for example, two of them can autonomously decide to create a new type for a common scientific project without having any impact on the settings of the third organization. In another example, a single organization may decide to create its own type for data that it does not want to share with anybody else. DTE, like any other security model that relies on a centralized access control system, requires a stricter coordination between the nodes of the network. In our case study, the impact on the existing partner security policy was limited. It was only necessary to create a special account to protect the encryption keys. The processes that are part of the TCB of the partner/domain policy implementation run under this account. To integrate exchangable information with the partner security policy, it was only necessary to set up permissions for the clinicians group so as to allow its members to handle identity type data.

Acknowledgments

I thank Frank Stajano, whose discussion of this paper has been invaluable. Without him this work would have not been possible. The development of the quality management project has been partially sponsored by Janssen-Cilag.

References

1. Council Directive 95/46/EC of the European Parliament and of the Council of 24 Oct. 1995 on the Protection of Individuals with Regard to the Processing of Personal Data and on the Free Movement of Such Data, Official Journal no. L281 **31** (1995). Available at http://europa.eu.int/comm/internal_market/en/media/dataprot/index.htm (visited November 7, 2000)
2. Recommendation No.R (97) 5 and Explanatory Memorandum of the Committee of Ministers on the Protection of Medical Data. The European Council (1997). Available at http://www.coe.fr/dataprotection/rec/r(97)5e.htm (visited July 29, 2000)
3. Gesetz zur Fortentwicklung der Datenverarbeitung und des Datenschutzes vom 20. Dezember 1990, BGBl. I S. 2954, 2955, zuletzt geändert durch das Gesetz zur Neuordnung des Postwesens und der Telekommunikation vom 14. September 1994, BGBl. I S. 2325. Available at http://www.rewi.hu-berlin.de/Datenschutz/Gesetze/bdsg.html (visited July 30, 2000)
4. Council of Europe, Convention for the Protection of Individuals with Regard to Automatic Processing of Personal Data, Jan. 28, 1981, EUR. T.S. No. 108, reprinted in 20 I.L.M. **377** (1981). Also available at http://www.coe.fr/eng/legaltxt/108e.htm (visited July 1, 2000)
5. O.E.C.D., Recommendations of the Council Concerning Guidelines Governing the Protection of Privacy and Transborder Flows of Personal Data, O.E.C.D. Doc. C58 (final) (Oct. 1, 1980), reprinted in 20 I.L.M. **422** (1981). Available at http://www.oecd.org/dsti/sti/it/secur/prod/PRIV-EN.htm (visited March 28, 1999)
6. Reidenberg, J.R., Schwartz, P.M.: Data Protection Law and On-Line Services: Regulatory Responses. European Commission (1998). Available at http://europa.eu.int/comm/internal_market/en/media/dataprot/studies/regul.pdf (visited July 29, 2000)
7. Anderson, R.J.: Clinical System Security: Interim Guidelines. British Medical Journal **312** (1996) 109-111. Available at http://www.cl.cam.ac.uk/~rja14/#Med (visited July 30, 2000)
8. Anderson, R.J.: A Security Policy Model for Clinical Information Systems. Presented at the 1996 IEEE Symposium on Security and Privacy. Available at http://www.cl.cam.ac.uk/~rja14/#Med (visited July 30, 2000)
9. Anderson, R.J.: Security in Clinical Information Systems. Published by the British Medical Association (1996). Available at http://www.cl.cam.ac.uk/~rja14/#Med (visited July 30, 2000)
10. Denning, D.E.: A Lattice Model of Secure Information Flow, Communications of the ACM, **19** (1976) 236-243

11. Badger, L., Sterne, D.F, Sherman, D.L., Walker, K.M., Haghighat, S.A.: Practical Domain and Type Enforcement for UNIX. Proceedings of the 1995 IEEE Symposium on Security and Privacy, Oakland May 8-10 (1995) 66-77
12. Badger, L., Sterne, D.F, Sherman, D.L., Walker, K.M., Haghighat, S.A.: A Domain and Type Enforcement UNIX Prototype. Proceedings of the 5th USENIX UNIX Security Symposium, Salt Lake City June 5-7 (1995) 127-140
13. Research and Development in Advanced Communication Technologies in Europe, RIPE Integrity Primitives: Final Report of RACE Integrity Primitives Evaluation (R2040). RACE (1992)
14. Denley, I., Weston Smith, S.: Privacy in Clinical Information Systems in Secondary Care, British Medical Journal **318** (1999) 1328-1331

Tower: A Language for Role Based Access Control

Michael Hitchens and Vijay Varadharajan

Distributed System and Network Security Research Group
School of Computing and Information Technology
University of Western Sydney, Nepean
{m.hitchens, v.varadharajan}@uws.edu.au

Abstract A language for specifying role-based access control (RBAC) policies is presented. The language is designed to support the range of access control policies of commercial object systems. The basic structures of RBAC, such as role, users and permission, are present in the language as basic constructs. Examples are given in the language of access control situations, such as static and dynamic separation of duty, delegation and joint action based access policies. The language is flexible and is able to capture meta-level operations. The language also provides a mechanism for tracking actions and basing access control decisions on past events.

1. Introduction

In a computing system, when a request for a certain service is received by one principal (an agent) from another, the receiving principal needs to address two questions. First, is the requesting principal the one it claims to be? Second, does the requesting principal have the appropriate privileges for the requested service? These two questions relate to the issues of authentication and access control (authorisation). Recently, there has been extensive interest in Role Based Access Control (RBAC) [11,3] as an alternative to the more traditional discretionary access control (DAC) and mandatory access control (MAC) approaches. In RBAC models the attributes used in the access control are the roles associated with the principals and the privileges associated with the roles.

An important aspect of an access control model is the type of policies that the model can support. The model must be flexible enough to support the variety of access control requirements of modern application environments. When the model is implemented using a particular mechanism that mechanism must retain the flexibility of the model. The implementation must not restrict flexibility by making unnecessary assumptions about pre-defined access policies and then building those policies into the access control mechanism. On the one hand, a mechanism can be used to support a number of policies while on the other hand, a policy may be supported by multiple mechanisms. A given mechanism should be able to specify and support a number of policies.

It has been claimed elsewhere that role based access control better suits the needs of real world organisations than MAC or DAC based approaches [10]. While we support this view, we believe that a number of issues in the design and implementation of RBAC systems have not been adequately addressed in previous work. Much of the work on RBAC models and systems has not addressed the issue of

M. Sloman, J. Lobo, and E. Lupu (Eds.): POLICY 2001, LNCS 1995, pp. 88–106, 2001.

how to express policies in a real world system. The power of defined languages to express complex relationships and structures has long been recognised. We therefore strongly believe that a language-based approach to authorisation is required to support the range of access control policies required in commercial systems. While some language-based proposals have been presented, eg., [6,13], these tend to either lack expressiveness or tend to be highly formal.

It has been recognised that RBAC systems need to deal with permissions which reflect the operations of the application (such as *credit* and *debit* in a financial system) rather than the more traditional approach of a fixed set of operations such as *read, write* and *execute* [9,13]. However the effects of this on the design of such systems is rarely addressed. Defining the level of granularity available for the specification of policies has an obvious effect on what policies can be expressed. The choice of the granularity of access control has obvious parallels with the ideas of object-oriented design.

In a previous paper [5] we discussed some of the issues which need to be considered in the design of a language for specifying RBAC policies. These issues include the basic constructs of the language, the question of ownership and the recording of the history actions so that access control decision may be based on past events. In this paper we present some of the details of the language Tower, which has been specifically designed for the expression of RBAC policies in object systems and which addresses these issues.

In the next section, we revisit the arguments for using a language to express RBAC policies. Section 3 describes the basic structure of the language. Section 4 outlines the basic constructs of Tower, including roles, users, and permissions. In section 5, we use the Tower language to specify some commonly used access policies such as standard role based access, separation of duty, joint actions and delegation. Finally section 6 concludes the paper with a brief comparison of our work with other proposals.

2. A Language Based Approach

Roles are intended to reflect the real world job functions within an organisation. The permissions that are attached to the roles reflect the actual operations that may be carried out by members of the role. The policies that need to be expressed in an RBAC system can therefore be seen to have the potential to be both extensive and intricate. The inter-relationships between structures of an RBAC system, such as role, user and permission, likewise have the potential to become complicated.

Languages, in various forms, have long been recognized in computing as ideal vehicles for dealing with the expression and structuring of complex and dynamic relationships. Therefore it seems sensible to at least attempt to employ a language for expressing RBAC. If the language is well designed, this will deliver a degree of flexibility superior to other approaches. Flexibility is a necessary requirement if the RBAC system is to be capable of supporting a wide range of access policies. Other work has recognised the possibility of using a language to express RBAC policies, for example [16].

While in theory a general purpose language could be used, a special purpose language allows for optimisations and domain specific structures which can improve conceptual design and execution efficiency. In particular, the notion of roles and other domain specific concepts are available as primitive constructs within our proposed language Tower. This should simplify the expression of access control policies. The permissions associated with a role tend to change less often than the people who fill the job function that the role represents. Being able to express the relationships between permissions and roles within the structure of the language should make the administration of the access control system simpler; this is a major advantage when it comes to management of authorisation policies. In fact, key aspects of any authorisation model are the ease with which one can change, add and delete policy specifications and the specification of authorities that are able to perform such operations. A language that does not support the necessary constructs will not fulfill this requirement.

In some sense the question of who can modify the policy setting determines whether something is discretionary or mandatory. In general, we feel that the traditional notions of discretionary and mandatory are not very helpful in that a policy may be discretionary to some and mandatory to others. For instance, consider a manager of a project group and a number of group members. A policy can be mandatory to the group as it is set by the manager but is discretionary to the group manager. Similarly at a higher level, a policy may be mandatory to the group manager but is discretionary to the laboratory manager above. This is typical of many organisations and is often true in large distributed systems. It is often the flexibility and management of the operations of the access control system itself which are significant when it comes to the applicability of such a system to practical real situations. The use of a language based policy approach helps us to better structure such policies. Some recent work such as [1] and [6] have considered the use of a logic based language in the specification of authorisation policies. This paper proposes a language theory based approach and is primarily targeted towards object based systems.

Of course, another reason for employing a special purpose language is that a general purpose language will include many constructs that are not required for access control. This would impinge on the efficiency, safety and usability of such a system.

3. Access Control Language: Tower

The most important structures in Tower are the definitions of users, roles, and permissions. The details of these structures are discussed in subsequent sections but first we wish to make the following general comments. Each structure is declared and is given a name. The name is used to identify the structure throughout the access control system. The problems of a single level name space are avoided by employing block structured scoping. Each of these names must be unique within a particular scope. A new structure instance may be created and assigned to a structure variable. The closure of a structure includes any variables declared in the same scope. The structures are immediately available upon creation for evaluating access requests. They may also have their values modified in code that is subsequently executed. In this paper we do not specify the management interface of the access control system. We envisage that both users and administrators can enter policies (in the form of Tower expressions) into the system. Whether this is in a form similar to the Adage VPB [16] or by some other means is not relevant to the design of the language itself.

For an access control system to function it will require some capacity for storing information about the objects it manages and the access policies to be enforced. The Tower language allows the specification of information internal to the access control system in the form of variables. There are two distinct categories of variables in Tower, which differ in the type of information stored, their scope and use. These categories are:

- Simple variables (henceforth referred to as variables)
- Structures

The types of (simple) variables supported are standard ones such as integer, real, boolean, string, userid (user identity) and sets. Tower

From the point of view of such variables, Tower is a block-structured language. A block consists of the definition of either a role or permission or statements between matching *begin* and *end* statements. Within a block, variables are declared before any roles, permissions or interior blocks. A variable is in scope within the block in which it is declared, within any structures declared within that block and within any interior blocks (except for further declarations using the same variable names) and any constructs defined within them. Variables declared within permissions or roles are only in scope within those constructs. Variable declarations have the following syntax:

```
var_name [= value], var_name [= value], ... : var_type
```

except for set variables, which are declared as

```
setvar_name [= value], setvar_name [= value], : set of element_type
```

A set variable of any set type may be empty.

The optional section after each variable name allows the value of variables to be initialised when declared. The value of variables can be altered in subsequent code, especially in the action sections of privileges (see below). The values of variables may be tested within condition expressions and constraints. Any attempt to access a value of a variable before it is initialised results in an error.

Each variable name may be followed by a * or a & (or both). These control the actual number of instances of the named variable and their effect within the current scope. If neither symbol follows the variable name in the declaration then only a single variable is created. If the variable name in the declaration is followed by either or both of these symbols then more than one variable, each with the same name, is (potentially) created within this scope. If a variable's name is followed by a *, then a separate such variable is created for each object covered by the permission(s) within the scope of the declaration. If a variable's name is followed by a &, then a separate such variable is created for each user whose access requests involve this scope. If both symbols occur, then a separate variable is created for each user/object pair. As it cannot be always known in advance which users and objects will be involved, these variables are created dynamically as required. As accesses to variables only occur when a request to a specific object by a specific user occurs, it is straightforward for the system to determine which variable is to be used.

Structure variables cover the following constructs within Tower: privileges, permissions, roles, users, ownership and blocks. Their values must be initialised before use (the exception to these provisions is blocks). The details of how values for these structures are created are covered in the following sections. Apart from the obvious differences between structures and variables in terms of syntax and value, the chief difference between them is the scope of structures. Unlike variables, which are only in scope within the block or structure within which they are declared, structures can be in scope within the entire access control system. The decision on scoping must be made when the structure variable is declared. Global scope is the default; if a structure's scope is not to be global then its name must be followed by a '@' character in the declaration. The unique user identification of the user who created the structure can be pre-pended to its declared name to ensure uniqueness.

The exception to the above are blocks defined by **begin** and **end** keywords. Any such block is considered to be global if it is not defined within another block. Blocks do not need declaration but can be given a name, as in *my_block* := **begin** ... **end.**

The name of a block can be used to add additional structures or variables to the scope it represents. That is, Tower is not a statically scoped language but to some extent is dynamically scoped. This is related to database schema evolution.

Many constructs within Tower are based upon sets. The language provides a number of operations upon sets for all of these constructs. The following standard set operations are provided in Tower:

- **union**,e.g.Set1:=Set2 + {element1,element2},
- **difference**, e.g. Set1 := Set2-Set3,
- **intersection**, e.g. Set1 := Set3/Set4,
- **test for inclusion**, e.g. element1 **in** Set1,
- **cardinality**, e.g. size(Set1),
- **equality**, e.g. Set1 = Set2, and
- **subset test**, e.g. Sett1 < Set2.

The operators are type-sensitive, i.e. the types of all the sets involved must match and the types of the elements must match the declared element type of the sets.

4. Basic RBAC Structures

In this section, we describe the representation of the basic RBAC elements in Tower. In a previous paper [5] we refined the basic RBAC model and proposed one which explicitly includes the objects to which access is being controlled. We also introduced another structure, for which we use the term *privilege*. Ownership of an object may be vested in a user, a role or any combination thereof. Permissions apply to one or more objects and privileges specify the methods to which the privilege grants access and the conditions under which they may be accessed. The model is illustrated in figure 1

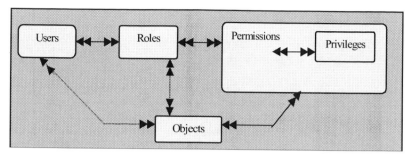

Fig. 1. Object-Oriented Role Based Access Control Model

4.1 Privileges

In an object-oriented system, it is reasonable to base the lowest level construct of the access control system at the method level. In Tower, a privilege is a triple, consisting of the set of names of the methods to which it gives access, the condition under which access is granted and any action to be taken within the access control system if access is granted. A new privilege is created as follows:

privilege_name := **privilege**
      [condition_expression]
      [action_statement,action_statement,...]
      {method_clause,method_clause,...}
 end_privilege

The condition expression and the set of action statements are optional. The condition expression is a Boolean expression (of arbitrary complexity) which must evaluate to true if any of the methods is to be invoked under the authority of this privilege. A condition expression can test both the values of parameters passed and access control system variables in scope. The action statement (or statements) is (are) executed if the invocation of any of the methods is allowed under the authority of the privilege (the default) or *whenever* the condition expression is tested, by preceeding each action statement to be executed with the keyword **always**. When an action statement is executed, the state of the access control system is altered.   A *method_clause* is either a method name or a set of method names.

Note that there is no specification within a privilege as to the objects to which it applies. This is handled at the permission level. While users will probably have access to multiple methods of each object, they will not necessarily be able to access those methods under the same condition. We therefore associate conditions and methods in privileges and group privileges together with a specification of which objects they apply to within the permissions. For those methods of an object to which the same conditions apply, they may be grouped together in the method set of a privilege.

4.2 Permissions

Permissions encapsulate the access to objects of a single class. A permission consists of a specification of the objects to which it gives access and how these objects can be accessed. The latter is specified as a set of privileges. A permission will give access to some subset of the objects of the class to which the permission applies. Normally the subset will be a proper subset and not all the objects of the class. This restriction reflects the observation that normally a user will not have access to all the objects of a class (unless they are the only user who can access objects of that class). It would be an unusual situation where, for example, a single user would have access to all spreadsheets or all text documents in a multi-user system. However, it is usually impossible to specify in advance the names (or other identifiers) of all the objects of a given class to which a user will have access. A permission can specify that it allows access to objects of a class owned by a given set of users. This allows access control to be specified for objects which have not yet come into existence. The syntax for a creating a new permission is as follows:

```
permission_name := permission
        class_name
        [owner]
        [users user_set]
        [roles role_set]
        [objects object_set]
        [variable_declarations]
        privileges {privilege_clause,privilege_clause,...}
end_permission
```

The *class_name* gives the name of the class of the object to which this permission grants access. After that, we have clauses specifying the objects covered by the permission. A permission may contain one or more of these clauses. These clauses are the first test on whether access will be granted by the permission.

The objects to which the permission will grant access may be specified in terms of their ownership. If the keyword **owner** is employed then the permission can grant access to objects of the named class owned (singly or jointly) by the user attempting to gain access. The permission may grant access to objects of the named class owned by any of the listed entities. This may be a set of explicitly named users or users which currently have the named role as an active role. The permission may be defined to give access to a set of existing objects by explicitly naming them. The permission can then be used to access those objects and no others. Finally the object set may be a named object set. Such a set can be updated independent of the permission. If an access to an object is attempted which is not to one of the specified objects then this permission will not grant access.

Of course, even if the object that is being accessed is one covered by the permission, access may still be denied according to the privileges included within the permission. Tests for ownership may also occur in the condition sections of privileges, but such tests are additional (not an alternative) to the permission level tests.

After the specification of the objects to which the permission applies any variables that are in scope within the permission are declared. Finally, there is a set of privileges which define the exact access allowed by the permission. A *privilege_clause* is either a privilege, a privilege set or a *privilege_expression*. A *privilege_expression* is an expression specifying changes to a privilege (such as adding or subtracting methods, conditions or actions).

The following gives an example of the initialisation of a permission and the effects of ownership. A user, *a*, wishes to access the objects of class *text_object* owned by user *b*. *a* enters the following code:

```
b_text := permission
    text_object
    users b
    {privilege,privilege,...}
end_permission
```

The code is syntactically correct and the permission will be created if both the owner of the class definition for *text_object* and user *b* give their permission. The method by which they would do this relates to the management interface and is outside the scope of this paper. The management interface and operations are addressed in a separate paper that is currently in preparation.

4.3 Roles

The syntax for creating a new role value is as follows:

```
role_name := role
    [variable_declarations]
    [authorised constraint_expression [[always] constraint_action]]
    [active constraint_expression [[always] constraint_action]]
    [session constraint_expression [[always] constraint_action]]
    [roles {role_clause,role_clause,...}]
    [permissions {permission_clause,permission_clause,...}]
end_role
```

Role constraints may be used to affect the roles of a user at three different levels:
- the roles that a user may be authorised to have as active,
- the roles that a user has active across concurrent sessions
- the roles that a user has authorised within a particular session

These are in increasing level of refinement – if a role specifies that no user can have both it and another role as authorised roles, then obviously the user can not have both those roles as active roles (either in the same session or in another one).

Constraints may be used to impose restrictions upon whether a user may have this role added to his/her set of roles, or whether a user may add another role while possessing this one. The constraint tests in a role are checked when a user to role mapping is made (the role is to become an authorised role) and when a session to role mapping is made (the role becomes active). The constraints are also checked whenever any relevant user mappings are altered. For example, this avoids the necessity of specifying exclusion in both roles. A constraint test is a Boolean function which must evaluate to true if the role is to be added. A short hand is provided for the common case of exclusion, which is that possession of the current role is mutually exclusive with the roles in the role set, eg., **exclude** *role_set*. This set can be explicitly listed in the constraint expression or represented by a set variable, allowing easier dynamic update.

The constraint action allows for updating of any variables relevant to the constraint. Variables have been discussed above. The role and permission sections define the access allowed by the newly created role. The definitions of *role_clause* and *permission_clause* are analogous to that of *privilege_clause* in section 4.2. Role inheritance is modelled by allowing roles to be formed, in part, from other roles. These roles may already exist, and are referred to by name, or are defined within the new role.

4.4 Users and Sessions

The syntax for creating a new user structure is as follows:

```
user_name := user
    name
    uuid
    [variable_declarations]
    [{role,role,...}]
    [{session,session,...}]
end_user
```

Note that the roles are those which the user may take on (known as the authorised roles of that user). When a new user is created this set may often be empty. In addition to explicitly naming roles, one or more role sets could also be given. The variable declaration section allows attributes [4] to be assigned to the user. The sessions of the user will only be updated by the system, reflecting the current sessions of the user.

For each log-in session of a user, it is also necessary to record the actual roles that are current (known as the active roles). It is the active roles that are used to check whether any attempted method invocation should be allowed. The syntax for a session is much the same as that for a user. Note that in some sense it is a conceptual syntax, as such structures would be implicitly created whenever a new user session is commenced. However, they have an actual existence and are used in checking role constraints as well as actual method invocation. Here the roles are the active roles for the particular session.

4.5 Ownership of Objects and Structures

The concept of ownership can simplify the expression of access control policies. Many systems limit ownership to a single user. This does not match many real world situations, where ownership is often equally shared between many people. For example, all members of the committee may jointly own a document produced by a committee. Vesting ownership in more than a single entity leads to the question of how many of these entities must co-operate for successful performance of actions restricted to an owner. Many discussions of RBAC ignore the question of ownership completely. In Tower we employ a relatively simple answer to the question: for each object, the number (or fraction) of the joint owners who must agree before an action can be performed is stored along with the ownership information.

Each object (and class specification) stored in the system has a corresponding access control structure. These structures record the owner(s) of the corresponding object and other related information (such as attributes). While the creation of the ownership structures is automatic on the creation of the corresponding object, they have a conceptual Tower syntax. This allows updating of the ownership information within the scope of the language.

```
name := object
    owners
    {uuid, uuid, ...} | {role, role, ...} | {uuid, uuid, ...} {role, role, ...}
    quorum positive integer | real between 0 and 1 | all
    creation {uuid, uuid, } | {role, role, } | {uuid, uuid, } {role, role, }
    [variable_declarations]
end_object
```

The name of the structure is the system dependent unique object identifier. The first clause specifies the owner of the object, as one or more specified users and/or the members of named roles. The second option allows for a dynamic concept of ownership, as it grants joint ownership to all users who currently have at least one of the named roles as an active role[1].

The second clause specifies how many of the owners must agree if any operation requiring owner approval is to be carried out. For an object there are only three such operations:

- changing any of the information stored in the ownership structure (including the specification of the owner),
- allowing the object (or class specification) to be referenced from within a permission, and
- revoking the allowance for the object (or class specification) to be referenced from within a permission.

The second operation prevents users from including objects within a permission when they do not own that object. The third operation allows for revocation of access.

The third *creation* clause specifies the owner of any object created as a direct result (i.e. without subsequent accesses to other objects) of access to this object. For example, while the owner of a text editor may be the system manager, any files created using the text editor can be specified as belonging to the user who accessed it.

The same principles of ownership can be applied to structures of the access control system (roles, permissions, privileges, users). The syntax is the same as that given above, except that keyword **object** is replaced with **structure**. The name of the ownership structure is that of the structure to which it applies, followed by the special character "^". This allows us to control access to the access control system itself in a conceptually efficient manner. Each structure in Tower has an associated ownership structure. The ownership information in such an ownership structure also applies to itself, avoiding infinite recursion. Thus it is possible to specify who owns each structure and can therefore modify it. This also allows us to restrict the use of access control structures; they can only be altered or used (included in the values of other structures) either by their owner, or with their owner's permission. In the case of

---

[1] While we could have simply allowed the role to be an authorised role, insisting that it must be an active role helps to protect untrusted code running used limited permissions.

removing one structure from another (such as removing a role from a user's list of authorised roles), the permission of the owner of either structure is sufficient.

4.6 System Evolution : Alterations to Structure Values

The previous sections have described how the various structures of the language are given their initial values. As the system evolves, any of these structures may need to have their values updated. Set operations may be applied to each of these structures, for example

```
P1 := P1 + {Pr1,Pr2}
```

Permission *P1* now has privileges *Pr1* and *Pr2* added to its set of privileges. The type of *Pr1* and *Pr2* (i.e., privilege) means that the update must be to the privilege set of the permission. Therefore we can simply use the permission name without further qualification. This applies to all the components of structures that can be unambiguously identified. Where a structure consists of two or more sets of the same element type, such as the record of the owners of an object and the owners of any new objects, further qualification, and updates occur as follows:

```
object1.owners := object1.owners + {michael}
object1.creation := object1.creation + {vijay}
```

The first statement adds the user *michael* to the set of users who own object *object1*. The second statement adds the user *vijay* to the set of users who will own any objects created using *object1*.

From the above, the set operations applied to a privilege alter the contents of its set of method names (as the only set contained in a privilege is the method set). Similarly, the roles and permissions which make up a role can be altered, as in the following examples:

```
R1 := {P1,P2}
```

The permissions in *R1* are now *P1* and *P2*.

```
R1 := R1 + {R2,R3}
```

R1 has *R2* and *R3* added to its roles

```
R1 := R1 - {R3}
```

R3 is no longer one of *R1's* roles

The system can determine if the roles or permissions of a role are being updated by resolving the names on the right hand side of the assignment statements.

The other information held in a structure may also be updated within assignment statements. Additions (for example) may be made to the condition within a privilege, as:

```
Pr1 := Pr1 + condition_expression
```

The new condition expression for the privilege is formed by joining the previous expression and that in the assignment statement with the and conjunction.

5. Examples

The basic constructs and structures of the Tower language can be used to specify a range of access control polices. This section gives a number of examples of solutions to common access control situations using Tower. In the interests of space, the examples do not include all the necessary preliminary declarations and initialisations. Nonetheless we hope they convey the required information.

5.1 Role Hierarchy

One of the most important advantages claimed for the role based approach is that it can model the structures of real world organisations. A simple (possibly simplistic) view of such structures is a hierarchical ordering of responsibilities, with more senior positions encompassing all the privileges of the more junior positions, plus some extra privileges. For example, consider a hypothetical structure for a bank branch, as shown in figure 2.

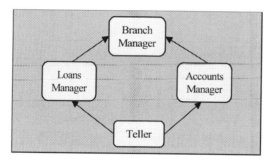

Fig. 2. An Example of Role Inheritance

Let *teller_role* be a role containing all the appropriate permissions and privileges needed for a teller to carry out his or her functions. Let *P1* and *P2* be permissions which contain the extra privileges required for an accounts manager. Let *P3* and *P4* be the permissions which contain the extra privileges required for a loans manager. Let permissions *P5* and *P6* contain the extra privileges required for a branch manager.

The roles for accounts manager and loans manager can be created as follows (we assume appropriate variable declarations):

```
accounts_manager_role := role
     roles teller_role
     permissions {P1,P2}
end_role
loans_manager_role := role
     roles teller_role
     permissions {P3,P4}
end_role
```

Note that both these roles inherit all the privileges of the teller role. The role for the branch manager can be created as follows:

```
branch_manager_role := role
    roles {accounts_manager_role, loans_manager_role}
    permissions {P5,P6}
end_role
```

Note that the privileges associated with the teller role are indirectly inherited by the branch manager role. While this may be considered a simplistic example, it does demonstrate role inheritance in Tower. More realistic examples, involving partial overlap rather then strict inheritance, can also be modelled.

5.2 Role Hierarchy with Private Roles

In the previous section, it was implicitly assumed that *all* actions possible to other staff were also possible for the branch manager. For example, there are no private files for correspondence and record keeping. While this may well be the policy for a bank, it could instead allow some privacy to its employees. In this case, not all permissions would be inherited. Permissions may need to be shared amongst all holders of a position but not inherited, or we may require permissions to be private to individual users.

For example, for permissions that are to be shared by all loans managers but not inherited by branch managers, each loan manager has their user structure defined as:

```
user_structure_name := user
    (name of loans manager)
    (uuid of loans manager)
    {loans_manager_role,private_loans_manager_role}
end_user
```

where *private_loans_manager_role contains* those permissions not to be given to branch managers.

A user can be allowed their own private permissions by creating a role for which they will be the only authorised user. For example, for a teller *michael*, a role called *michael_private_role* could be created and their user structure would be

```
michaels_user_structure := user
    michael
    (uuid of michael)
    {teller_role, michael_private_role}
end_user
```

5.3 Separation of Duties

Static Separation of Duty Consider a class where one group of users is allowed to add items to an object and another is allowed to remove items from the object; for example, items are produced by one group of users and submitted for certification by another. Between creation and certification, the items are held in a container object. This situation is a simple example of static separation of duties and can be represented in Tower as follows:

```
create_privilege := privilege          certify_privilege := privilege
    {create}                               {certify}
end_privilege                          end_privilege


create_permission := permission        certify_permission := permission
    container_class                        container_class
    objects {container_object}             objects {container_object}
    privileges {create_privilege}          privileges {certify_privilege}
end_permission                         end_permission


creator_role := role                   certifier_role :=role
    authorised exclude certifier_role      authorised exclude creator_role
    permissions {create_permission}        permissions {certify_permission}
end_role                               end_role
```

Only one constraint expression is actually necessary. For completeness, a constraint expression is included in both roles.

Dynamic Separation of Duty Tower can also handle dynamic separations of duty. Consider a class of cheque objects, which may be accessed by members of the role accountant. However, the same user may not both issue and authorise the same cheque.

```
begin
    issuing_user* : userid
    issue_privilege :=privilege
        issuing_user := user
        {issue}
    end_privilege
    authorise_privilege := privilege
        issuing_user <> user
        {authorise}
    end_privilege
    cheque_permission := permission
        cheque_class
        privilege {issue_privilege,authorise_privilege}
    end_permission
    accountant := role
        permissions {cheque_permission}
    end_role
end
```

Note that one copy of the variable *issuing_user* is created for each object covered by the *cheque_permission* and its privileges. The value of the variable is set in the action part of the *issue_privilege* and checked in the condition part of the *authorise_privilege*. The role accountant does not need to be declared within the block, but placing it within the block aids readability.

5.4 Chinese Wall Policy

The Chinese Wall policy [2] can be viewed as a special form of dynamic separation of duty. In this policy, objects are grouped together into different sets which reflect conflicts of interests. If a user has accessed an object in a set, then the user is not allowed to access any other object within that conflict of interest set. For example, if company A and company B are in the same conflict of interest set and if a user is acting as a consultant to company A, then s/he is not allowed to act as a consultant to company B.

The operations for each company are placed in a separate role. A conflict of interest set is represented by the set of each of these roles. The constraint expression for each role must reflect, on a per user basis, the actual role which has been accessed.

```
begin
    companyA, companyB : role
    user_company& = {} : set of role
    companyA := role
        authorised user_company= {} or user_company = {companyA}
        user_company:={companyA}
        permissions {permissions for company A}
    end_role
    companyB := role
        authorised user_company = {} or user_company = {companyB}
        user_company:={companyB}
        permissions {permissions for company B}
    end_role
end
```

Objects may affect more than one conflict of interest set. Consider the example where the users are consultants to various firms. One conflict of interest set is accounting firms and another the mining companies. An object which holds information about both a mining company and an accounting firm should involve checks on both conflict of interest sets for a user. As the labels associated with objects and users are global in such systems they can be handled in Tower by including all conflict of interest variables and roles in a single Tower block.

5.5 Delegation

Delegation within Tower is handled by dynamically assigning and de-assigning roles. While roles are usually thought of as broad concepts covering complete job descriptions, they can also be used in a much more fine-grained manner. The permissions representing the delegated authority can be placed in a new role. This role can be added to the authorised role of the user (which may represent a real world user or some active system entity) to whom the authority is to be delegated. When the delegated actions are completed, the role can be removed.

5.6 Joint Action Based Policies

Joint action based policies [14] are used in situations where trust in individuals needs to be dispersed. Often this arises due to the fact that individuals are trusted according to their expertise which in turn maps the concept of trust to a specific set of actions. In delegation, there is a partial or complete granting of privileges whereas in joint actions, agents may acquire privileges by working together in tandem which none posses in isolation. For instance, consider the following examples:

Admission of a patient: A patient is admitted to the hospital if the patient and a doctor agree. The doctor and the patient jointly own a patient's record. Every doctor and patient has the following permission and privileges.

```
patient_record_permission := permission
    patient_record
    owner
    doctor_id* = 0, patient_id* = 0 : userid
    privileges {admit_privilege,...}
end_permission
admit_privilege := privilege
    doctor_id <> 0 and patient in user and user <> doctor_id
    or
    patient_id <> 0 and doctor in user and user <> patient_id
    always
    if doctor in user then doctor_id := user
    else patient_id := user
    {admit}
end_privilege
```

The above example depends on ownership specified in the *patient_record* as only specific members of the roles *patient* and *doctor* could act on specific patient records. Note that the first attempt to admit the patient (by either doctor or patient) will fail – the access control system cannot predict future access. If actions are assumed to be sequential, the first attempt must fail.

Consider another example involving the authorisation of payment for goods: Any member of the role *buyer* and any member of the role *accountant* can authorise the payment. The two roles are assumed to be mutually exclusive.

```
payment_record := permission
    payment
    authorising_buyer* = 0, authorising_accountant* = 0 : userid
    privilege {authorise_permission,...}
end_permission
authorise_permission := permission
    (authorising_buyer <> 0 and accountant in user) or
    (authorising_accountant <> 0 and buyer in user)
    always
    if buyer in user then authorising_buyer := user
    else if accountant in user then authorising_accountant := user
    {authorise}
end_permission
```

5.7 Limiting Number of Accesses

Sometimes one user will wish to give access to another user, but limit that access to a certain number of operations. Such situations can be handled in Tower as follows.

User a wishes to give user b access to method m of object o but wishes to impose a maximum number of times (say 5) that b may call m.

```
couermission := permissionnting_p
    o_class
    object o
    count = 5 : integer
    permissions {m_permission}
end_permission
m_permission := permission
    count > 0
    count := count -1
    {m}
end_permission
```

If the user wished to have more than one permission, then count would apply to all calls on the object. If the requirement was to limit the number of calls to each method individually, then a separate variable would be required for each method. If the limit was to be over a number of objects, then the variable could be declared within a block and used within the permission for each object, which would also have to be declared and initialised within the block. As the count variables can be updated, within the action parts of the permission, the exact limiting of the access can be quite flexible.

6. Implementation

Implementation of Tower is in its early stages. We rejected any implementation on top of other access control mechanisms, such as access control lists, as being too inefficient and probably incapable of supporting the full expressive power of the language. Instead we have chosen to directly implement it. The chosen vehicle is the CORBA interceptor mechanism [8]. This allows the access control to be independent of the rest of the system while still being able to allow or deny access.

The implementations in each ORB can communicate, allowing distributed access control. However, several of the issues related to implementation of RBAC management in a distributed environment still need to be solved. We will report on the implementation when it is completed.

7. Brief Comparison with Other Work

The language described above is far from the first attempt at expressing role based access control. Other proposals have been put forward which allow the access control policies to be expressed in a systematic manner for role based or related systems. These proposals range from the formal one such as in [6] to more practical ones such as [13] and [15] to related mechanisms such as in [7]. While formal languages such as the ASL in [6] can have good expressive power, they suffer from a resistance amongst real users, due to their highly intricate nature. For example, these languages often depend upon their users having a reasonable level of understanding of logical principles. This is not always found amongst real world users, even those entrusted with the management of access control policies for a system. Their syntax will often contain symbols not commonly used, limiting their appeal. While it is true that such languages are not generally written for widespread use, this simply perhaps strengthens the argument that a different approach should be used for the expression of access control policies in real world systems. Another drawback of some such proposals is the attempt to be too general. While it may be useful in a theoretical language to be able to cover a number of access control approaches, in the real world, it is more important to be able to address those that are used in practice and to develop tools tailored to support them. The language described in this paper is intended to address this practical issue and does not assume an overly high level of theoretical ability.

Furthermore, in the language that has been proposed in this paper, we have considered meta-variables and role constraints, which few of the other proposals have included. For example, [13] attempts to use an assortment of predefined functions to fulfil the functionality that we address using meta-variables. A set of predefined functions is highly unlikely to present a sufficient degree of flexibility and capability. It is far better to provide the user needing to specify the access control policies with flexible mechanisms (such as those we provide) and allow them to construct structures for expressing their policies. Finally, some other earlier work such as that in [7] is limited in their expressiveness; it does not address concepts such as time or object attributes and the syntax is also somewhat limited targeted at specific operating systems.

Consideration has been given elsewhere to the use of RBAC structures in the management of RBAC policies [12]. We believe that the structures of Tower could be used in this manner but leave detailed consideration of this to future work

8. Concluding Remarks

In this paper, we have proposed a language based approach to the specification of authorisation policies. We believe that such an approach is required to support the range of access control policies used in commercial systems. We have presented the details of a language for role based access control systems. The proposed language focuses in particular on object-oriented systems. The notion of roles is used as a primitive construct within the language. It is often the flexibility and management of the meta-level operations, which are significant when it comes to the applicability of an access control system to practical real situations. The use of a language based policy approach helps us to better structure such meta-level policies. In this paper, we have described the basic constructs of the language and used the language to specify several access control policies. In particular, we have described policy example scenarios involving role hierarchy, separation of duties both static and dynamic, Chinese Wall policy, delegation as well as joint action based access policies.

References

1   Bai, Y., and Varadharajan, V.: 'A logic for state transformations in authorization policies", Proceedings of the 10th IEEE Computer Security Foundations Workshop, Rockport MA, USA, 1997, IEEE Computer Society Press, pp. 173-183.

2   Brewer, D. and Nash, M.: 'The Chinese Wall security policy'. Proceedings of the IEEE Symposium on Security and Privacy, Los Alamitos CA, USA, 1989, pp. 206-214.

3   Ferraiolo, D., and Kuhn, R.: 'Role based access controls', Proceedings of the 15th NIST-NCSC National Computer Security Conference, Baltimore MD, USA, 1992, pp. 554-563.

4   Hilchenbach, B." 'Observations on the real-world implementation of role-based access control", Proceedings of the 20th National Information Systems Security Conference, Baltimore MD, USA, 1997, pp. 341-52.

5   M. Hitchens & V. Varadharajan, "Issues in the Design of a Language for Role Based Access Control", ICICS'99, pp. 22-38.

6   Jajodia, S., Smarati, P., and Subrahmanian, V.: 'A logical language for expressing authorizations", Proceedings of the IEEE Symposium on Security and Information Privacy, Oakland CA, USA, 1997, pp. 31-42.

7   Karger, P.: 'Implementing commercial data integrity with secure Capabilities', Proceedings of the IEEE Symposium on Security and Privacy, Oakland CA, USA, 1988, pp. 130-39.

8   Object Management Group (OMG), "CORBAservices: Common Object Services Specification" and "Security Services in Common Object Request Broker Architecture", 1996-98.

9   Sandhu, R., Coyne, E., Feinstein, H., and Youman, C.: 'Role-based access control: A Multi-Dimensional View", 10th Annual Computer Security Applications Conference, Orlando FL, USA, 1994, IEEE CS Press, pp. 54-61.

10 Sandhu, R., and Feinstein, H.: 'A three tier architecture for role-based access control'. Proceedings of the 17th NIST-NCSC National Computer Security Conference, Baltimore MD, USA, 1994, pp. 34-46.

11 Sandhu, R., Coyne, E.J., and Feinstein, H.L., 'Role based access control models', IEEE Computer, 1996, 29, (2), pp. 38-47.

12 Sandhu, R.: 'Role Activation Hierarchies', Proceedings of the 3rd ACM Workshop on Role Based Access Control, Fairfax VA, USA, 1998, pp. 33-40.

13 Simon, R., and Zurko, M.: 'Separation of duty in role-based environments'. Proceedings of the 10th IEEE Computer Security Foundations Workshop, Rockport MA, USA, IEEE CS Press, 1997, pp. 183-94.

14 Varadharajan, V. and Allen, P.: 'Joint action based authorisation schemes', ACM Operating Systems Review, volume 30, (3), July 1996, pp. 32-45.

15 Varadharajan, V., Crall, C., and Pato, J.: 'Authorization for enterprise wide distributed systems: Design and application", Proceedings of the IEEE Computer Security Applications Conference, ACSAC'98, Scottsdale AZ, USA, 1998.

16 Zurko, M., Simon, R., and Sanfilippo, T.: 'A user-centered, modular authorization service built on an RBAC foundation', Proceedings of the IEEE Symposium on Security and Privacy, Oakland CA, USA, 1999. pp. 57-71.

Translating Role-Based Access Control Policy within Context

Jean Bacon, Michael Lloyd, and Ken Moody

University of Cambridge Computer Laboratory
New Museum Site, Pembroke Street
Cambridge CB2 3QG, UK
Tel: +44 1223 334600
{Firstname.Lastname}@cl.cam.ac.uk

Abstract. The motivation for this work derives from a study undertaken with a view to providing ubiquitous access to Electronic Health Records (EHRs) held within the National Health Service in England. Any implementation must guarantee confidentiality. In October 1999 the Cambridge Computer Laboratory's Opera group joined a consortium within the Eastern Regional Health Authority to propose an experimental architecture which included role-based access control (RBAC). Specifying a policy for role-based access has two aspects: first, the conditions for entering each role must be established; secondly, the access privileges associated with each role must be defined. Access control policy must implement public policy and its expression must be transparent to computer non-specialists. We have therefore designed and implemented a pseudo-natural language framework sufficient for both of these purposes. Policy statements are translated into first-order logic, with side conditions which are evaluated by consulting a context-dependent database, and subsequently into access control procedures.

1 Introduction

The research thrust of the Opera Group in the Computer Laboratory has been to develop a Middleware architecture in which individual services retain autonomy. Key components are the Cambridge Event Architecture (CEA) [1, 11], which offers support for generic registration and notification of events, and the role-based access control model OASIS (Open Architecture for Securely Interworking Services) [5]. The implementations of these components are interdependent; an overview can be found in [1]. A crucial practical advantage of making services autonomous in such matters as access control is that they can be managed independently; this is vital in any wide-area application that comprises a federation of independent partners.

Autonomy is not however the whole story. In such applications it is usual to find overall guidelines that each partner must respect. For example, health records contain personal data, and are subject to the provisions of the Data Protection Act. The Health Service is administered independently in England,

M. Sloman, J. Lobo, and E. Lupu (Eds.): POLICY 2001, LNCS 1995, pp. 107–119, 2001.
© Springer-Verlag Berlin Heidelberg 2001

Wales, Scotland and Northern Ireland, and each province has established its own Patient's Charter. Amongst other things, each charter establishes the patient's right to determine who may access their health records. In this paper we describe a strategy that will allow cooperating partners to express local role-based access control policy in pseudo-natural language, using the same process to specify the conditions for role entry and the access privileges associated with each role.

A prototype translator has already been built, and we describe the design principles underlying it [9]. The output of language translation is a specification in higher-order logic (HOL). This HOL specification may then be translated into first-order predicate calculus (FOPC), and also be represented in the Horn clause form required by OASIS. Java classes are then generated to enforce the policy specified; we refer to such an executable form as a (procedural) guard. In general, guards established at a local service must also take any overall policy guidelines into account.

In practice the OASIS model of RBAC is insufficient in itself to meet the needs of applications such as EHRs, in which individual patients may express additional conditions restricting access to their records. The experience in the UK is that most patients who override default policy wish to deny access to named individuals, either relatives or particular health care workers. In OASIS access *privileges* are associated with *roles*, and denial of access cannot be expressed directly; instead, RBAC policy must be supplemented by exception lists stored with individual health records. We expect that the default RBAC will be sufficient for most patients and that any exception lists will be short.

Provided that all the policies which determine local access are expressed in the OASIS model they are necessarily consistent, since the possession of additional roles can only increase a principal's privileges. More generally the component policies which contribute to the generation of a local guard must be expressed in a common logical formulation so that they can be checked for potential inconsistency. A general approach to resolving conflicts between policies in a distributed system is described in [10]. The guard generated should implement the synthesis of the policies expressed, and should carry a version number sufficient to identify the high-level policy sources from which it is derived. In an environment as complicated as the NHS it will only be possible to ensure that the policies enforced are current if guards can be generated automatically. We intend to store policies and their logical representations in active databases, and to use the CEA to ensure that changes are propagated throughout the system. At present we have prototypes for a number of components, but a great deal of work remains to be done.

2   Electronic Health Records: A Federated Management Problem

The UK National Health Service (NHS) has been underfunded over a long period, and is recognized as being in crisis. The new Labour government that took office in 1997 has made reviving the NHS one of its prime goals [14]. [15] outlined an implementation strategy intended to lead progressively to the integrated storage of health data, with access from all health care points. The strategy was based on bottom-up deployment, and there was no clear explanation of the mechanisms that would ensure compatibility across the country as a whole. The Opera group joined a consortium (EREHRC) formed by health care providers within the Eastern Region, coordinated by the Clinical and Biomedical Computing Unit based at Addenbrooke's Hospital in Cambridge. The EREHRC submitted a proposal to the NHS for a "pan-community demonstrator", focussing on what we see as the main obstacles to the introduction of EHRs: heterogeneity, local autonomy, and above all continuing local evolution - of hardware and software, management structures, and medical practice and taxonomy. The proposal was not funded, but it was well received, and there is some evidence that the NHS IT Authority is now more aware of the difficulties of a once-off deployment. In July 2000 a long White Paper [16] appeared just as Parliament was going into recess, presenting a new plan for reviving the ailing Service, but without emphasis on ubiquitous access to EHRs.

2.1 Browser-Based Access to Virtual Health Records

The EREHRC proposal contained a separate technical appendix developed by the Opera group, together with a sabbatical visitor, John Hine, from the Victoria University of Wellington, New Zealand. Specific proposals for a certificate authority suitable for supporting OASIS in a health care environment are described in [6]. An overview of the architecture is given in Figure 1.

A patient's Electronic Health Record (EHR) comprises many patient records, each relating to some aspect of treatment and stored by the provider of the unit of treatment. A crucial feature of the design is the use of a **virtual health record**, essentially an index structured according to a medical ontology, containing references to all the patient records relating to a given individual. The Index service of Figure 1 is responsible for storing and maintaining these virtual health records and for ensuring they are highly available. By law every access to an individual's EHR should be recorded, and we provide for an asynchronous audit, noting the identity of the data item, the principal accessing it, and the context. This context must include information sufficient to identify the policy that was current at the time of access.

2.2 Privacy Requirements for Virtual Health Records

The architecture developed by the EREHRC requires that each elementary patient record held at a provider service be given a unique identifier. This is essential for subsequent location of the record via the index service (a Universal Resource Name (URN) might be included) and for the records of the Audit service. Provider services report new data items to the Index service as they are generated; each item is incorporated in the index structure corresponding to the

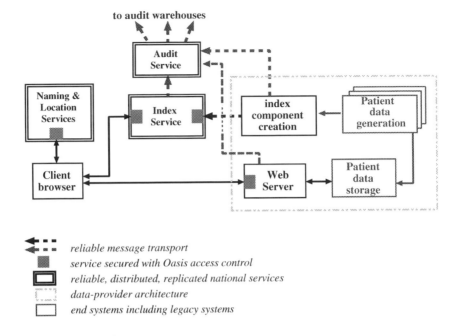

reliable message transport
service secured with Oasis access control
reliable, distributed, replicated national services
data-provider architecture
end systems including legacy systems

Fig. 1. An Architecture for an Electronic Health Record Service

patient in question. The Index service is essentially a replicated and highly available directory service; it must be reliable, but there is no need for immediate update as new records are created.

How suitable is the OASIS model of RBAC for expressing access control policy in this context? We believe that the model is suitable for many of the services that store patient records, and the language design experiments reported in later sections address this need. Preferences expressed by individual patients relate to their own health records, and it is natural to store exception lists with the index structures, which serve as a complete description of the electronic health data held for each individual. RBAC may be sufficient for expressing the default policy at the Health Record service, but other mechanisms will be needed for explicit denial of access.

2.3   Legal and Ethical Constraints Governing Access

Health records are personal, and therefore subject to the provisions of the Data Protection Act. The Patient's Charter [13] guarantees a patient's general right to restrict access to their health records. Ideally an access control guard should respect this regulatory framework as well as explicit policy, but it is hard to express law within logic [7]. Recent advances in biology are undermining the assumptions lying behind the patient's right to determine access; knowledge of one's genotype can affect one's kin as well as oneself. Genetic counsellors report that cases in which family members disagree are becoming more frequent, and a committee has been set up to look at the ethics relating to such shared medical data. When it becomes commonplace for genome data to be part of every health record, access control policy will need to take note of the ethical criteria that are established.

3   Role-Based Access Control: Horn Clause Logic

In OASIS each service is responsible for classifying its clients into named roles. A role definition language (RDL) is provided so that services may specify precise conditions for clients to enter each role. Figure 2 shows a service secured by OASIS access control. Policy is checked on role entry and on service use.

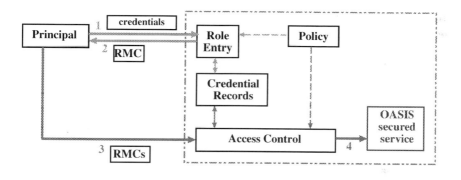

Fig. 2. A service secured by Oasis access control

RDL is a formal logic based on Horn clauses. A client becomes authenticated by presenting credentials to a service that enable the service to **prove** that the client conforms to its policy for entry to a particular role, and the client is then issued with a role membership certificate (RMC). The RMC may include parameters identifying aspects of the client, for example a local user identifier on a log-in certificate; a digital signature is generated to protect the parameter values and to ensure that the certificate is useless if stolen.

In OASIS services authorise clients by specifying the methods that they may invoke. A formal language, also based on Horn clauses, expresses the privileges associated with each role; the policy may include constraints which must be checked when access is attempted.

RBAC has a number of advantages. Permissions are expressed in terms of roles that may be adopted by principals. The policy governing role entry is decoupled from the rights associated with each role, which may be modified at a generic level. This leads to essentially scalable policy management, and incidentally enables secure access by anonymous principals, should this be desired.

3.1   Checking Constraints on RMC Parameters

The OASIS model includes provision to check side conditions on the parameters supplied with RMCs, typically by database look-up. For example, in a primary care context a group of doctors, called General Practitioners (GPs), share premises but have individual registered patients. Access to some information may be restricted to the patient's own GP rather than anyone who has the role GP in that practice. Side conditions will be evaluated within each environment, and the procedural guards at each service will consult a local database.

Two services which administer equivalent resources may recognize the same roles, and be made subject to the same policy; thus, the haematology departments of two hospitals within the same health authority may be managed according to a single policy. On the other hand different health care workers will be employed at the two hospitals, and side conditions will be evaluated in separate environments.

3.2   Failure of Expressive Power in OASIS RBAC

Individual access can be authorised within RBAC provided that the identity of the principal is available as well as the roles that the principal has entered. For example, in OASIS an RMC is issued to a principal on role entry. The encryption-protected fields of the certificate must contain the role name and issuing service but may also include additional parameters. It is possible to include a role that establishes a global name for the principal, and to require that this RMC is presented at every access. A possible name is the NHS-identifier that each patient and employee may soon carry on a smart card.

Within the strict OASIS model it is not possible to deny access in accordance with a patient's expressed wishes even if the identity of the client is known, since the model is permission based. In addition, there is no mechanism for expressing role conflicts [12], though it should be fairly straightforward to handle dynamic separation of duties by extending the semantics of the side conditions in RDL.

4   Managing Policy for Role-Based Access Control

4.1   Expressing Policy for Role Entry (Authentication)

Role Entry is expressed in the Role Definition Language. Formally, Role Entry statements are Horn clauses taking the form:

$$RoleName(arg,..) \leftarrow RoleRef(arg,..)[\wedge RoleRef(arg,..)]$$
$$[: SideCondition(arg,..) \wedge ..]$$

For example:

$$SeniorHaematologist(x) \leftarrow Haematologist(x) \wedge SeniorDoctor(x)$$

which states that a principal in the roles of Haematologist and Senior Doctor can take on the role of Senior Haematologist. The arguments may be either constants or variables when the policy is stated in this form. The values of variables will be instantiated at the time of role entry from information about the user established at log on, or from auxiliary information that is retrieved by database look-up.

4.2   Expressing Policy for Method Invocation (Authorisation)

Authorisation of clients is also expressed by Horn clauses in an identical form:

$$MethodRef(field, owner, invoker) \leftarrow RoleRef(arg,..)[\wedge RoleRef(arg,..)]$$
$$[: SideCondition(arg,..) \wedge ..]$$

This establishes a right for clients who hold the nominated RMCs to invoke the stated method, subject to the side condition expressed. This side condition may link the parameters of the method invocation to parameters of the RMCs. Note that any service interface may be authorised in this way, and data access is not restricted to read and write. For example

$$append(haematology\text{-}field, y, x) \leftarrow SeniorHaematologist(x)$$

4.3   Side Conditions and Database Lookup

Restrictions can be imposed by having constants, or matching variables, in the argument for the role or method references. This forces matching at the time of a principal's role entry or data access request. Further restrictions in the form of side conditions are also required to provide enough expressive power. These side conditions will take the form of relations or methods that will be looked up in a local database. For example:

$$Invoke\text{-}read(contact\text{-}details, y, x) \leftarrow GP(x)[gp\text{-}of(x,y)]$$

establishes a right for clients who hold the role GP to read the contact details of their patients.

5   Expressing Policy in Pseudo-natural Language

Access control policy must implement public policy and its expression must be transparent to computer non-specialists. By defining a subset of full English that can be deterministically translated into logic, policy statements intelligible to non-specialists can be defined. Such a subset of English defined in this way has been named Controlled English. Controlled English has been described in [3] and its use as a front-end to a model generation method is described in [4].

5.1   Language Design Using Controlled English

It is impossible to restrict the grammar of Controlled English to eliminate ambiguity without reducing the expressive power to an unusable degree. Where ambiguous sentences can be expressed there is a choice of approaches. Either two or more readings can be returned to the user who then makes a selection, or a fixed interpretation can be forced on readings. The role-entry and access policy statements must be formal and unambiguous so we favour a hard definition, allowing a deterministic interpretation from the natural language statements as originally written. The designer of the grammar should however attempt to ensure that ambiguity is kept to a minimum, and that where an interpretation must be forced it is the more common one.

Role-based access control by its nature restricts the type of English statements that need to be expressed. One of the most important restrictions is in the universal nature of statements; they must say something about **all** principals in a role. Furthermore, in access policy, the statements must say something about all fields of a certain type that may be accessed. The statement:
"A GP can read all his patients' details"
should not be used in such a policy expression. In addition to the statement's contextual ambiguity, in the conventional logic of natural language it only implies that there is a single GP who can read all his patients' details. All statements must therefore start with the words "every" or "all", and not "a".

5.2   Representing Policy in Higher Order Logic

The form of higher order logic that has been chosen for the initial conversion from the Controlled English statements is Discourse Representation Theory [8]. This form of logic has distinct advantages over more traditional Webber style logics. Clearer, more compact representations result from pronouns, and "donkey sentences" (e.g. "every farmer who owns a donkey beats it") can be translated.

Discourse Representation Structures (DRSs) are built up compositionally through a unification based grammar. We use a subset of Controlled English; in particular, only universal quantification can occur. Both the grammar and the lexicon are therefore restricted, which in turn limits the DRS structures that can arise. This simplifies the later conversion to FOPC.

Initially the DRSs may contain unresolved pronoun constructs. During the first pass, when constructing the logic, potential antecedents for pronouns are threaded through the syntax tree, and the possible alternatives are stored for each pronoun appearing in the statement. The pronoun references are then resolved according to set rules.

5.3 Translation to First-Order Predicate Calculus

DRSs are essentially equivalent in expressive power to (function free) first order predicate calculus. Translation from the DRSs to FOPC is simple. Take for example the statement:

"Every GP can read all his patients' contact details"

The resolved DRS for this statement is shown in Figure 3.

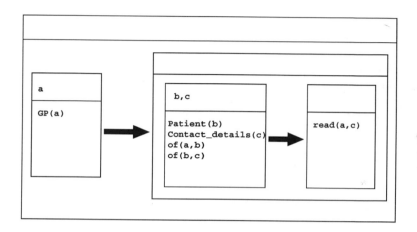

Fig. 3. An example Discourse Representation Structure (DRS)

A set of simple rules translates this into the FOPC formula:

$$\forall a.(GP(a) \Rightarrow \forall bc.(Patient(b) \wedge Contact\text{-}details(c) \wedge of(a,b) \wedge of(b,c) \Rightarrow read(a,c)))$$

This formula is equivalent to:

$$\forall abc.(GP(a) \wedge Patient(b) \wedge Contact\text{-}details(c) \wedge of(a,b) \wedge of(b,c) \Rightarrow read(a,c))$$

Converting the original FOPC formula to Horn clauses is made simpler by the limited nature of the HOL structures that can be formed from the grammar. In fact these structures can be enumerated, and it is possible to convert to the authorisation language directly by simply recognising the DRS pattern. The natural language makes explicit that b references some patient, and that the contact details of that patient may be read. The natural language side conditions that establish these relationships are subsumed by the field selector in the method invocation, and they must be discarded when generating the side conditions to be checked by the procedural guard.

The example above would be translated to:

$$Invoke\text{-}read(contact\text{-}details, b, a) \leftarrow GP(a)[Patient(b) \wedge of(a, b)]$$

It is useful to do some preprocessing on the statement in this form. There are two common problems that arise. First, the "of" side condition that results from the possessive needs to be expanded. This can be done simply by examining the referent of the "of" condition and altering it accordingly. This would result in:

$$Invoke\text{-}read(contact\text{-}details, b, a) \leftarrow GP(a)[Patient(b) \wedge gp\text{-}of(a, b)]$$

The second problem is conditions that are implicit in the context, for example $Patient(b)$ in the statement above. If we generate a check to look up (a, b) in the $gp\text{-}of$ relation, and this check is satisfied, then we can infer from the database schema that b **must** be a patient. The final form of the translation into the authorisation language becomes:

$$Invoke\text{-}read(contact\text{-}details, b, a) \leftarrow GP(a)[gp\text{-}of(a, b)]$$

6   Monitoring System Behaviour and Managing Policy Change

The policy language family described above is particularly suitable for expressing OASIS authentication and authorisation, and we shall investigate its use in specific contexts. The guards generated at services which administer patient records will check that each client has presented certificates which together satisfy a set of preconditions for the access requested. By law the access made and the principal requesting it - here represented by the credentials supplied - must be written to the audit trail. Guards must be kept up to date, and the audit record should be sufficient to identify the policy context under which access was authorised.

6.1   Design and Use of Audit Records

One strength of the OASIS model is that whenever access takes place the procedural guard proves that it is authorised. The context in which the proof takes place includes the arguments to the method invocation, the certificates presented and a representation of the current policy. When a patient record is read, the audit record should identify the patient, the specific data item, the certificates on which the proof depends and a code sufficient to identify the local and higher-level policies from which the procedural guard was derived.

The audit trail so established contains a lot of information about the way the service operates. In the EHR example, it is easy to imagine a number of audit warehouses, each serving a different function. There is a statutory requirement to ensure that patients can know who have seen their health records, and accesses will be indexed by patient identity. It is equally important for health workers to be aware that every access will be recorded, both to inhibit casual curiosity and to restrain them from being subverted by agents of interested parties such as insurance companies and journalists.

In [2] a system is described which allows staff throughout a hospital to access EHRs. In an emergency any health care worker can enter a role which overrides the normal privacy checks. This has worked well, because staff really believe in the effectiveness of the audit trail, and there has been no abuse of the emergency privileges that are available.

6.2   Responding to Changes of Policy

Access to an individual's EHRs is regulated in a variety of ways. In particular, records are personal, and therefore subject to Data Protection legislation, as enacted in both the UK and European parliaments. In each UK province there is also a Patient's Charter, which among other things makes explicit the right of each patient to determine who may access their health records [13]. Health authorities will express policies in terms of the role and seniority of their staff, and the nature of the data that is to be accessed or service that is to be managed. Specialist departments will recognize professional skills in addition to seniority.

All of these sources of policy must be respected when generating procedures (Java classes, in our case) to implement the access control guards on databases which contain patient records. For each high-level source non-specialists should be able to express policy intuitively; the large scale of an application such as the NHS means that guards on the individual databases must be generated automatically. Audit records must identify the policy regime under which each access has been authorized.

7   Evaluation and Future Work

Although this work is in its early stages it has shown that the use of roles in policy specification leads to economical expression of generic policies. We have focussed on access control policy, using a National Electronic Health Record application as an example. We have demonstrated that, starting from the expression of policy in a pseudo-natural language, it is feasible to generate code which carries out access control checks automatically.

We already favour RBAC as the most promising approach for meeting the access control requirements of large scale, continually evolving applications comprising independently developed, heterogeneous components. We have developed a RBAC system OASIS, an open architecture for securely interworking services, and have used the OASIS role entry policy, enforced through its role definition language (RDL), in the work reported here.

We have explored the limits to the expressive power of RBAC; in some situations individuals need to be named explicitly. OASIS easily meets this requirement since its encryption protected certificates may include any number of protected fields, including the holder's name, if identification rather than anonymity is required. At the level of policy expression, such requirements are expressed as side conditions on the parameter values. Alternatively, for an application such as the NHS where identification is a universal requirement, it may be preferable to create an explicit role for the purpose. Principals then hold a principal-specific role membership certificate which proves their authenticated identity for the duration of a session.

This is work in progress. A three-year EPSRC grant starting in October 2000 will develop active policy stores, so that local resource monitors can be updated automatically when a primary policy source is modified. The initial validation of the work will be for access control, but we have other applications in mind, including Service Level Agreements with major communications vendors. We intend to store both primary policies and their intermediate representations in active object-orientated databases, and will make access control to the policy store an essential part of the project. The high bandwidth and reliability of modern communications make it inevitable that applications will be federated across a wide area, with individual management domains interacting subject to a high-level regulatory framework. Many problems remain to be solved before automatic enforcement of expressed policy can become a reality.

8   Acknowledgements

We acknowledge EPSRC's support for the continuation of this work under GR /N35786 "Access Control Policy Management". We are grateful to Steve Pulman for his guidance on Natural Language Processing theory and practice and to Walt Yao for sharing his experience of OASIS implementation. We thank the anonymous referees for generally constructive criticism and for pointing out several errors of detail.

References

[1] Bacon, J., Moody, K., Bates, J.,Hayton, R., Ma, C., McNeil, A., Seidel, O., and Spiteri, M.: Generic Support for Asynchronous, Secure Distributed Applications. IEEE Computer Vol. 33(3) (March 2000) 68–76

[2] Denley, I., and Weston Smith, S.: Privacy in clinical information systems in secondary care. British Medical Journal 318 (May 1999) 1328–1331

[3] Fuchs, N.E., Schwertel, U., and Schwitter, R.: Attempto Controlled English - Not Just Another Logic Specification Language. Lecture Notes in Computer Science, Vol. 1559. Springer Verlag, Berlin, Heidelberg and New York.(1999) 1–20

[4] Fuchs, N.E., Schwertel, U., and Torge, S.: Controlled Natural Language Can Replace First-Order Logic. Proceedings 14th IEEE International Conference on Automated Software Engineering, IEEE Computer Society Press, (1999) 295–298

[5] Hayton, R., Bacon, J. and Moody, K.: OASIS: Access Control in an Open, Distributed Environment. Proceedings IEEE Symposium on Security and Privacy. IEEE CS Press, Los Alamitos, Calif. (1998) 3–14

[6] Hine, J.H., Yao, W., Bacon, J. and Moody, K.: An Architecture for Distributed OASIS Services Proceedings Middleware 2000, Lecture Notes in Computer Science, Vol. 1795. Springer-Verlag, Berlin, Heidelberg and New York. (2000) 107–123.

[7] Jones, A.J.I., and Sergot, M.J.: On the Characterisation of Law and Computer Systems:The Normative Systems Perspective In Deontic Logic in Computer Science: Normative System Specification Meyer,J.-J.Ch., and Wieringa, R.J.(eds), John Wiley and Sons (1993)

[8] Kamp, H., and Reyle, U.: From Discourse to Logic: Introduction to Modeltheoretic Semantics. In Natural Language, Formal Logic and Discourse Representation Theory, Vol.1 and 2, Kluwer (1993)

[9] Lloyd, M.: Conversion of NHS Access Control Policy to Formal Logic. MPhil in Computer Speech and Language Processing, University of Cambridge, (2000)

[10] Lupu, E. and Sloman, M.: Conflicts in Policy-Based Distributed Systems Management. IEEE Transactions on Software Engineering Vol. 25(6) - Special Issue on Inconsistency Management, (Nov/Dec 1999) 852–869

[11] Ma, C., and Bacon, J.: COBEA: A CORBA-based Event Architecture. In Proceedings of the 4th Conference on Object-Oriented Technologies and Systems (COOTS-98), USENIX Association, Berkeley, (April 1998) 117–132

[12] Simon, R. and Zurko, M.: Separation of duty in role-based environments. In Proceedings of the 10th IEEE Computer Security Foundations Workshop, Rockport, Mass., (June 1997) IEEE CS Press, Los Alamitos, Calif. 183–194.

[13] The Patients's Charter (for England), January 1997
see http://www.doh.gov.uk/pcharter/patientc.htm

[14] UK Government White Paper, "The New NHS: Modern, Dependable", December 1997
see http://www.doh.gov.uk/nnhsind.htm

[15] UK Government White Paper, "Information for Health", September 1998,
see http://www.doh.gov.uk/nhsexipu/strategy/index.htm

[16] UK Government White Paper, "The NHS Plan - A Plan for Investment, A Plan for Reform", July 2000,
see http://www.nhs.uk/nationalplan/

Model-Based Tool-Assistance for Packet-Filter Design

Ingo Lück [1], Christian Schäfer [2], Heiko Krumm [2]

[1] Materna Information & Communications, Voßkuhle 37, D-44141 Dortmund, Germany
Ingo.Lueck@materna.de
[2] FB Informatik, LS IV, Universität Dortmund, D-44221 Dortmund, Germany
Krumm@cs.uni-dortmund.de

Abstract. The design of suitable packet-filters protecting subnets against net-work-based attacks is usually difficult and error-prone. Therefore, tool-assistance shall facilitate the design task and shall contribute to the correctness of the filters, i.e., the filters should be consistent with the other security mechanisms of the computer network, in particular with its access control schemes. Moreover, they should just enable the corresponding necessary traffic. Our tool approach applies a three-layered model describing the access control and net-work topology aspects of the system on three levels of abstraction. Each lower layer refines its upper neighbour and is accompanied with access control models. At the top level, role based access control is applied. The lowest level specifies packet filter configurations which can be implemented by means of the Linux kernel extension *IPchains*. The derivation of filter configurations is substantially supported by tool assistance in the course of an interactive design process.

Keywords. packet filter, policy hierarchy, model-based management, firewall design

1. Introduction

Comprehensive intranets and their connections to a growing internet require special protection against network-based attacks. Therefore, firewall technology is usually applied for filtering the network traffic between subnets and furthermore to and from the outside world. The filters, however, cannot perform their task in isolation. They interfere with other security and management mechanisms, in particular with the existing access control and network topology schemes. On the one hand, the filters must not disable traffic which conforms to admissible resource accesses. On the other hand, they should protect against attacks on unknown vulnerabilities and therefore should preferably enable only the necessary traffic. Consequently, the design of suitable filter configurations, i.e., of the placement of filters and of the filtering rules applied, has to consider that context. The filters have to be seamlessly integrated into the general security architecture which is defined in terms of security policies, services, mechanisms, and tasks of proper management.

Security policies describe the critical resources and their users. They explain how the users' access to the resources should be regulated. Moreover, they list the organi-

M. Sloman, J. Lobo, and E. Lupu (Eds.): POLICY 2001, LNCS 1995, pp. 120-136, 2001.

zation's security goals and declare responsibilities and other security-relevant organizational issues [Pfl97]. Typically, like general management policies, security policy statements can have different levels of abstraction forming a policy hierarchy [Mof93, Wie95]. Business-oriented corporate policy statements are at the top of this hierarchy. Each lower level refines the statements of its upper neighbour and may introduce additional information. Finally, at the bottom, rules of technical network and system management directly guide the actions of administrators and define operational network and system parameters.

The other elements of the security architecture serve for the purpose of policy implementation. They form three corresponding abstraction layers. Security services – like authentication, access control, monitoring, and auditing – should provide for the secure operation of the system even under presence of threats. Below, a suite of security mechanisms implements the services, e.g., the access control mechanisms of the network nodes' operating systems can contribute to the implementation of the access control service. Moreover, at the bottom, the technical service and mechanism management has to take care of the proper operation of the systems.

Due to that extensive context, the design of suitable firewall configurations can be difficult and error-prone. Therefore, our approach aims to special tool-assistance. In particular, the tool should provide functions for automated filter-design. Since the fully automated derivation of detailed filter rules from abstract policy statements is not possible, the tool should support a step-wise design process which starts from abstract policy statements, gradually asks for additional information, derives consistent refinements of the policy, and checks the completeness of the result. By using the tool, the definition of policies and system information should be facilitated in order to make it comfortable and clear. By that, it supports the correct understanding of the design and enables efficient interactions between administrators and tool.

We developed a tool-assistance approach which itself is based on a combination of three approaches. Firstly, it applies object-oriented modelling as it is proposed by the Unified Modelling Language approach [Uml97]. In particular, object class and object instance diagrams are used allowing for the graphical specification and manipulation of models. Secondly, we follow up the approach of model-based management [Lüc99] supporting the development of systems for automated network, system and application management. The development starts with the design of a model of the system which should be managed. Thereafter the model is refined. Additional information for the modelling of management objectives and functions is introduced. Finally, the model serves as a starting point for derivation of the management application. The management application also has a model representation at it's disposal which directly supports automated management functions at run-time. Thirdly, our work is based on the notion of management policies and policy hierarchies [Mof93, Slo94, Wie95]. We propose a corresponding policy hierarchy for packet-filter design and represent the policy statements by model extensions. Accordingly, packet-filter design coincides with step-wise model and policy refinement. The tool-assistance is provided by an interactive design tool. Like the *POWER prototype* recently proposed in [Cas00], the tool supports the integration of policies into the practical management: "It enables the refinement of abstract policies and their eventual mapping into an appropriate configuration for controlling devices in the managed system". While the *POWER tool* applies an information and system model in combination with policy templates and policy wizard engines, our tool relies on a homogeneous modelling of policies, rules and managed system.

The approach can be applied for the integral design of whole suites of access control and traffic control mechanisms. Here, we report on a special exemplification concentrating on the design of packet-filters. An implementation of the approach and a corresponding experimental design tool were developed which are particularly attended to configurations of *IPchains*, the packet-filtering extension of the Linux kernel [Lin99].

Besides from the approaches already mentioned, our work is strongly related to role based access control RBAC [San96, Fer99] which had a forming influence on our abstract access control model. Moreover, the modelling is oriented at elements and views of the firewall reference model introduced in [Sch97]. Furthermore we have to mention that also others were aware of the difficulty of filter design. Commercial firewall products are already accompanied with comfortable management tools (e.g., [Cis99]). Those tools, however, concentrate on comfortable filter definitions and do not yet support the automated derivation of filtering rules from abstract policy statements. Nevertheless, an approach has been presented recently which has quite similar objectives and functions as our approach. The Firmato, firewall management toolkit is also based on the application of a system model [Bar99]. In Firmato, an entity-relationship model reflects the hosts, services, server-roles, zones, and connections of the system. The models are specified by means of a model definition language for which a compiler is supplied. It automatically translates model definitions into corresponding filtering rules. Additionally, an illustrator tool shows the resulting filter rules. Compared to Firmato, our approach models the system not only on one, but on three different levels of abstraction. Due to the extended scope of modelling, the filtering rules cannot be derived completely automatically and the refinement steps profit from automated derivations as well as from user interactions.

In the sequel we first outline the approach of model-based management and give a short introduction into the Linux packet-filter kernel extension *IPchains*. Thereafter, we explain the system model with its three layers. The layers correspond to three levels of abstraction. Assignment and correlation elements connect the layers. The next section describes the process of interactive filter design. The initial model and the refining transformation steps are discussed. Then, a software tool supporting this design process is presented. Finally, the conclusion reports about the broader context of the work and particularly outlines pending extensions.

2. Model-Based Management

Due to the growing complexity and extent of networks, systems and applications, their efficient technical management depends more and more on suitable automation. On the one hand, the administrators should be relieved of routine-tasks. Management applications should therefore incorporate automated functions which automatically control the managed system. The applications should have a description of the management objectives at their disposal, should monitor the system and – when the managed system deviates from the objectives – they should compute and execute suitable correcting reactions. On the other hand, the reduction of the development efforts for such specialized and extensive management applications is of high interest.

The approach of model-based management offers support with respect to both aspects [Lüc99]. A model of the managed system is utilized here twice. Firstly, at development time, the model supports the derivation of management applications. Secondly, a run-time representation of the model is available to the management application supporting the detection of deviations and the computation of reactions. Moreover, tool-assistance shall be available for the comfortable and quality-ensured development of the model. For those purposes, the model has to represent different aspects of the managed system and its context. It has to represent the abstract nominal behaviour of the managed system, the working points and functions of the management application, the internal structure and dependencies of the system, as well as the necessary elements and functions of the system's environment. Therefore, the scope of the model is beyond that of static information models which mainly describe the scheme of the management information base (e.g., CIM [Cim98]).

For the step-wise and well-structured modelling of the system [Lüc99] proposes a combination with the approach of service-oriented management [Mcb98, Haw98]. The model development begins with the modelling of the services which have to be provided by the managed system defining a relatively abstract view of the system at the top of the model. At the bottom of the model, the services to be used by the system are described. In the middle, the internal structure of the system is specified by storing information about system components and the dependencies between components, provided and used services (cf. [Rod97]). This hierarchically structured system model is completed by additional model parts which describe the management functionality and apply the approach of policy hierarchies [Mof93, Wie95, Hei96]. Abstract policies specify the nominal behaviour of the system. On lower levels, more detailed policies and management rules define working points of automated monitoring and reaction.

Our approach of model-based tool-assistance for packet-filter design is a special variant of this model-based management. The management objective is the packet-filtering of network traffic. The special management system consists of packet-filters. They are supplied by filtering rules which are parts of the model and generated by the assisting modeller tool.

3. Linux IPchains

IPchains [Lin99] is an IP packet filter tool integrated into the Linux kernel. Thus, a Linux system can be used as a simple firewall which can provide access control and auditing at the boundary of internet and intranet as well as between segments of the intranet.

A packet filter is a piece of software which looks at the header of packets as they pass through, and decide the fate of the entire packet. It might decide to accept the packet (e.g. let the packet go through), deny the packet (e.g. discard the packet as if it had never received it), or reject the packet (like "deny", but telling the source of the packet that it has done so).

The kernel starts with three lists of rules; these lists are called firewall chains or just chains. The three chains are called input, output and forward. When a packet comes the kernel uses the input chain to decide its fate. If it survives that step, then the kernel decides where the packet is sent to next. If it is destined for another machine, it consults the forward chain. Finally, just before a packet is about to go out, the kernel consults the output chain.

A chain is a checklist of rules. Each rule says "if the packet header looks like this, then here's what to do with the packet". If the rule doesn't match the packet, then the next rule in the chain is consulted. Finally, if there are no more rules to consult, then the kernel looks at the chain policy to decide what to do. In a security-conscious system, this policy usually tells the kernel to reject or deny the packet. In our work, we only use rules which accept packets. Furthermore, our chain policies are configured to deny packets.

A rule can specify:
- source and/or destination IP addresses:
  by full name, by IP address or by specification of a group of IP addresses
- the protocol:
  by name or by number
- for the particular case where a protocol of TCP or UDP is specified:
  source and/or destination port (as one port or a range of ports)
- for the particular case where the TCP protocol is specified:
  match only packets with the SYN flag set
- for the particular case where the ICMP protocol is specified:
  type and/or code
- the name of an interface
- match only the second fragment and the following ones
- a rule can be configured to log matching packets

Most parts of a rule can also be used inverted (e.g. all protocols except TCP can be specified).

For each rule there is a byte and a packet counter. If a packet matches a rule, the byte counter for this rule is increased by the size of the packet (header and the rest) and the packet counter for this rule is incremented by one. Counters can manually be set back to zero.

4. Model

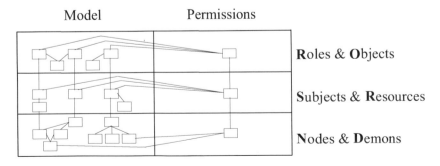

Fig. 1. Model overview

As it is shown in Fig. 1, there are three levels of abstraction (Roles & Objects, Subjects & Resources and Nodes & Demons) in our model. Each level is a refinement of the superordinated level in the sense of a "policy hierarchy" [Wie95]. The uppermost level represents the business-oriented view of the network whereas the lowest level is related to the technical view. The vertical subdivision differentiates between the actual model on the left side and the permissions on the right side. Each of these permissions refer to the model components of the same level.

4.1 Level RO

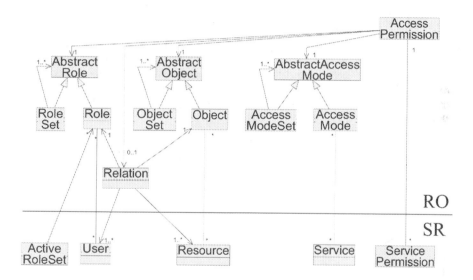

Fig. 2. Level Roles & Objects

The three main classes of level RO (see Fig. 2) are *Role*, *Object* and *AccessMode*. Objects of theses classes represent:

Role: Roles in which people act who are working in the modelled environment.

Object: Objects of the modelled environment which should be subject to access control.

AccessMode: Ways of accessing objects.

An *AccessPermission* allows the performer of a *Role* to access a particular *Object* in the way defined by *AccessMode*. In comparison with [Fer99] *AccessPermissions* combine privileges (associating operations and objects) and their association with roles.

In order to reduce the amount of necessary *AccessPermissions*, the classes *RoleSet*, *ObjectSet* and *AccessModeSet* were introduced. They facilitate merging of *AccessPermissions* without extending the RBAC concept.

For example there can be many different "printer" *Objects* and *AccessPermissions* associated with the printers. If some of these *AccessPermissions* have the same *Role* and *AccessMode* associations, they can be merged into one *AccessPermission* by grouping the printers in an *ObjectSet*.

The cause for introducing the class *Relation* becomes clear when looking at several examples for business-oriented policies and their representation by *AccessPermissions*. The first two examples work without *Relation*:

"Employees are allowed to use the central printer." "Employee" is represented by an object of the class *Role*, "central printer" by an object of the class *Object*, "use" by an object of the class *AccessMode*.

"Administrators are allowed to administrate the print server." Similar to the first example, an *AccessPermission* is created which refers to "administrator", "print server" and "administrate" objects.

"Dial-in-users are allowed to use the Workstation in their offices." This policy should enable employees being at home to use the Workstation in their office via dial-in server. Here, each role performer is allowed to use the Workstation especially associated with him or her. The required *AccessPermission* has to consider the relation between "dialInUser" as a *Role* object and "Workstation" as an *Object* object. For this purpose, there is the object "associatedWorkstation" of the class *Relation*. The *AccessPermission* which was created for this policy refers to the objects "dialInUser", "associatedWorkstation", "Workstation" and "use".

Of course a *Role* can be part of more than one *AccessPermission* (not shown in the examples above). The concept of role inheritance is not implemented in the current prototype.

4.2   Level SR

The level SR (see Fig. 3) consists of a more complex set of classes. Objects of these classes represent:

User: People working in the modelled environment; e.g.: Ms Miller, Mr Smith.

Subject: Subjects acting on the user's behalf carrying out his or her requests; e.g.: Mr Smith can have different subjects. One of them represents him while working at the Workstation in his office, another one while working at home via dial-in-server.

ActiveRoleSet: Set of roles which are appropriate for the associated *Subject*; e.g.: the *Subject* representing Mr Smith at his Workstation has a different *ActiveRoleSet* compared with his dial-in *Subject*. With that, he acts in different roles depending on the way he enters the network. As a possible result, he can get restricted rights while working at home.

Host: Hosts in the network, e.g.: Ms Miller's Workstation, Mr Smith's Workstation. All *Subjects* are associated with Hosts

Service: Services in the network which are used to access resources. A service has references to all resources which it is able to access, e.g. a print service with reference to a printer as a *Resource* or a remote login service with a computer as *Resource*.

Resource: Resources in the network; either real resources, e.g. printers or files, or *Services* which in turn can be used as *Resources* by other *Services*. With that, chains of *Services* can be modelled which are necessary to access to actual *Resources* finally.

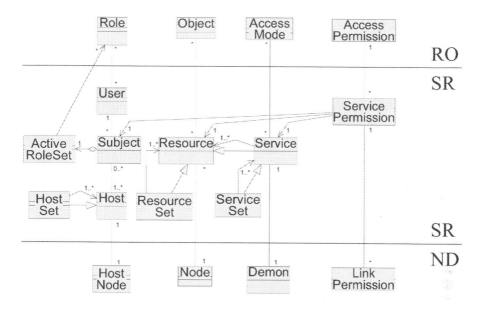

Fig. 3. Level Subjects & Resources

A *ServicePermission* allows a subject to access a resource by using a service. In our model, the term subject is used in accordance with the definition in the RBAC-concept ([Fer99]: "All requests by a user are carried out by subjects acting on the user's behalf."). But there is a difference in the permissions we define for subjects. RBAC associates a subject with the permission of its active roles. We extend that approach and combine the transition from roles to subjects with an additional refinement of operations and objects to services and resources. By that, we change all permission components from a business-oriented view into a more technical one.

As well as in level RO, this level contains additional classes in order to reduce the amount of necessary *ServicePermissions* which are *HostSet*, *ResourceSet* and *ServiceSet*.

4.3 Level ND

In the level ND (see Fig. 4), there are even more classes than before. Objects of these classes represent:

Node: This class is abstract, thus, there are no objects. It is the parent-class for all nodes of the network.

HostNode: Typically, a Workstation which is used by only one employee. A *HostNode* has a single interface.

TransitNode: The generalization of all network nodes which pass on data in the network, e.g. bridges, switches, router. A *TransitNode* has at least two interfaces.

Interface: Each interface has exactly one *IPAddress* and is connected with a physical link. *PhysicalLink*: A connection between two or more interfaces, e.g. a single cable or a hub connecting interfaces.

FilterNode: A subclass of *TransitNode* representing one of the *IPchains* Hosts for which packet filter rules are generated.

VirtualNode: Apart from special cases, a Node does not really exist. It represents an arbitrary set of IPAddresses, e.g. all IPAddresses existing outside the intranet.

IPAddressRange: A range of *IPAddresses* specified by an upper and lower limit.

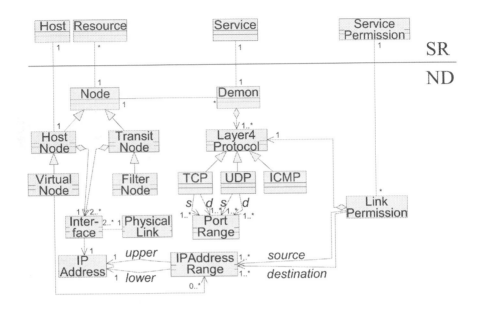

Fig. 4. Level Nodes & Demons

Demon: A process running on a Node in the network which communicates by using one or more Layer4Protocols, e.g. an HTTP server using TCP or a DNS server using TCP and UDP.

Layer4Protocol: This class is abstract, thus, there are no objects. It is a parent-class for all layer-4-protocols.

TCP, UDP, ICMP: Special *Layer4Protocols* containing attributes in order to specify particular features of each protocol, e.g. the side which initialises the connection can be specified for TCP.

PortRange: A range of port numbers used by *TCP* and *UDP* to specify source and destination ports.

A link permission allows the transition of IP packets for a particular *Layer4Protocoll*. Moreover, the allowed source and destination ranges can be defined. Thus, a link permission refers to one Layer4Protocol and two *IPAddressRanges* (source and destination).

5. Interactive Filter Design

The process of interactive filter design is structured into four phases:

  1: system modelling,
  2: association between abstraction levels,
  2: access control definition,
  4: permission derivation.

Fig. 5 shows an example where the first three phases have been carried out. Below we will describe all four phases in general and with regard to this example. Fig. 6 shows the icons and model classes used in the example.

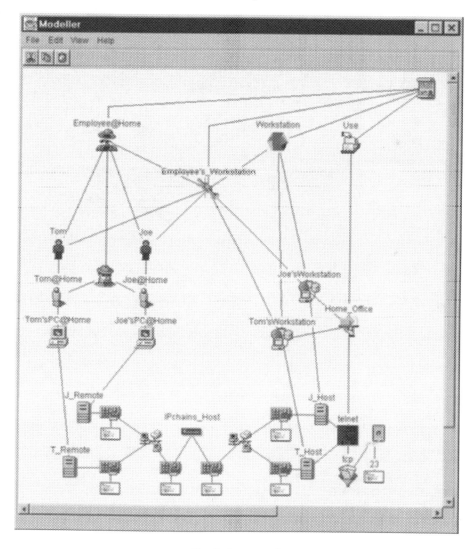

Fig. 5. An example

In the system modelling phase the filter designer successively considers the existing system on the three different levels of abstraction. On each level, he specifies the corresponding objects and their associations. Only those associations, however, are modelled which connect objects of the same abstraction level. Therefore, the three steps of system modelling can be performed separately. Thus, the designer can firstly concentrate on the role-based access control creating the RO-part of the model. He introduces objects of type *Role*, *Object*, *and AccessMode* as well as the connections between these objects. Thereafter, he designs the SR-part in terms of objects of type *User*, *Subject*, *Host*, *Resource*, and *Service*. Finally, the ND-part of the model directly reflects the existing network structure.

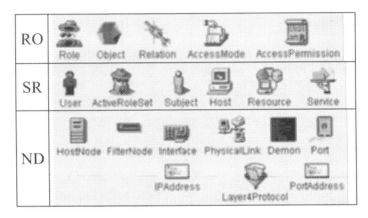

Fig. 6. Symbols for model classes

To keep our example clear we look only at a small part of the whole system. The RO-part of the model consists of the following objects (see Fig. 5):
- "Employee@Home" *Role*: For all employees who are allowed to work at home.
- "Workstation" *Object*: A workstation owned by the company.
- "Use" *AccessMode*: To model usage of a workstation.
- "Employee's_Workstation" *Relation*: Each employee has a Workstation in his office that is exclusively used by him. This *Relation* associates every employee with the workstation in his office. So, in the first phase it is associated with the "Employee@Home" *Role* and the "Workstation" *Object*.

In the SR-part we have the following objects:
- "Tom", "Joe" *User*: Tom and Joe in the model.
- "Tom@Home", "Joe@Home" *Subject*: The system-representation of Tom and Joe when they are working at home.
- An *ActiveRoleSet*: To be associated with all roles that Tom and Joe are allowed to act in when they are at home. (In this example it will only be one role as we'll see later.)
- "Tom'sPC@Home", "Joe'sPC@Home" *Host*: The PCs that are located at the homes of Tom and Joe respectively.
- "Tom's Workstation", "Joe's Workstation" *Resource*: The Workstations that are located in the offices of Tom and Joe respectively.

- "Home_Office" *Service*: A service that enables remote access to workstations to use them from home. So this *Service* is associated with the workstation *Resources* in our example.

The ND-part of the model consists of the following objects:

- "T_Remote", "J_Remote" *HostNode*: There is a gateway server to enable access to the system by modem. After authenticating the caller it represents him to the network by usage of an individual IP address. Thus, for all other components in the network it looks as if the caller is a host in the net. Therefore we represent Tom's and Joe's remote access by *HostNodes*. Each of them is associated to an individual *IPAddress* through its *Interface*.
- "IPchains_Host" *FilterNode*: It has two *Interfaces* that connect it to the remote *HostNodes* on the one and to the local *HostNodes* on the other side.
- "T_Host", "J_Host" *HostNode*: The workstations in Tom's and Joe's offices.
- "telnet" *Demon*: Both Tom's and Joe's workstation have a telnet demon process running. So there are associations between this *Demon* and the two *HostNodes*. Telnet communicates using tcp on port 23. Hence there is an association to a *Port* that is associated with *Layer4Protocol* "tcp" and *PortAddress* "23".

The next phase introduces the associations between the three abstraction levels of the system model. The first step is attended to the transition from RO to SR. Here, the associations between *User* and *Role* objects directly reflect the relations of the role-based access control. Additionally, the filter designer has to specify the relation between abstract *Objects* and their implementing sets of localizable *Resources*. Finally, abstract *AccessModes* have to be associated with *Services*. For that purpose, the tool identifies the existing *Object-AccessMode*-pairs of RO-level. Each pair corresponds to a certain abstract operation, e.g., "usage of central printer", and the designer has to define which *Service-Resource*-pairs implement the operation, e.g., that "print service" under access of "printer1" is a possible implementation of "usage of central printer". In this case, the *Object* "central printer" is mapped to the *Resource* "printer1" and the *AccessMode* "use" is mapped to the *Service* "print service". The second step defines the associations between SR and ND. It connects *Hosts* with the corresponding *HostNodes* of the existing network, *Resources* with the *Nodes* where the resources reside, and finally *Services* with the implementing *Demons*. For instance, the resource "printer1" may be local to *HostNode* "pshost" and the "print service" may be provided by a *Demon* which is allocated at *HostNode* "pshost", as well.

Let us have a look at our example (Fig. 5) again. First, we introduce the associations between objects of level RO and level SR:

- The *Role* "Employee@Home" is associated with the *Users* "Tom" and "Joe" who should be allowed to act in this role. Furthermore, it is associated with the *ActiveRoleSet* object to express that the *Subjects* "Tom@Home" and "Joe@Home" have to act exactly in this *Role*.
- The *Object* "Workstation" is associated with the *Resources* "Tom'sWorkstation" and "Joe'sWorkstation".
- The *AccessMode* "Use" is associated with the *Service* "Home_Office".
- The *Relation* "Employee's_Workstation" is associated with the *Users* "Tom" and "Joe" and with the *Resources* "Tom'sWorkstation" and "Joe'sWorkstation". It is stored in the *Relation* object that

"Tom'sWorkstation" is related to "Tom" and "Joe'sWorkstation" is related to "Joe".

As the second step of phase two the associations between objects of level SR and level ND are introduced:

-   The *Hosts* "Tom'sPC@Home" and "Joe'sPC@Home" are associated with the *HostNodes* "T_Remote" and "J_Remote" respectively.
-   The *Resources* "Tom'sWorkstation" and "Joe'sWorkstation" are associated with the *HostNodes* "T_Host" and "J_Host" respectively.
-   The *Service* "Home_Office" is associated with the *Demon* "telnet".

The third phase defines the abstract access control rules. The designer inputs the *AccessPermisssions* by creating all corresponding triples of *Role*, *Object*, and *AccessMode*.

In our example (see Fig. 5) we have just one *AccessPermission*. It is associated with the *Role* "Employee@Home", the *Relation* "Employee's_Workstation", the *Object* "Workstation" and the *AccessMode* "Use". It models an abstract rule that can be written as: "An employee working at home is allowed to use the workstation in his/her office."

The last phase utilizes the information having been supplied so far for the automated derivation of the *IPchains* filtering rules. The first step analyses the RO- and SR-parts of the model in combination with the *AccessPermissions* in order to create the *ServicePermissions*. For each *AccessPermission* it traces the associations of the contained *Role*, *Object*, and *AccessMode*. The associations reach *Subjects*, *Resources*, and *Services*. The tool is able to compute all possibly implementing combinations resulting in the definition of the *ServicePermissions*. The example *AccessPermission*, that employees are allowed to use the central printer, in this way is translated to a set of *ServicePermissions* which grant the access to "printer1" via "print service" to each subject containing "employee" in its *ActiveRoleSet*. The second step translates *ServicePermissions* to *LinkPermissions*. The tool traces the associations from *Hosts* and *Resources* via *HostNodes* to *IPAddressRanges*, and from *Services* via *Demons* to *Layer4Protocols*. Moreover, it looks for link routes between *Subject*-site *HostNodes* and *Demon*-Site *HostNodes*. For each direction, subroute, and sub-*IPAddressRange* of a ServicePermission, the set of resulting *LinkPermissions* is created. They contain additional parameters – i.e., special protocol options (e.g., TCP-flags, type and code of ICMP packets) – to be supplied by the designer interactively. Eventually, the resulting set of *LinkPermissions* is subject to optimisation which eliminates duplicates and merges compatible *LinkPermissions* with overlapping address ranges. In our example of printing employees, the generated *LinkPermissions* open the routes between the IP-addresses of those *HostNodes*, which can be accessed by employee-subjects, and the *HostNode* where the printing service demon is located.

The next step of the last phase checks the correctness of the derived set of *LinkPermissions*. The permissions should enable just that traffic which corresponds to admissible object accesses of the abstract model. One part of this condition – all necessary traffic shall find an enabled route – is ensured by construction since the translation of *AccessPermissions* via *ServicePermissions* to *LinkPermissions* comprises all *AccessPermissions*. In contrast, the other part of this condition – all traffic should be suppressed which does not correspond to an *AccessPermission* – is of course usually not true since packet filters are a very restricted means for the implementation of general access control. In particular, the filter rules apply to IP-addresses and protocol type information. This information only correlates with users, roles, objects, and operations if the network is explicitly designed accordingly, e.g., if nodes and their IP-addresses are exclusively associated with certain users and services. Moreover, the network topology, the number of *FilterNodes* and their placement in the given network topology has to support the necessary traffic restrictions.

Nevertheless, it is of interest for the filter designer to be informed about the differences between access control and packet filters. Possibly, a slight restructuring of the network reduces the risks. Furthermore, the information can help to focus on additional security mechanisms. Therefore, the tool performs a model-based analysis of the generated *LinkPermissions*. For each *Demon* it computes the set of possible client *Nodes* which can reach the demon via the network. The *HostNodes* correspond with sets of possible *Subjects* and *ActiveRoleSets* in the SR-part of the model, the *Demons* correspond with sets of *Resources* and *Services*. In a next step, these object sets are mapped to *Roles*, *Objects*, and *AccessModes* of the RO-part of the model. Possible triples which do not directly correspond to *AccessPermissions* are reported to the filter designer.

Finally, in a very last step the back-end of the tool generates the **IPchains** filtering rules. Each *LinkPermission* is directly translated to a positive filtering rule. Additionally, the tool produces filtering rules which correspond to fixed patterns and support helpful general traffic restrictions, e.g., protection against IP-spoofing at the borders to the outside world.

For the *AccessPermission* in our example (see Fig. 5) the tool generates two *ServicePermissions* (not shown to keep the figure clear). One of them is associated with the *Subject* "Tom@Home", the *Resource* "Tom'sWorkstation" and the *Service* "Home_Office". It allows "Tom@Home" to use "Home_Office" with "Tom'sWorkstation". The other *ServicePermission* is similar but for "Joe@Home", "Joe'sWorkstation" and "Home_Office". In the next step, the tool derives two *Link-Permissions* from the *ServicePermissions*. The *LinkPermission* derived from the *ServicePermission* dealing with Tom is associated with the *IPAddress* related to "T_Remote", the *IPAddress* related to "T_Host" and the *Layer4Protocol* "tcp". It allows "T_Remote" to communicate with "T_Host" on "tcp" port 23. The other *Link-Permission* derived from the *ServicePermission* dealing with Joe is similar. In this example, there is exactly one *LinkPermission* derived from each *ServicePermission*. However if a *Service* is distributed among different *HostsNodes* one *ServicePermission* leads to many *LinkPermissions*. As a last step the tool evaluates the *LinkPermissions* to generate **IPchains** filtering rules as shown below. We used the following IP addresses for our example:

"T_Remote" = 128.123.3.1 , "T_Host" = 128.123.1.1
"J_Remote" = 128.123.3.2 , "J_Host" = 128.123.1.2

The tool produced the following filter configuration file for the IPchains_host. At the beginning, it sets up the default chain policy "REJECT". Thereafter, positive rules enable the inbound and outbound telnet traffic for each of the two remote entries T_Remote and J_Remote.

```
#flush all chains
ipchains -F

#default policy REJECT on all chains
ipchains -P input REJECT
```

```
ipchains -P forward REJECT
ipchains -P output REJECT

#inbound path
ipchains -A input    -i eth0 -p tcp
         -s 128.123.3.1 -d 128.123.1.1 23 -j ACCEPT
ipchains -A forward -i eth1 -p tcp
         -s 128.123.3.1 -d 128.123.1.1 23 -j ACCEPT
ipchains -A output   -i eth1 -p tcp
         -s 128.123.3.1 -d 128.123.1.1 23 -j ACCEPT

#outbound path
ipchains -A input    -i eth1 -p tcp
         -s 128.123.1.1 23 -d 128.123.3.1 -j ACCEPT
ipchains -A forward -i eth0 -p tcp
         -s 128.123.1.1 23 -d 128.123.3.1 -j ACCEPT
ipchains -A output   -i eth0 -p tcp
         -s 128.123.1.1 23 -d 128.123.3.1 -j ACCEPT

#inbound path
ipchains -A input    -i eth0 -p tcp
         -s 128.123.3.2 -d 128.123.1.2 23 -j ACCEPT
ipchains -A forward -i eth1 -p tcp
         -s 128.123.3.2 -d 128.123.1.2 23 -j ACCEPT
ipchains -A output   -i eth1 -p tcp
         -s 128.123.3.2 -d 128.123.1.2 23 -j ACCEPT

#outbound path
ipchains -A input    -i eth1 -p tcp
         -s 128.123.1.2 23 -d 128.123.3.2 -j ACCEPT
ipchains -A forward -i eth0 -p tcp
         -s 128.123.1.2 23 -d 128.123.3.2 -j ACCEPT
ipchains -A output   -i eth0 -p tcp
         -s 128.123.1.2 23 -d 128.123.3.2 -j ACCEPT
```

6. Tool

Our Tool primarily consists of a graphical editor (see Fig. 5) with following functions:
- Load/save the model
- Import of textual model-descriptions
- Interactive construction of the model by choosing and positioning of model-elements and associations
- Organization of model-elements in folders
- Check of Model-dependent constraints
- Configuration of attributes by means of inspect dialogues
- Guided derivation of different permission variants through the model-hierarchy levels

The editor allows the selection of classes from each level of the model. So, an object is created whose graphical representation can be placed freely in the drawing area. An invisible grid leads to an ordered alignment. Folders can be created in which model elements can be organized. Attributes for which get- and set-methods are available in the model classes can be configured ("Inspect"-Dialog). If an association between two objects should be modelled, it is done by drawing an edge using the mouse.

This will be possible if the source object has a suitable set-method for the class of the destination object.

The tool supports the initial import of a textual model description. By that, information from external management applications can be utilized, e.g. a list of user names or used IP-addresses. The input format which is shown in the following example can be easily read and edited:

```
[Interface]
interface_label
*IPAddress: ipaddress_label

[IPAddress]
ipaddress_label
Address: "192.168.0.1"
```

By selecting the menu point "Check Constraints", the tool checks whether the model is complete in the sense of given constraints. Dialogues indicate that constraints are violated e.g., "Host needs to have a name set", "Interface needs a reference to an IPAddress", etc. Moreover, dialogues ask for input where information for a model refinement is missing e.g., "Which *Service* is needed for *AccessMode* 'modify' of *Resource* 'database' ?". These steps support interactive derivation of *ServicePermissions* from *AccessPermissions*, *LinkPermissions* from ServicePermissions and an *IPchains* configuration file from *LinkPermissions*.

7. Concluding Remarks

We reported about a tool approach assisting in the design of *IPchains* packet filter configurations. Though the developed special tool already provides very helpful support, we presently study a more general modelling which additionally represents access control mechanisms and application gateways. Thus, the design of gateway-based firewall configurations will be supported and the tool can perform more specialized correctness checks. Ultimately, our aim is the integral modelling of all relevant security mechanisms and system components of a computer network in order to support a combined management of security services, security mechanisms, and network elements.

Furthermore, there is another direction of work which will directly extend the present tool. Up to now, the tool is used at design time only. The proper operation of packet-filters, however, depends also on managing actions at run-time. In particular, continuous monitoring and auditing shall support the detection of attacks. It is usually based on the log-files of the packet-filters which provide large sets of low-level information. Our current work therefore utilizes the layered model and the associations between the layers for the transformation of low-level log-statements into corresponding high-level reports.

References

[Bar99]   Y. Bartal, A. Mayer, K. Nissim and A. Wool: Firmato: A Novel Firewall Management Toolkit. In Proc. IEEE Computer Society Symposium on Security an Privacy, 1999.

[Cas00]   M. Casassa Mont, A. Baldwin, C. Goh: POWER Prototype: Towards Integrated Policy-Based Management. in Proc. of the IEEE/IFIP Int. Symposium on Network Operations and Management NOMS 2000, IEEE, 2000.

[Cim98]   Desktop Management Taskforce: Common Information Model - Specification 2.0; Desktop Management Taskforce Inc. DMTF, 1998, available via http://www.dmtf.org/spec/

[Cis99]   Cisco Systems, Inc: Delivering end-to-end security in policy-based networks. http://www-uk.cisco.com/warp/public/cc/cisco/mkt/enm/cap/tech/deesp_wp.htm , 1999.

[Eji96]   M. Ejiri, S. Goyal (eds.): Proc. of the IEEE/IFIP Int. Symposium on Network Operations and Management NOMS'96, IEEE, 1996.

[Fer99]   D.F. Ferraiolo, J.F. Barkley and D.R. Kuhn: A Role Based Access Control Model and Reference Implementation within a Corporate Intranet. ACM Transactions on Information Systems Security, Volume 1, Number 2, February 1999.

[Haw98]   M. Haworth: Service Management and Availability Planning for Data Backup and Recovery; HP Open View Service Management Solutions, White paper, Hewlett-Packard Company, Palo Alto, 1998.

[Hei96]   K. Heiler, R. Wies: Policy Driven Configuration Management of Network Devices. In [Eji96] , pg. 674-689, 1996.

[Laz97]   A. Lazar et al. (eds.): Integrated Network Management V, Proc. 5th IFIP/IEEE Int. Symposium on Integrated Network Management, Chapman & Hall, London, 1997.

[Lin99]   Linux documentation: IPchains HowTo, 1999.

[Lüc99]   I. Lück, M. Schönbach, A. Mester and H.Krumm: Derivation of Backup Service Management Applications from Service and System Models. In: R. Stadler, B. Stiller (Eds.), Active Technologies for Network and Service Management, Proc. DSOM'99, pages 243-255, Zürich, Oct. 1999, LNCS 1700, Springer-Verlag.

[Mcb98]   D. McBride: Successful Deployment of IT Service Management in the Distributed Enterprise; White paper, Hewlett-Packard Company, Palo Alto, 1998.

[Mof93]   J. Moffet, M. Sloman: Policy Hierarchies for Distributed Systems Management. IEEE Journal on Selected Areas in Communications, 11, 9, 1993.

[Pfl97]   C.P. Pfleeger: Security in Computing (second edition). Prentice-Hall, Inc. 1997.

[Rod97]   G. Rodosek, T. Kaiser: Determining the Availability of Distributed Applications; in [Laz97], pg. 207-218, 1997.

[San96]   R. Sandhu, E. Coyne, H. Feinstein, Ch. Youman: Role-Based Access Control Models. IEEE Computer 29(2), pg. 38-47, 1996.

[Sch97]   C.L. Schuba and E.H. Spafford: A Reference Model for Firewall Technology. First Annual Sprint Applied Research parTners Advanced Networking (SPARTAN) Symposium, March 1997.

[Slo94]   M. Sloman: Policy Driven Management for Distributed Systems. Journal of Network and Systems Management, Plenum Press, Vol. 2, No. 4, 1994.

[Uml97]   G. Booch, J. Rumbaugh, I. Jacobson: The Unified Modelling Language User Guide; Addison-Wesley, Reading, 1997.

[Wie95]   R. Wies: Using a Classification of Management Policies for Policy Specification and Policy Transformation. In Proc. of the 4th IFIP/IEEE Int. Symposium on Integrated Network Management, Santa Barbara, 1995.

Policy Based SLA Management in Enterprise Networks

Dinesh Verma, Mandis Beigi, and Raymond Jennings

IBM Thomas J Watson Research Center
PO Box 704
Yorktown Heights, NY 10598, USA
{dverma,raymondj,mandis}@us.ibm.com

Abstract. The Differentiated Services Architecture defines the mechanisms that are needed to offer multiple classes of services in an IP network. While this model offers significant scaling advantages over the signaling-oriented approach of Integrated Services, the management of a differentiated services network remains a complex problem. Since the operation of a differentiated network involves numerous access routers, core routers and servers, a consistent operation is difficult to achieve by independently configuring each device. In this paper, we explore a scheme to enable a network administrator to manage and configure DiffServ networks from a central location and also abstract away the specific details of device configuration, and allow him/her to express the management of the network in terms of application-oriented performance metrics. This leads to a simplification of network management task, which can be exploited to support business needs of an enterprise network, such as honoring Service Level Agreements provided to its customers.

1. Introduction

The IP networks of today are transitioning from a best-effort service model to one that can provide different service levels in the network. The interest and activities of the technical community in the area has led to the development of two standards for Quality of Service (QoS) -- the RSVP signaling (IntServ/RSVP) approach [1], which was followed by the differentiated services (DiffServ) approach [2]. Integrated services with RSVP signaling approach attempts to provide per-flow QoS assurances with dynamic resource reservation, where a flow corresponds to a transport session (such as a TCP connection or UDP stream to a multicast address group). In order to avoid the scaling issues associated with the per-flow state needed in the RSVP approach, the DiffServ approach attempts to provide different service levels to traffic aggregates, and the service level of each packet is identified by means of a 6-bit field in the IP header. Each distinct value of the field identifies the processing to be done for a specific level, which are called Per Hop Behavior (PHB) in DiffServ terminology.

The DiffServ standards can be deployed by an Internet Service Provider (ISP) to offer different service levels to its customers, or by an enterprise network operator to offer different classes to the various applications running over an enterprise intranet. An

M. Sloman, J. Lobo, and E. Lupu (Eds.): POLICY 2001, LNCS 1995, pp. 137-152, 2001.

ISP has to resolve the complex issues associated with pricing of different service levels. In an enterprise environment, the pricing issue is relatively less important, and classes of services are more likely to be defined in terms of the perceived importance a traffic to the business needs of the enterprise. In both types of deployment, the tricky issue arises in the management of the differentiated services network.

A sample deployment of the differentiated services in an enterprise network is illustrated in Figure 1. We assume that the wide area network (WAN) is bandwidth-constrained, and consists of routers that support DiffServ. The WAN is connected to two LANs, one hosting several clients, and the other hosting some servers. The access routers examine the 5-tuples (source and destination IP address, source and destination port numbers and the protocol) in a packet headed towards the WAN and mark then with a specific value of the DS field. The core routers look at the different markings and process the packets accordingly. Marking can also be done by the servers in the network. In this case, the access router at the server site needs to examine only the DS field of the packets entering the WAN and optionally changing it.

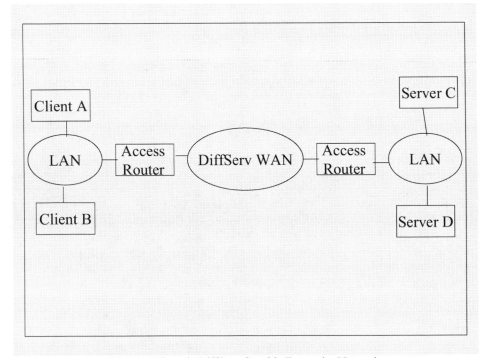

Fig. 1. A Sample DiffServ Capable Enterprise Network

In a typical enterprise, the number of servers and routers runs into hundreds and thousands. Independent configuration of all these devices in order to map one application (e.g. clearing credit card transactions) to a higher service level than another application (e.g. email) is tedious and can easily lead to missed devices and inconsistent configuration. Furthermore, the amount of resources to be reserved at a specific core router for any specific PHB (or service level) is dependent on routing topology and the performance associated with the service levels. The determination of the appropriate resources needed at specific routers needs to be done by means of an automated tool.

As a result, the network administrator in an enterprise needs tools that allow configuration of networks at a higher level of abstraction than that offered by individual configuration of the network devices. In this paper, we present a management tool for Differentiated Services, which we have built to simplify managing DiffServ in an enterprise environment. With relatively minor modifications, the same tool can be used in an ISP environment.

Section 1 (this section) introduced the problem and provides the background. In Section 2, we present the architecture of the QoS management tool that we have developed. Section 3 describes the view of QoS management that a network operator sees, as well as the view of QoS management that devices in the network experience. Section 4 provides details on how the network operator's views are transformed into device configuration and Section 5 provides details on the other components that comprise the management tool. Section 6 gives an example of managing the tools in an enterprise, including some screen views associated with the tool. Finally, we identify open issues and areas of future work.

2. The QoS Management Tool

The QoS Management tool is software used by a network administrator to configure and administer the DiffServ components in an enterprise network. The components of the management tool are as shown in Figure 2.

The QoS management tool consists of five major components:

- The *Graphical User Interface* is the means by which an administrator can input the objectives for deploying QoS in the network. The objectives constitute the business Service Level Agreements (SLAs) that the network is required to meet to satisfy the performance needs to its customers. The SLAs are specified in terms of the performance that is expected from each of the applications in the network.
- The *Resource Discovery* component is responsible for determining the topology of the network and the users and applications that are operational in the network. The component is also responsible for identifying the capabilities of each device in the network, e.g. the set of PHBs that are supported at the core routers, or the capabilities of a server to retrieve configuration information stored in the network. Some servers (e.g. IBM System 390) and routers (e.g. Nways 2216) are capable of obtaining configuration information stored in a network directory and configure themselves.
- The *view transformation logic* component is responsible for ensuring that the business SLAs that are specified by the network administrator are mutually

consistent, correct and feasible with the existing capacity and topology of the network. It also translates the business SLAs into device configuration information[1] that can be distributed to the different components.

- The *Configuration Distributor* is responsible for ensuring the device configuration is distributed to the various devices in the network. The distribution of the configuration can be done in a variety of ways. One way would be by storing them into a repository from where different devices can retrieve it[2]; making a configuration file and copying it over to the device. Another way is to have a program, which can log into the device console remotely and issue commands to configure it appropriately.
- The *performance monitor* keeps track of the performance of the network, and compares the performance obtained by different traffic flows in the network. It determines whether the business SLAs specified by the network administrator are being satisfied or not. Our current prototype only validates SLA compliance. We are exploring adaptive models that exploit feedback from the performance monitor.

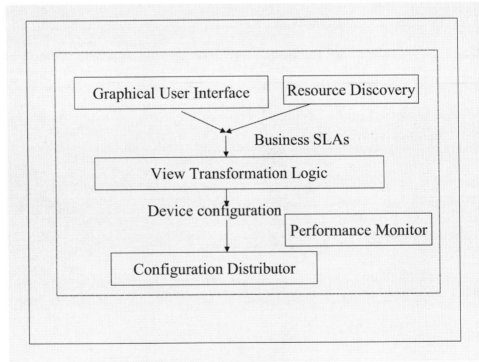

Fig. 2. Components of the QoS Management Tool

---

[1] The device configuration in terms of PHBs is abstract in the sense that it is not mapped to how a router actually implements a PHB (and can be called an abstract policy). In this paper, we would use configuration due to its clarity.

[2] The technique for storing configuration information in a repository follows the preferred architecture of policy framework working group within IETF [8].

Both the business SLAs and device configuration are specified in XML using a specialized DTD. The configuration distributor is responsible for the translation of the XML tags into the specific notation used in the configuration files, or for the schema used within the LDAP directory.

There are several advantages of using XML for the representation of SLAs and configuration information. XML provides a human-readable format for representing information, which is useful in the debugging and deployment of the tool. Due to the wide availability of parsers and validators for XML documents, the effort needed in the development of the QoS management tool is reduced. Furthermore, due to the flexibility of information representation in XML, adding new types of information is relatively easy.

3. QoS Views

As described earlier, there are two views of QoS management, one corresponding to business SLAs, which is manipulated by the network administrator, and one corresponding to the individual device configuration. Both the business level SLAs and device configuration information consists of a number of tables. The tables of the SLA information can be populated by the network administrator or by means of the resource discovery module, while the tables of device configuration information are generated by the logic component. Business SLAs are manipulated by the network administrator, while the device configuration view is used by the configuration distributor. The business SLA view would be easier for the network administrator to specify while the device configuration view would be the easier one for devices in the network to interpret.

The business SLA information manipulated by the network administrator consists of the elements shown in Figure 3. Each element in Figure 3 corresponds to a table, which is populated with details specific to the enterprise network. Arrows indicate tables that contain links to other tables, and some significant attributes in each table are outlined. Similarly, the device configuration view is shown in Figure 4.

The network administrator sees two types of active entities in the network: users and applications. Each of these can be grouped into user groups or application groups. A user is characterized by the machine name or an IP address. If a user does not have a static IP address, the machine name is specified rather than the IP address. A user group is essentially an alias for a group of IP addresses. A user group may be defined as a collection of different users, or as a range of IP addresses. Thus, a user group may be defined for a department such as accounting which uses IP addresses from the subnet with addresses from the class C network address of 9.2.75.0. Individual machines from accounting may use DHCP to assign addresses dynamically within this network.

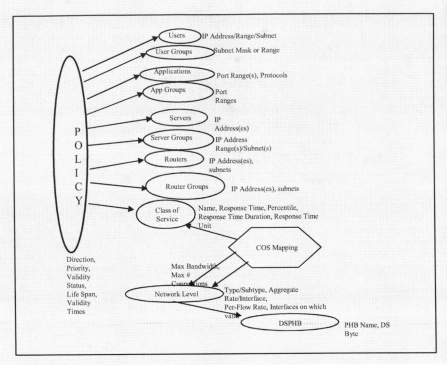

Fig. 3. High Level View for QoS Management

An application is characterized by a class of TCP or UDP port numbers that it uses. This model works well for applications that run on well known ports, or can be configured to use port numbers that are dynamic but constrained to take port numbers between a specific range. This characterization does not work for applications that use dynamic port ranges without any constraints.

The topology of the network enumerates the servers and routers that are present in the network. The goal of the topology generation is to determine the devices that need to be configured in the network, and to generate the appropriate configuration information for the listed devices. With some distribution mechanisms, the need to determine network topology can be avoided. However, the availability of network topology results in a better configuration information for the devices.

The administrator can define several classes of service in the network. The class of service measures the responsiveness of traffic flows belonging to that class. The responsiveness of a service is characterized by the round-trip delay experienced by packets in the network. This metric is readily available for TCP-based applications where the round trip time estimates can be obtained from the server's stack measurements. For UDP-based applications or the ISP environments, this metric can be obtained by statistical probing techniques (see [3] for an example of such a probing technique).

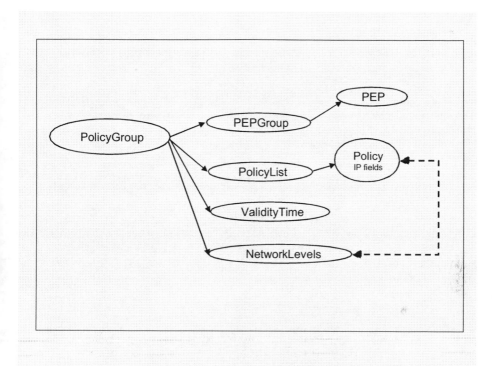

Fig. 4. Low Level View for QoS Management

A policy is defined for a user (or user group) accessing an application (or application group) running on a server (or group of servers). The policy maps this traffic aggregate into a class of service. A policy also has a life-span, which defines the period when the policy is active. A life-span has a beginning time and an ending time. In addition to the life-span, the policy may be further restricted to occur only on specific days or dates by specifying a validity-time field.

The last step of managing application level performance is defining the class of service (COS) in terms of the PHBs that are supported at the different network devices. A list of the PHBs that are supported at the different devices is obtained by means of resource discovery. A table of COS mappings defines how each class of service is to be implemented in the network. COS mappings can be defined differently at different servers or routers in the network. The COS mapping table defines limits on the amount of resources that each class of service should enforce, e.g. limits on the network bandwidth, or bounds on the total number of connections belonging to that class should be permitted at a server.

Like the business level view, the device configuration view consists of a set of tables. These tables are divided into several groups, each group consisting of three tables. Within each group, the first table enumerates the set of devices, which constitute the group. The second table enumerates the set of PHBs, which are supported in all the devices in the group. The third table specifies the device configuration rules that map specific traffic aggregates to specific network PHBs. All devices in the group are configured identically and support the same set of PHBs. The device configuration rules consist of the fields in the protocol headers that define a traffic aggregate. Such a traffic aggregate can be defined by means of a 6-tuple, which consists of a subset of the source and destination IP addresses (or subnets), protocol, source and destination port address ranges, and the incoming DS field. Instead of the source and destination IP addresses, domain names may be specified to accommodate hosts that use DHCP and do not have a static IP address. This eliminates the need to recomputed device configuration when DHCP leases expire or change.

4. View Transformation Logic

The view transformation logic validates the information provided in the business SLAs, and transforms them into the configuration of devices in the network. The logic furthermore ensures that the policies specified are mutually consistent and cover all aspects of interest to the network administrator.

The view transformation logic takes a parsed XML tree [4] representing the business level view and validates its semantic correctness. The validation of the syntax of the policy specification is done automatically by XML parsers/generators given the document type definition (DTD) which defines the syntax of the business level specification. The semantic validation consists of the following three types of checks:

- *Bounds Checks*: This check validates that the values taken by any parameter in the policy specification in within the specific constraints determined by the network administrator. As an example, a network administrator should be able to specify that all response times in any defined class of service be less than 1000 ms.
- *Constraint Checks*: This check validates that the values taken by any two parameters in the policy specification are within constraints that make sense. For example, two attributes of a class of service are response time and the duration over which the response time has to be measured. The latter must be larger than the former, and the network administrator should be able to specify how large the response time ought to be.
- *Consistency Checks*: These checks ensure that each traffic flow is mapped onto exactly one service class, and that each service class is properly defined at all the interfaces. These checks are applied in the manner described below.

The three types of checks can be looked upon as validating an entry in a table, a row in a table, and resolving conflicts between two rows in a table.

The approach taken for consistency checking is to map each row of a table into a region in a hyper-space defined by the columns of the table. The scheme is best illustrated by means of simplified policy table, which consists of only three columns, a user group, an application group and a service class. Two of these columns, the user group and the application group form the two axes of a 2-dimensional space. Any row, which specifies the user groups and application groups forms a region in the 2-

dimensional space. This region is marked with the service class described in the row. If there is any region, which is marked with two service classes, there is a potential conflict.

With the representation of policies used in the business SLAs, the space being compared consists of six dimensions comprising of: the clients (user or user groups), the application (or application group), the server (or server groups), the life span, the validity time and the conflict resolution priority. The class of service is the column used for marking the regions in hyper-space. If two policies are found to be conflicting, the user is asked to change the conflict resolution priority to eliminate the conflict.

To determine if classes of service are mapped properly to network PHBs, the space of comparison consists of two dimensions: the class of service being mapped and the set of interfaces for which the mapping is valid. The network PHB, which the class of service is being mapped to, is used for marking the hyper-space. If the same class of service is being mapped to different PHBs at the same interface, it is an error, which must be corrected by the network administrator.

After validating that SLAs are consistent and well-formed, the view transformation logic translates the SLAs into device configuration information. The step essentially maps applications to corresponding port number ranges, users/user groups to the corresponding IP addresses and the class of service to corresponding PHBs at each of the interfaces in the network. After the device configuration rules are obtained, they are grouped to reduce the number of irrelevant rules that may be applied to a device.

In order to group the device configuration rules, each rule is considered to be either relevant or irrelevant to a server or router. To a server, a rule is relevant if the source or destination IP address range contained in the device configuration rule contains the IP address of the server. For a router, a device configuration rule is considered relevant only if the shortest-hop[3] route taken between the source and destination IP addresses passes through an access router. In most of the configuration, this rule applies only when the source or the destination IP address range is behind that access routers.

After the generation of rules associated, the devices in the network are divided into several groups. Two devices are placed in the same group if and only if they support the same set of network PHBs and have the same set of relevant policies. The device configuration rules are then distributed to the individual devices.

One function that is needed by the policy tool is the determination of the bandwidth needed for each PHB in the core routers. This requires linking up the bandwidth requirement of each class of service with the current routing topology in the network. Unlike the case of determining the relevance of a policy, we need to determine whether a router lies on the current route taken by a traffic flow, as opposed to

---

[3] An implicit assumption is that OSPF or RIP routing protocols and the shortest hop path is used for routing IP packets in the network.

whether a router could potentially be on one of the possible shortest hop paths. Our implementation is not currently linked to a routing daemon in the network.

5. Component Description

Although the view transformation logic is the most crucial portion of policy management, other components, namely configuration distributor, resource discovery, performance monitoring and the user interface are essential for its operation. These are described in the following sections.

5.1 Configuration Distributor

The distribution of device configuration rules to the individual devices may be done in a variety of ways. Among the possible methods that can be used are:

− *Populating a Repository*: The management tool can write out the device configuration rules into a configured repository in the network. Individual servers and routers pull the configuration information from the repository and configure themselves. The repository supported in our implementation is an LDAP directory server   [5].

This approach provides the easiest option for the QoS management tool. However, it does require that the devices in the network be capable of pulling QoS configuration information out from the *LDAP directory*. All devices may not be capable of such a function. Furthermore, since many common LDAP server implementations do not support asynchronous notification to a client when an entry changes, there is a lag between the time when a policy is entered at the management tool and when it becomes effective at a device.

An alternative repository would be a *web-server* with servlets or cgi-bin *scripts* that implement functions such as populating an LDAP directory, pushing configuration files to the devices, or invoking command line scripts. This approach can address most of the issues associated with managing policies using an LDAP directory.

− A provisioning protocol such as COPS can be used to distribute the configuration in an standard manner. Another alternative is to use SNMP for configuration. These approaches are being explored by the various working groups within the IETF [9] [10].

− *Distributing Configuration Files*: The QoS management tool can generate the configuration files that would be needed at each device and copy them remotely over to the appropriate router and server. The approach works for all types of devices, and does not require any specific software to be running at the device. However, the QoS management tool has to understand each type of device and the format of configuration file that can be used with it. Most servers support configuration of differentiated services by means of configuration files.

- *Command Line Interfaces*: Most routers permit the ability for remote administration by means of a telnet session and specific command lines. The QoS management tool can use automated scripts to specific routers and control the configuration of the router using commands specific to the router. As in the case of configuration files, the QoS management tool has to understand the scripts that can be used for different types of routers.

Regardless of the choice of the distribution mechanism, care must be exercised when configuring devices that unstable network behavior is not introduced while transiting from one network configuration to another.

5.2 Resource Discovery Mechanisms

Resource discovery identifies the set of active routers, applications and users in the network. It is included as part of the QoS manager to simplify the task of the network administrator.

The most basic form of resource discovery is by means of manual configuration by the operator. This requires that all users, applications, user groups, application groups and the network topology be input by the user. In a large network, such a manual input is rather tedious.

Fortunately, automation can assist in discovering the various entities in the network. The network topology (servers and routers) can be determined automatically using an SNMP manager. The exploration mechanism would work provided an SNMP agent is active at all routers and servers. This is usually true in an enterprise environment. Workstations and desktops usually do not have SNMP enabled, but their discovery is not crucial for the purpose of policy management. Some other topology discovery mechanisms that can be used are described in [6]. While the resource discovery by SNMP can yield information about the servers and routers in the network, the grouping of the servers into administrative domains needs be done manually.

In order to locate the users and user groups in an organization, one can look up the corporate directory. While most corporate directories list the users and their grouping into organizations, the information related to the machines or the set of addresses being used by a specific user is not readily available. Finally, the set of applications needs to be discovered. This information can be obtained automatically by looking at the network configuration of the servers that are running at different machines, which provides information about the applications that may be running at the server, and the ports they are configured to use. We are currently investigating tools that can be used to automate the discovery of users, their machines, and applications.

5.3 Performance Monitoring and GUI

The SLAs offered in the enterprise QoS are provided in terms of the TCP round-trip delays, which are present in the network. The conformance to business SLAs can be determined by monitoring the performance recorded by the stack of the servers. On the S/390 and AIX servers, the stack is augmented with a performance monitoring agent as per the architecture described in [7]. Among the attributes measured by the performance monitoring agent, the round trip delay observed by packets belonging to a specific policy class is maintained. This information can be obtained by an SNMP manager which is included as part of the QoS manager. Our current implementation does not include an SNMP manager, and does not support performance monitoring.

The GUI which is included as part of the QoS manager allows the user to manipulate the different tables that are included as part of the business SLA view. It also allows a user to view the device configuration that is generated as a result of the view transformation process, and to look at the entries in the LDAP repository which is used for configuration distribution.

6. Sample QoS Configuration

In this section, we present a simple example of a network in which QoS using DiffServ can be implemented. The network is as shown in Figure 5. It consists of a core network (WAN) and three client sites labeled as Research, Accounting, and Engineering. The three client sites access a server site with two main servers, labeled as eComm and CICS.

The active applications in the network consist of a web-server running on port 80, a mail server using ports 11-13, a video server configured to use port ranges between 4000-6000, and applications that run legacy transactions on the server. These applications use SNA encapsulated in IP using either the DLSW protocol which uses TCP and port 265, or the IBM Enterprise Extender protocol which uses port 300 and is UDP-based. DLSW and Enterprise Extender based applications are considered business-critical, while the mail server is considered an office support application. The video server and the web-server are defined as staff utility applications.

As part of the business policies, the network administrator has defined three classes of services in the network, the bronze service is the default one and has a round trip response time of less than 1 second. The silver service has a response time of less than 0.5 seconds while the Gold service has a response time of less than 100 ms. The network administrator wants to enforce the following policies in the network:
- Any access to CICS server gets the silver service.
- Business critical applications on eComm Server get the gold service.
- Engineering access to office support applications on eComm Server gets the silver Service.
- Staff utility applications get the bronze service.
- The default service is the bronze service.

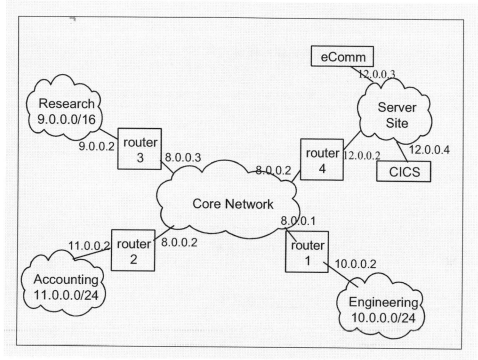

Fig. 5. Sample Enterprise Network for QoS Example

The five policies expressed above are input by means of the GUI panel shown in Figure 6. The blank entries have an implied semantics of any application group or user group.

The last column in the panel is the conflict resolution priority for policies that may conflict with each other. While the above set of policies may appear to be just fine, there is a conflict between the first and fourth policies as both of them can be applied to the case of an access to a staff utility application running on the CICS Server. The tool is capable of determining these conflicts. One can correct the conflict in a variety of ways, e.g. by deleting the fourth policy (which is redundant due to the default service class) or by changing the conflict resolution priority of one of the rules to a higher value (which is the approach shown).

These business policies are translated into the device configuration view. With this particular setting, the device configuration policies fall into two groups, one that applies to the eComm Server, and the other that applies to the CICS Server and all the four routers in the network. The device configuration view is as shown in Figure 7. This reflects the classic 5-tuple classifier found in the description of Differentiated Services.

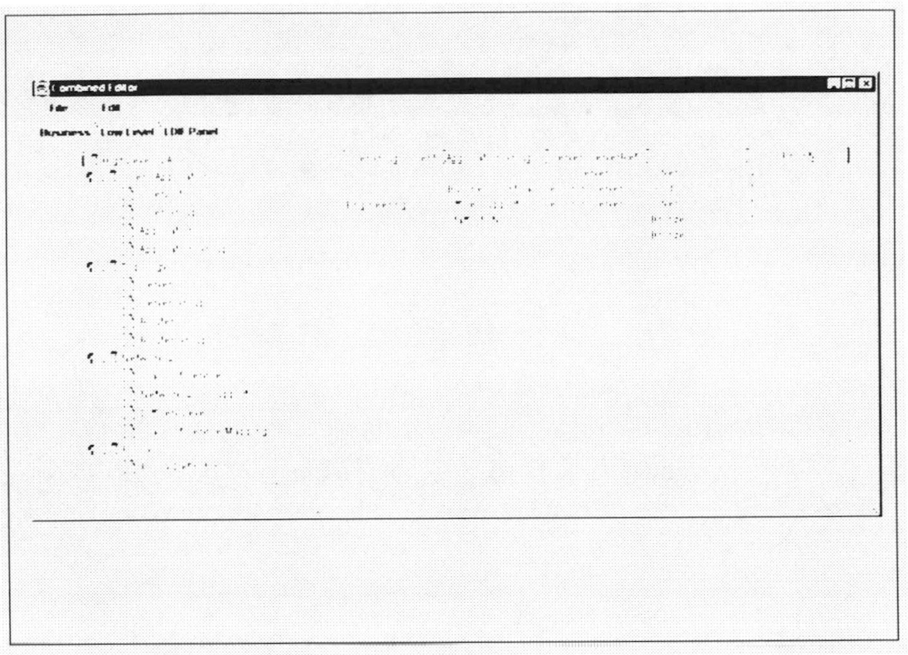

Fig. 6. GUI Panel for Entering High Level Policies

The final view (which we do not show due to the length constraints of the paper), consists of the entries that will be stored in the LDAP repository. Even with the simple set of policies shown in the network above, there are close to 50 entries stored in the directory for the set of 5 policies described above. For a real enterprise, the number of entries that need to be stored in the directory would be much bigger. Thus, tools offering a higher level view of QoS management would be of great help in simplifying the management of QoS in networks.

7. Conclusions and Future Work

In this paper, we have described a scheme that can simplify the task of managing Quality of Service in Differentiated Services networks. This scheme provides an abstraction of the network that deals with applications, customers and classes of service rather than the specifics of the PHBs that are required of individual routers. Such a high-level view can offer significant simplification of the task of QoS administration. In addition to the support for differentiated services, a similar mechanism can be used for configuring RSVP support in network.

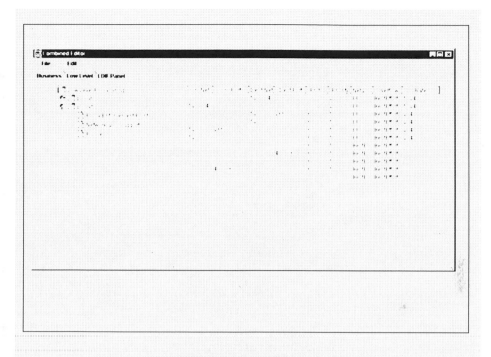

Fig. 7. GUI Panel for Low Level Policies

We are currently working to extend a similar high-level management for security in enterprise networks. Some areas of the tool remain to be finished, including the integration of a performance monitoring component and the investigation of effective resource discovery mechanisms for applications and servers. Similarly, our support for dynamic port numbers and dynamic host addresses needs further work. Despite these limitations, we believe such a tool can offer significant advantages to a network administrator, and assist in keeping track of business SLAs and network performance.

8. Acknowledgements

This work has evolved due to several discussions with many colleagues, including Jay Aiken, Roy Brabson, Arvind Krishna, Dilip Kandlur and Edward Ellesson. Vishal Bhotika was instrumental in coding significant portions of the management tool in a very short amount of time.

References

1. R. Braden, L. Zhang, S. Berson, S. Herzog, and S. Jamin, *Resource ReSerVation Protocol (RSVP) Version 1 Functional Specification.* RFC2205, Sept. 1997.
2. S. Blake et. al. , *An Architecture for Differentiated Services,* Internet RFC2475, December 1998.
3. M. Beigi et. al, *Low Overhead Continuous Monitoring of IP Network Performance,* Proceedings of Symposium on Performance Evaluation of Computer and Telecommunication Systems, July 1999.
4. W3C XML Specifications, available at URL http://www.w3.org/TR/REC-xml.
5. M. Wahl, T. Howes and S. Kille, *Lightweight Directory Access Protocol V3,* RFC 1997, March 1995.
6. R. Siamwalla, R. Sharma, and S. Keshav, *Discovering Internet Topology*, July 1998. http://www.cs.cornell.edu/skeshav/papers/discovery.pdf.
7. A. Mehra et al., Policy-Based Differentiated Services on AIX, Internet Computing Magazine, October 2000.
8. Ineternet Engineering Task Force Policy Framework Working Group, Charter available at URL http://www.ietf.org/html.charters/policy-charter.html.
9. The IETF Resource Allocation Protocol Working Group, charter available at URL http://www.ietf.org/html.charters/rap-charter.html.
10. The IETF SNMP Configuration Working Group, charter available at URL http://www.ietf.org/html.charters/snmpconf-charter.html.

Integrating Goal Specification in Policy-Based Management

Mark Bearden[1], Sachin Garg[1], and Woei-jyh Lee[2]

[1] Avaya Labs, Avaya Inc., Basking Ridge, New Jersey
{mbearden,sgarg}@avaya.com
[2] University of Maryland, College Park, Maryland
adamlee@cs.umd.edu

Abstract. Current products and emerging IETF standards for policy-based management do not clearly distinguish the goal (the "what") of management from the rules or procedures that specify "how" to achieve the goal. This paper defines an information model that allows direct specification of management goals in addition to policy rules. We extend the IETF's draft "Policy Framework Core Information Model" and integrate it with our goal specification information model. Further, following the IETF's refinement of the core information model into a QoS information model, we show how the general goal information model is extended to specify specific types of goals, including service-level QoS goals. The relationship of goals and rules in policy specification is considered. A prototype implementation of a management server that uses the given information model to specify and enforce QoS goals on a per-user, per-application basis is also discussed.

1 Introduction

Most emerging policy-based management (PBM) solutions require system administrators to specify policies as declarative rules of the form if *event/condition* then *action* [7,17,18,19]. From a system administrator's viewpoint, such rules represent the specification of "what" needs to be achieved in terms of the network/system behavior. However, from the viewpoint of an end-user, such rules specify "how" the desired system behavior is to be achieved. The end-user's view of *what* should be achieved is often quite different from the system administrator's view. For instance, a typical enterprise service user U is interested in QoS goals such as "U's transaction failure rate should be less than 0.5%" or "U's transaction delay should be less than 2s" for a given networked service such as SAP. User U is not likely to specify or take interest in a policy rule such as if $(User = U \ \& \ Service = SAP)$ then (Set DSCP = 16). The rule itself is specified by an administrator who assumes that assigning Diffserv priority codepoint of 16 will achieve the QoS goal [1]. In other words, from the end-users' perspective, current enterprise PBM solutions and emerging PBM standards only support the specification of *how* desired network and application behavior is achieved as part of policies. There is no support for specifying end-user service level goals

M. Sloman, J. Lobo, and E. Lupu (Eds.): POLICY 2001, LNCS 1995, pp. 153–170, 2001.

distinctly from policy rules. Even if the management goals in a PBM system do not pertain to an end user (for example, "Bandwidth utilization on all Routers should be less than 85%"), it is beneficial to allow the distinction between the specification of goals and policy rules.

In this paper we describe an information model, or policy representation schema, that makes an explicit distinction between the *what* and the *how* in PBM. This enables the following:

- direct specification of end-user service level (e.g. parts of a service level agreement) and other types of goals as part of management policies;
- specification of the relationship between management goals and policy rules—for instance, specifying that a specific goal G is potentially achieved by a specific set of policy rules;
- automated verification of the effectiveness of policy rules, by comparing specified goals to measurements or estimates of achieved service;
- modification of policy rules—by an expert off-line, or automatically on-line—to better achieve required goals, based on comparison of measured/estimated achieved service and specified goals;
- exchange of goal information among different components of a single management service—such as monitoring, control, event correlation, and decision making components;
- sharing of goal information among multiple and multi-vendor management services—such as service level measurement software and policy specification and enforcement software.

We also describe the architecture of a prototype management server that implements the goal information model. The rest of the paper is organized as follows. Section 2 describes related previous work in the specification of policies. Specifically, current IETF work towards a QoS schema serves as a baseline for our information model. In Section 3, we describe the information model to incorporate goals as propositions alongside declarative policy rules. An example is given to show the use of the schema in describing goals. Section 4 gives a description of a prototype management server implementation that utilizes the goals and rules schema. Section 5 concludes with a summary.

2   Related Work

Much previous work has defined network management policy as a set of rules with the form if E then A, where E represents some detectable event or network state, and A represents an action to be taken when E is detected. Examples of this approach are the currently emerging IETF standards for policy specification [9,11,14] and recently introduced PBM products from Cisco [17], Avaya [18], Nortel [19], Orchestream [20], and IPHighway [21]. A rule-based approach to defining policy is also taken by the designers of HP Labs' Generalized Policy Model [3] and Bell Labs' Policy Description Language [7].

The concept of distinct high-level and low-level representations of management policy is discussed informally in [5,6,8,13,15]. In these works, "high-level" policy generally refers to a declarative statement of *what* the end-user wants, i.e. a proposition or a single action. "Low-level" policy representations are generally procedural and specify the logic of *how* to achieve a goal, e.g. as rules or program control flows that are evaluated to determine a sequence of actions that should be taken. The sense of the present work is that when goals and rules are seen as distinct, then rules are intuitively "low-level" and goals are "high-level" policy specifications. In practice, it may be convenient to describe multiple "higher" or "lower" levels. An example is distinguishing a device-independent policy rule specification [9] from a yet "lower" level device-specific rule format. Yet in both cases, policy rules maintain the sense of "how" to achieve a management goal. The ISO RM-ODP [16] defines a policy as a set of "obligations, permissions, and prohibitions", without specifying how obligations, etc. should be represented, whether as high-level propositions to be satisfied or low-level procedures to be evaluated.

Finally, the present work utilizes the concept of policy domains in a way similar to the work in [2,5,10].

3   Information Model

In this section, we describe a schema for representing management goals. The schema is presented as an extension of the IETF's proposed schema for policy rules [9]. The goals schema is specified at two levels, first as a core schema and subsequently as a set of schema refinements, following the presentation style adopted by the IETF in [9] and [11] respectively. The core schema defines and organizes top level goal objects that are applicable to specifying a wide range of goals. At the refinement level of specification, the core schema is extended to define goal objects in a manner specific to different types of management goals (quality of service, resource utilization, security, etc.).

At present, there is no generally agreed upon definition of the term *policy*, which is alternately defined as a specification of a management goal or as the strategy to achieve a goal [5,14,15]. Here we define a *policy* to be a collection of policy goals and/or policy rules that express desired system behavior. An intuitive description of the difference between goals and rules is as follows. A policy goal specifies what system behavior is desired. In other words, goals describe the desired system state, but not how to reach the desired state. A policy rule, on the other hand, specifies action(s) to be taken to approach a desired state. A natural relationship exists between goals and rules: A set of policy goals may be associated with a set of policy rules which, when enforced, will cause execution of actions that are expected to cause the given goals to be satisfied.

3.1   The Core Goals Schema

Figure 1 shows the combined core schema for policy rules and policy goals. The shaded classes given on the left-hand side of the figure are given in [9]

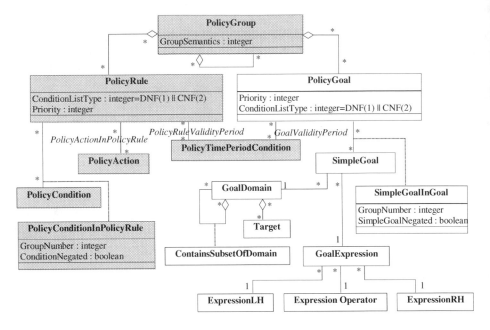

Fig. 1. Core schema for policy goals and rules.

and comprise the IETF's proposed core schema for policy rules. We extend the core schema for rules by defining the classes (not shaded) shown on the right-hand side of Figure 1. The attribute `GroupSemantics` is also added to the class `PolicyGroup`, as explained below.

An instance of the `PolicyGoal` class represents a boolean expression evaluated with respect to the achieved system behavior. A policy goal is defined by associating a set of `SimpleGoal` instances with a `PolicyGoal` instance. Each `SimpleGoal` instance is a proposition evaluated with respect to a particular goal domain, i.e., a set of system resources and users. The set of `SimpleGoal` instances associated with a policy goal are combined to define a boolean expression, using the attributes of the `SimpleGoalInGoal` association class in conjunction with the value of the `ConditionListType` attribute of class `PolicyGoal`. For a detailed description of how these attributes are used, see the discussion in [9] regarding the combining of `PolicyCondition` instances to define a `PolicyRule`. Briefly stated, the `ConditionListType` flag of the `PolicyGoal` class specifies the use of either disjunctive (DNF) or conjunctive (CNF) normal form for combining the associated simple goals into a single expression, while the `GroupNumber` attributes of the `SimpleGoalInGoal` associations are used to group the simple goals into distinct subexpressions within the larger expression.

As an extension of [9], the `PolicyGroup` class is (re)defined as an aggregation either of other `PolicyGroup` instances, or else of a combination of `PolicyRule` and/or `PolicyGoal` objects. We extend `PolicyGroup` with an attribute called `GroupSemantics` that indicates the relationship between goals and rules in the

Value of GroupSemantics	PolicyGroup can be Associated With	Relation of Associated Rules and Goals
RULES_ONLY	Only PolicyRule instances	-
GOALS_ONLY	Only PolicyGoal instances	-
GOALS_AND_RULES	PolicyRule and PolicyGoal instances	The specified rules may be independent of the goals, and vice versa. The intended policy is interpreted to be the union of the goals and the rules.
RULES_FROM_GOALS	PolicyRule and PolicyGoal instances	Rules are dependent on and derived from goals. The intended policy is defined to be the set of associated goals.
GOALS_FROM_RULES	PolicyRule and PolicyGoal instances	Goals are dependent on and derived from rules. The intended policy is defined to be the set of associated rules.

Table 1. Possible values for `GroupSemantics` attribute of class `PolicyGroup`.

same `PolicyGroup` instance. The values and the associated interpretations of the `GroupSemantics` attribute are listed in Table 1[1].

For instance, if the value of `GroupSemantics` for a given `PolicyGroup` instance is RULES_FROM_GOALS, the instance can aggregate both goal (`PolicyGoal`) and rule (`PolicyRule`) objects, and the rules are interpreted to be inferred from the goals. That is, the rules in the policy group should be generated such that they will ensure satisfaction of the goals in the same policy group, while the goals are specified by an administrator. Note that neither necessity nor sufficiency is implied in the set of rules being able to satisfy the goals. Instead, the implication simply is to update the set of rules (by adding, deleting or modifying constituent `PolicyRule` objects) if the goals are not satisfied at some point in time. For example, if a policy group contains the goal "User U requires average DNS lookup response time of under 1 second", and if the value of `GroupSemantics` is RULES_FROM_GOALS, then it is expected that the same group should contain a rule such as "If network traffic is a DNS lookup from U, then assign said traffic priority P" such that P is a high enough priority value to satisfy the response time goal. If the goal becomes unsatisfied at a certain time, then either a human administrator or an automated management system ought to change the rule until the goal becomes satisfied. Continuing the example, such a change could be increasing the priority value P.

A simple goal is defined by a *goal expression* and a *goal domain*, represented by `GoalExpression` and `GoalDomain` objects respectively, as shown in the lower part of Figure 1. A goal expression represents a comparison between a left-hand side value (`ExpressionLH`), and a right-hand side value (`ExpressionRH`), using an operator (`ExpressionOperator`). An example is "$AvgTransactionDelay \leq 100ms$". A goal domain is defined to be an aggregation of *targets*, where a target is some (logical or physical) system element associated with the evaluation of the

---

[1] The last case, GOALS_FROM_RULES, seems less intuitive than the others but is listed for completeness.

goal expression. Each target is represented by an instance of the `Target` class. For example, the expression "$AvgTransactionDelay \leq 100ms$" needs to be evaluated with respect to some specific service S and user U. S and U are each represented by a `Target` instance, and a `GoalDomain` instance associated with these two `Target` instances is in turn associated with the `SimpleGoal` instance, along with the `GoalExpression` instance that represents "$AvgTransactionDelay \leq 100ms$". The resulting simple goal's interpretation is "U's average transaction delay, when accessing S, is at most 100ms.".

Goal domains may be defined as containing not only targets that are directly associated with the goal domain, but also subsets of other goal domains. We do not explore here the details of representing these subsetting relations between goal domains. For a detailed study on specification of domains, see [10].

As in [9], we assume the existence of a policy repository that defines a number of `PolicyGroup` objects and a set of (reusable) `GoalExpression`, `ExpressionOperator`, `GoalDomain`, `Target`, etc. objects that may be shared between `PolicyGroup` objects. Each policy goal has an associated priority attribute to be used for determining enforcement precedence, or for resolving conflicts between satisfying multiple policy goals. Each policy goal object also has an association with a `PolicyTimePeriodCondition` object defined in [9] that indicates when the policy goal is expected to be satisfied.

3.2   Schema Extension for Application-Level QoS Goals

The core goal schema of Figure 1 is refined to produce schema extensions for specific management areas. We give here four possible extensions which serve to validate the generality of the core schema. The first extension, given in Figure 2, is for specifying application-level QoS goals. Class `AppLvlQosGoalExpression` defines a desired system state expressed in terms of application QoS. The left-hand side of the expression is given by `AppLvlQoSVariable`, which is a subclass of `ExpressionLH` from the core schema. Likewise, `QoSValue` is subclassed from `ExpressionRH` to form the right hand side of the expression. A `QoSValue` instance may specify either a constant or a reference to another instance of `AppLvlQoSVariable`. Class `GoalDomain` is extended to define `AppLvlQoSGoalDomain`, which is associated with one `Client` instance, up to one `Application` instance, and up to one `Server` instance. Clients and servers can be identified by a platform-dependent combination of name and/or network address. Applications are identified by port numbers and/or name. Due to the wide range of existing applications and application-level QoS metrics, we do not attempt to define here specific values for `AppLvlQoSVariable`. For possible values, see the types of application QoS measurements supported by commercial application-level QoS monitoring products such as Lucent's VitalSuite [22] or Concord's eHealth [23].

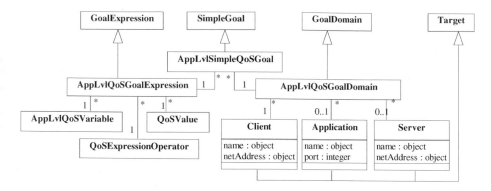

Fig. 2. Extended information model for application-level QoS goals

3.3   Schema Extension for Network-Level QoS Goals

Figure 3 gives a second schema extension for network-level QoS goals, similar to the application-level QoS extension given above. The main difference is that the targets in the goal domain (class `NetLvlQoSGoalDomain`) are a set of source and destination nodes that define a communication channel such as a TCP connection. An example of network level QoS goal is: Packet loss between source node (IPaddr = 135.104.25.58) and destination node (IPaddr = 135.104.26.120) should be less than 2%. In this example the loss of packets applies to all IP traffic from the source node to the destination node.

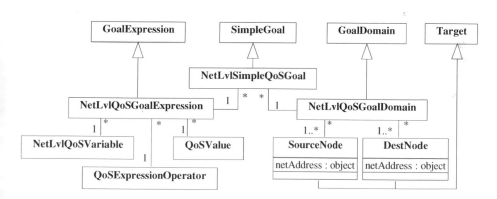

Fig. 3. Extended information model for network-level QoS goals

3.4   Schema Extension for Resource Utilization Goals

Figure 4 gives a third extension to the core goals schema, for representing resource utilization goals. In this extension, the goal domain is a set of resources, and the left-hand side of the goal expression is a variable representing a measure of resource utilization. Examples for `ResourceUseVariable` include resource load, local throughput, unused capacity, error rates, etc.

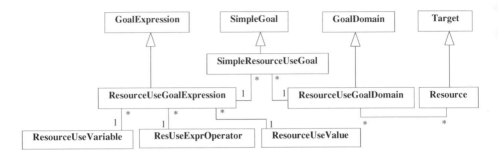

Fig. 4. Extended information model for resource utilization Goals

3.5   Schema Extension for Resource Access Permission Goals

Figure 5 gives a fourth extension to the core goals schema for representing simple resource access permission (security) goals. In this extension, the goal domain identifies a client and a resource. The left-hand side of the goal expression is a variable representing a defined mode for accessing the resource, for example "ConnectAccess", "AdministrativeAccess", "Readable", "Writeable", etc. The `AccessModeValue` object for an instance of `AccessGoalExpression` is a boolean value. `AccessModeValue` equals true (alternately "permit", "allow", etc.) if the given access mode is enabled, or false if not enabled. The omitted expression operator part of this expression is implicitly "is equal to".

Our position here is that an access permission goal is just like other goals in that it may or may not be satisfied at any given point in time. As an example, an administrator might specify a `SimpleAccessPermissionGoal` instance that states a given user should have read access to a given resource. Yet the given resource might have an inbuilt constraint that allows only a limited number of clients to have simultaneous read access. If a management system is unable to satisfy the access permission goal, perhaps because the maximum number of users have been granted access, then it is meaningful to associate a false value (not satisfied) with the `SimpleAccessPermissionGoal` instance. Thus `SimpleAccessPermissionGoal` can model not just a set of security/access goal parameters but also the *goal* of ensuring that the given security/access parameters are *successfully* applied in a system. Another interesting aspect of access goals is that the distinction between "what" and "how" may not always clearly exist. For instance, a router or a firewall may take access control lists (ACL's) as direct input to implement access permissions. This implies that the access goals might be themselves policy rules which are directly passed on to the network device without any conversion. It is up to the administrator to model ACL's as either policy goals or policy rules.

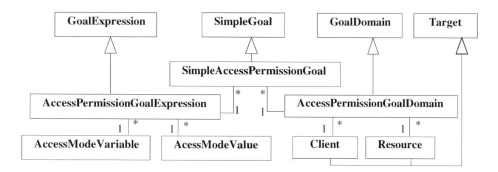

Fig. 5. Extended information model for resource access permission goals

3.6   Other Possible Extensions

The four schema extensions given here represent only a few of the potentially useful refinements of the core schema. The given refinements do not provide all necessary implementation details, but they demonstrate the extensibility of the core goals schema and exemplify a methodology for future policy schema development. Other useful refinements of the core goals schema might include extensions for specifying availability/fault-tolerance goals at the application or network level (Web-server uptime should be greater than 99% or , number of redundant paths between a source and destination IP host should be equal to two), or resource access on a user and application basis (User U should be denied the use of a server for an application A, but should be allowed to use it for another application B). The pervasive idea in extending the core schema is to model the requisite set of targets and goals by subclassing appropriately from `GoalExpression` and `GoalDomain` classes in the core schema.

3.7   Schema Applied to Example Goals

Consider the following example policy specification problem that is used to illustrate the application of the above goals schema. An organization has three sets of users with different assigned responsibilities. The first group contains users A and B whose critical responsibilities require access to desktop applications that access a financial application A_F over the organization's intranet. Application A_F is running replicated on two server hosts $Host_1(A_F)$ and $Host_2(A_F)$, each of which can accept or reject remote user requests over communication port $port(A_F)$. The other two user groups contain users $\{A,C\}$ and $\{D,E\}$ respectively, whose assigned tasks require timely access to the organization's Web servers. (User A is in two groups.) In order that an administrator may log in to one of the two servers and execute administrative tasks without experiencing the delay of a fully utilized server, the following additional resource utilization constraint is given. At least one of the hosts in $\{Host_1(A_F), Host_2(A_F)\}$ should always have a CPU utilization of less than 75%. We assume that the incoming request can be redirected to either one of the servers to achieve the given load-balancing.

A high-level description is given in Table 2 for a set of policy goals that correspond to the above example. Column one gives the management targets, i.e. users or resources, for which each policy goal is defined. The priorities are assigned assuming that if resources are insufficient to simultaneously satisfy any

Policy Targets	PolicyGoal Description	Priority
A, B, A_F, $Host_1(A_F)$,$Host_2(A_F)$	Each user should be allowed access to restricted application A_F, and 95% of the user's A_F transactions should complete within 2 seconds.	Highest
A, C any HTTP server	75% of each user's HTTP transactions should be established (first byte of response received) within 2 seconds.	Intermed.
D, E any HTTP server	50% of each user's HTTP transactions should be established within 3 seconds.	Lowest
$Host_1(A_F)$ $Host_2(A_F)$	One or more of the servers hosting the application A_F should have CPU load less than 75% at any given time.	Intermed.
default	Users are not allowed access to restricted application A_F unless explicitly given access. Unless otherwise specified, any user can access any service and receives "best effort" quality of service.	-

Table 2. Example management goals.

two different policy goals, then just the goal that has the higher priority should be satisfied alone, if possible. The policy goals in Table 2 could be determined internally by the organization's management, or by a formal SLA (service level agreement) [12] established between the organization and an external application service provider. The default system policy, applicable only in the absence of contradictory policy goals, is described in the bottom row of the table.

We proceed to show how the extended core schema can be used to represent the above policy goals. For each of the three defined groups of users and resources, a `Goal` object and associated set of `SimpleGoal` objects are defined in a policy information repository. These are identified in Table 3. Each simple goal defined in the second column is either an application-level performance (QoS) goal, a resource utilization goal, or a security (access) goal. For each simple goal case, the expression and domain are identified, as well as the subclass of `SimpleGoal` that is used. The `Application` part of each application-level goal domain identifies the port of the application, either $port(A_F)$ or 80 for HTTP. $Any(T)$ is a special value that indicates any target of type T. RT_p is a left-hand QoS variable defined to be the smallest value such that p percent of the transactions for a particular application, during some measurement period, have end-to-end response time of less than RT_p. The security goal expressions in the example have the form <CONNECT,{PERMIT,DENY}> to indicate that the indicated client should or should not be permitted access to the application. The two rightmost columns give the attribute settings used to combine the simple goals into policy goal expressions; "Grp." and "Neg." specify group numbers and negation of the simple goals. All the simple goals are logically AND'ed together, except for the two `ResourceUseQoSGoal`'s, which are OR'ed. The bottom row of the table gives the default system behavior translated into a policy goal with lowest priority.

Policy Goal Name	SimpleGoal (GoalExpression,GoalDomain)	SimpleGoal Subclass	Priority, Cond. List Type	Grp., Neg.
Goal1	RT_95 < 2s, $\{A, port(A_F), Any(Host)\}$	AppLvlSimpleQoSGoal	3, CNF	1, F
	RT_95 < 2s, $\{B, port(A_F), Any(Host)\}$	AppLvlSimpleQoSGoal		2, F
	<CONNECT,PERMIT>,$\{A, port(A_F)\}$	SimpleAccessPermissionGoal		3, F
	<CONNECT,PERMIT>,$\{B, port(A_F)\}$	SimpleAccessPermissionGoal		4, F
Goal2	RT_75 < 2s, $\{A, 80, Any(Host)\}$	AppLvlSimpleQoSGoal	2, CNF	1, F
	RT_75 < 2s, $\{C, 80, Any(Host)\}$	AppLvlSimpleQoSGoal		2, F
Goal3	RT_50 < 3s, $\{D, 80, Any(Host)\}$	AppLvlSimpleQoSGoal	1, CNF	1, F
	RT_50 < 3s, $\{E, 80, Any(Host)\}$	AppLvlSimpleQoSGoal		2, F
Goal4	CPU_Load < .75, $\{Host_1(A_F)\}$	SimpleResourceUseGoal	1, DNF	1, F
	CPU_Load < .75, $\{Host_2(A_F)\}$	SimpleResourceUseGoal		2, F
default	<CONNECT,DENY>, $\{Any(Client), A_F\}$	SimpleAccessPermissionGoal	0, CNF	1, F
	<CONNECT,PERMIT>, $\{Any(Client), \neg A_F\}$	SimpleAccessPermissionGoal		2, F
	Any = Best Effort, $\{Any(Client),Any(App),Any(Host)\}$	AppLvlSimpleQoSGoal		3, F

Table 3. Example management goals expressed using schema.

It is interesting to note that the definition of policy goals and simple goals depends on what is being measured or monitored. For instance, consider Goal4 in Table 3, which consists of two simple goals that are OR'ed. This assumes that the CPU load on each host $Host_1(A_F)$ and $Host_2(A_F)$ is being measured and reported separately to the management system. If the monitoring/measurement tool was such that it measured the CPU loads and reported only the minimum of the two (represented by $minLoad(Host_1(A_F), Host_2(A_F))$ to the management system, then Goal4 would be reduced to a single simple goal with GoalExpression being $minLoad(Host_1(A_F), Host_2(A_F)) < .75$ and the GoalDomain being $\{Host_1(A_F), Host_2(A_F)\}$.

3.8   Modeling Enforcement Domains and Validity Constraints

Enforcement of a policy may require specifying the *enforcement domain* for the policy. This is the the the set of resources that are involved in enforcing the goals and/or rules contained in a policy group. An enforcement domain can specify a set of targets that should enforce the policy. These targets can include network elements and services such as routing devices, firewalls, load balancing traffic redirectors, application servers, name lookup servers, etc. Alternately, an enforcement domain may specify as targets a set of networks or subnetworks where policy should be enforced. Most commercial PBM products require the

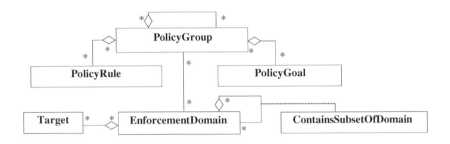

Fig. 6. Representation of enforcement domain for a policy group.

specification of enforcement domains, but no known standard for modeling enforcement domains is yet proposed. The core schema modification given in Figure 6 suggests a possible way of representing the enforcement domain for a policy group very similar to representing the goal domain (`GoalDomain` class) in our core schema. A detailed study on the specification of enforcement domains is given in [10].

4   Prototype Implementation

In this section, we describe a prototype implementation of a management system that utilizes the application-level QoS part of the proposed goals schema. Figure 7 shows the high-level architecture of the management system. The bottom most layer represents devices which may include client machines, routers, switches and servers. In our terminology, these devices, or software running on these devices, are "targets" that are monitored and/or controlled by the management server.

The management server itself is shown in the top left portion of the figure. It is implemented as a Java program that runs inside a single Java virtual machine. The server has a graphical user interface that is used by an administrator to define and modify user-centric application-level QoS goals as per the extension schema presented in Section 3.2. The server's basic control loop includes monitoring of achieved QoS by communicating directly with the targets and/or with third-party service level monitoring software. Our prototype currently interfaces with Lucent's VitalSuite [22], which is a tool for monitoring application level QoS. VitalSuite requires deploying agents on clients' desktop computers, which measure and report end-to-end application-level QoS for dozens of popular applications including Web, Oracle Financials, SAP, email, Telnet, and FTP. Our management server interfaces via SQL with a centralized VitalSuite database that contains QoS data gathered from client agents. The monitored data is used to evaluate whether the specified goals are satisfied.

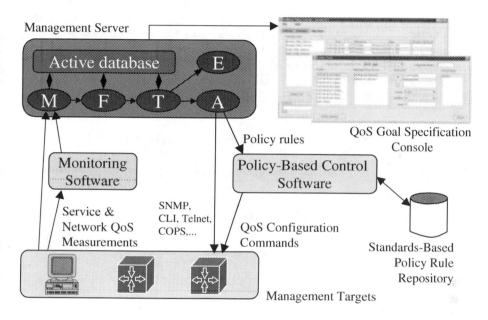

Fig. 7. Architecture of a management server.

The second basic function of the management server is to actively control the behavior of target elements, basing the control actions on the evaluation of whether or not specified goals are satisfied. As with monitoring, this can be done via direct communication with targets or via interfacing with third-party control software. In our prototype we have thus far followed the latter approach, which enables us to leverage existing rule-based commercial PBM products. The management server interfaces with Avaya's Cajun Rules (CR) [18] via an LDAP interface. This enables the server to retrieve the policy rules that have been defined using CR's graphical interface and to issue changes in policy rules which are pushed to CR. The CR software then generates low-level (vendor specific) device configuration commands via SNMP, LDAP or other protocols to affect the behavior of supported target elements.

4.1   Graphical Interface for Goal Specification

Figure 8 shows two frames of the GUI provided by the management server. The foreground frame is a dialog window used to define simple goals. The background frame displays both defined simple goals and a set of policy goals comprised of simple goals. Each simple goal is defined by selecting from among a set of defined user hosts, services, and simple goal expression components. The dialog window shows a selected simple goal definition with user "135.104.25.49", service "HTTPserver", and expression "ResponseTime ≤ 200 (ms)". The set of users and services are discovered on behalf of the management server by the third party monitoring software (VitalSuite). The set of application-level QoS metrics that can be measured and used in simple goal definitions are also automatically imported from the VitalSuite software. Sets of simple goals are grouped into policy goals that are displayed on the left-most panel of the background frame. For example, the three simple goals shown on the right-hand panel of the frame are part of a (highlighted) policy goal identified as "Silver_Web_Service".

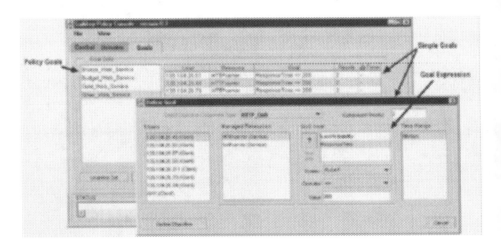

Fig. 8. Graphical interface for goal specification

Enforcement domains consisting of management targets (network devices and server hosts) that may be controlled to enforce the QoS goals are declared in a separate part of the UI, not shown. A list of network devices that may be included in enforcement domains is automatically imported from the Cajun Rules software.

After policy goals are defined, the system administrator uses a separate control panel of the UI to indicate whether each defined goal should currently be enforced, and what enforcement domain should be used. Once this is done, corresponding management logic, which encapsulates monitoring and control of elements specified in the enforcement domain, gets activated for the specified goal. As noted before, our implementation allows the management logic to monitor and control targets either directly or via interfacing with third-party software tools.

4.2   Use of Software Components for Policy Enforcement Logic

Most current PBM software systems support a limited set of protocols and devices. As new protocols and devices are introduced in the market, the PBM software also needs to be upgraded. The design of the prototype management server addresses extensibility and enables software reuse by utilizing "component-based" software architecture. Policy enforcement logic contained in the server is implemented as a set of communicating software objects called "policy components". Policy components separate the complete functionality of management logic into sub-parts that can be individually replaced or modified without replacing the rest of the logic. Two examples of such components are an object that implements MIB-II monitoring via SNMP, and an object that controls class-based-queuing settings on a Cisco router. Such reusable components may be written and integrated by device vendors, vendors of policy-based control software, other third-party management tools vendors, or by system administrators themselves. The management server allows an administrator to:

– Load a packaged set of components into the management server. This step instantiates each component inside the management server's JVM.
– Activate a package after the administrator specifies the goal and the domain parameters required by the components in the package. This step activates the management logic that enforces the specified goal.
– Deactivate, unload, and reload packages of policy components. This enables the administrator to upgrade or extend the capabilities of the management server.

The management server provides a set of services that load and unload policy components, maintain shared component state and configuration state, schedule internal tasks, display a graphical console interface for the operator, and generate status or error messages intended for the operator. A basic policy component interface associates no specific management functionality with a component, defining instead just an interface that is common to all components. The defined interface includes methods for activation and deactivation as well as methods for accessing common management information such as goals, rules, targets, domains and other defined variables as per the core and extended schema. Although the specified interface does not restrict the functionality of a component to being either a monitoring component or a control component, additional interfaces have been developed to do so. Table 4 lists a set of component interface types, along with their functionality, that we have found thus far to be useful in programming management server logic. The small modules shown inside the management server in Figure 7 represent loaded components that are labeled with the one-letter abbreviations given in the table.

The active database shown inside the management server in Figure 7 is an in-memory database constituted of instances of the core and application-level

QoS extension schema classes. The active database is used by loaded policy components to define and retrieve management information, including targets,

Component Type	Functionality
Collector (C)	Monitor the state of targets via polls or traps. Also store monitored data in a schema compliant local repository for use by other components
Filter (F)	Receive state change notifications from collector components and/or other filter components and determine whether these notifications should be passed. Used to reduce the amount of state change notifications between components.
Trigger (T)	Embodies conditional logic that determines what actions should be invoked when predefined state changes are observed. The input to a trigger is the output from one or more collectors and/or filters.
Evaluator (E)	Compute values, such as dynamic thresholds for triggers. Also to implement various optimization criteria for computing parameters for actions, such as ToS values for setting priority.
Action (A)	Translate internal control decisions into external control signals applied (directly or indirectly) to managed elements. The parameters may be received from an evaluator component.
Initializer	Perform miscellaneous operations on other components in a package, for example, informing components of which identifiers they should use to read/write shared variables stored in the active database. Each packaged set of policy components contains at least one initializer component.

Table 4. Classification of policy components

goals, policy rules etc. In addition, it serves as the medium for inter-component communication via its event notification interface. Any component can register with the active database as a listener for changes in the stored state. For example, goal specifications and the status of delivered QoS have objects that can be listened to. When a state change occurs, the active database notifies all the registered listeners of the change. The methods for instantiating, initializing, retrieving and updating objects in the active database, which are compliant with the proposed schema, are exported in an API to enable third-party developers to write components.

5   Summary

This paper proposes a core information model for specification of management goals in policy based management systems. The information model embodies the intuition that there should be a distinction between the goals ("what") of management and the logic ("how") that achieves the goal. In the draft IETF policy core information model, as well as in commercial PBM products, no such distinction is made; a policy is defined to be a set of `if` condition `then` action rules. From the perspective of an end user, such rules specify "how" rather than "what" (though they may be interpreted as "what" to achieve from the perspective of a system administrator). We chose to use the draft IETF schema for policy rules as a baseline, extending the model to include goal specification as well as rules. To validate the extensions to the core information model, a set of refinements are presented for specifying goals in specific management areas, such as application-level QoS, resource management, and resource access. The architecture of a prototype management server that implements the proposed schema is discussed. The server features a component based architecture for extensibility and reuse, and a graphical user interface for specification of application-level QoS goals.

References

1. S. Blake, D. Black, M. Carlson, E. Davies, Z. Wang and W. Weiss, "An Architecture for Differentiated Services", IETF RFC 2475, December 1998.
2. N. Damianou, N. Dulay, E. Lupu, M Sloman, "The Ponder Policy Specification Language", Workshop on Policies for Distributed Systems and Networks (Policy2001), Bristol, UK, Jan 2001.
3. M. Dekhil, V. Machiraju, K. Wurster, and M. Griss, "Generalized Policy Model for Application and Service Management", Policy Workshop 1999, November 1999, Bristol, U.K.
4. M. Hasan, B. Sugla, and R. Viswanathan, "A Conceptual Framework for Network Management Event Correlation and Filtering Systems", in *Proceedings of the Sixth IEEE/IFIP International Conference on Integrated Management* (IM'99), May 1999, Boston, Massachusetts.
5. A. Langsford and J. D. Moffett, *Distributed Systems Management*, Addison-Wesley, Wokingham, England, 1993, 307 pp.
6. L. Lewis, "On the Integration of Service Level Management and Policy-Based Control", Policy Workshop 1999, November 1999, Bristol, U.K.
7. J. Lobo, R. Bhatia and S. Naqvi, "A Policy Description Language", in *Proc. 16th National Conference on Artificial Intelligence* (AAAI'99), Orlando, FL, July 1999.
8. J. D. Moffett, "Specification of Management Policies and Discretionary Access Control", chapter seventeen in *Network and Distributed Systems Management*, ed. M. Sloman, Addison-Wesley, Harlow, England, 1994, pp. 455-480.
9. B. Moore, E. Ellesson, J. Strassner, and A. Westerinen, "Policy Framework Core Information Model – Version 1 Specification", IETF Internet-Draft, October 2000. http://www.ietf.org/html.charters/policy-charter.html.
10. M. Sloman and K. Twidle, "Domains: A Framework for Structuring Management Policy", chapter sixteen in *Network and Distributed Systems Management*, ed. M. Sloman, Addison-Wesley, Harlow, England, 1994, pp. 433-453.
11. Y. Snir, Y. Ramberg, J. Strassner, and R. Cohen, "Policy Framework QoS Information Model", IETF Internet-Draft work in progress, April 2000. http://www.ietf.org/html.charters/policy-charter.html.
12. R. Sturm, W. Morris, and M. Jander, *Foundations of Service Level Management*, Macmillan: Indianpolis, Indiana, 2000, 272 pp.

13. D. Verma and B. Wijnen, "SLAs and Policies", Policy Workshop 1999, November 1999, Bristol, U.K.
14. A. Westerinen, J. Schnizlein, J. Strassner, Mark Scherling, et al., "Policy Terminology", IETF Internet-Draft (Informational), July 2000. http://www.ietf.org/html.charters/policy-charter.html.
15. R. Wies, "Policies in Network and Systems Management: Formal Definition and Architecture," *Journal of Network and Systems Management* 2(1), March 1994, pp. 63-83.
16. *Reference Model of Open Distributed Processing Part 2*, ITU-T X.902, ISO/IEC 10746-2, 1996.
17. Cisco QoS Policy Manager product documentation, Cisco Systems, Inc. http://www.cisco.com/.
18. Cajun Rules product documentation, Avaya Inc. http://www.avaya.com/.
19. Optivity Policy Services product documentation, Nortel Networks, Inc. http://www.nortel.com/.
20. Distributed Policy Engine product documentation, Orchestream. http://www.orchestream.com/.
21. Open Policy System product documentation, IPHighway. http://www.iphighway.com/.
22. VitalAgent and VitalSuite product documentation, Lucent Technologies, http://www.lucent-networkcare.com/software.
23. eHealth product documentation, Concord Communications, http://www.concord.com/.

Taxonomy and Description of Policy Combination Methods

Yasusi Kanada

IP Network Research Center, Research & Development Group, Hitachi, Ltd.
Totsuka-ku Yoshida-cho 292, Yokohama, 244-0817, Japan
kanada@crl.hitachi.co.jp

Abstract. To control complicated and decomposable networking functions, such as Diffserv, two or more policies must cooperate. Combining two or more mutually dependent policies for a specific purpose is called policy combination. Methods of passing information between combined policies can be classified into real tags and virtual tags, or labels and attributes. Policy combinations can be classified into concatenation, parallel application, selection, and repetition. Explicitly specifying policy combinations makes policy systems semantically clearer and better suited to general use, extends the range of functionality, and improves the possibility of optimization. If policy combinations can be specified in a policy system, two types of policy organizations can be distinguished: homogeneous and heterogeneous. Heterogeneous organization is more service-oriented and seems to meet service-management requirements, but homogeneous organization is more device-oriented and may provide better performance.

1. Introduction

In policy-controlled networks, networking functions such as access, QoS, and security function are specified in a device-independent method and customized for individual customer or group of customers. Network service is managed based on service-level agreements (SLA). SLA can be regarded as a policy specifications or high-level policies. High-level policies are broken down into low-level policies and stored into policy servers.

If the functions controlled by policies are simple, the policies can be independent of each other. In contrast, to control functions that are complicated and decomposable, such as Diffserv (Differentiated Services) [Ber 99], the relationships between policies must be taken into account. For example, marking and queuing policies in Diffserv must work together. If related policies are deployed to different targets (e.g., network devices or device interfaces), the application order may be naturally constrained. However, if policies are deployed to the same target, the order is not explicitly determined or determined in a device-specific way. This makes the semantics of policies vague, and makes the policy system less useful. Thus, the relationships between policies should be clearly defined, and these relationships should be controllable for network operators and administrators. For example, if marking and queuing policies are deployed to a network interface in a router, the marking policy

M. Sloman, J. Lobo, and E. Lupu (Eds.): POLICY 2001, LNCS 1995, pp. 171-184, 2001.
© Springer-Verlag Berlin Heidelberg 2001

must be applied before the queuing policy. This means that mechanisms to define the relationships between policies and to control the relationships in the policy description language must be supplied.

Kanada [Kan 00b][Kan 00a] previously proposed two architectures for combining building-block policies: *label-connection architecture* and *pipe-connection architecture*. Both architectures are based on declarative programming languages used in artificial intelligence and knowledge engineering. Thus, in these architectures, policies are regarded as programs. This is because they control the behavior of network nodes or a network. Label-connection architecture is a direct extension of policies that consists of if-then (condition-and-action) rules used in commercial policy servers. Pipe-connection architecture offers significant advantages in terms of semantics and parallelism. However, it is still in an early stage of research. Label-connection architecture offers its own advantages and can be implemented by using currently available technology [Kan 00b]. This paper focuses on label-connected architecture. Most of the results discussed in this paper can, however, be applied to pipe-connected architecture too.

In this paper, the term *policy combination* refers to combining two or more mutually dependent policies for a specific purpose. Our focus is on lower-level (implementation-level) policies. Means of passing information between two policy rules are classified in Section 2. Methods for combining policies are classified in Section 3. Methods for organizing combined policies are classified and explained in Section 4 using Diffserv examples. Problems and possible solutions associated with these forms of policy combination are discussed in Section 5.

2. Methods for Passing Information

A policy consists of if-then rules. To make two or more policy rules that belong to different policies cooperate, the information must be transferred between them. A single piece of information transferred between rules is called a *tag*. Tags can be *real*, i.e., in the packet, or *virtual*, i.e., outside of the packet (see **Fig. 1**).[1] A tag causes a *data dependence* [Kuc 81] between policy rules.

Tags can be categorized into the following two.

1. *Labels*: A tag may be used for selecting a rule from a policy. This type of tag is called a label. A label connects one rule to another (i.e., the label assigned by one rule specifies the next rule to be applied). DSCPs (Diffserv code points) [Nic 98] are used as real labels. Virtual labels, called VFLs (virtual flow labels), were introduced by Kanada [Kan 99]. Examples of labels are described in Section 3.

2. *Attributes*: A tag might not only be used in the action part of the rule, but not in rule selection. This type of tag is called an attribute [Kan 00b]. Virtual attributes are useful for hierarchical scheduling, shaping, and policing. An example of hierarchical shaping is described in Section 3.4.

---

[1] A virtual tag may be transmitted by additional data lines in the network device hardware, by a value in a register of the hardware or a variable in the software, or by the location in the hardware circuit. So a virtual tag cannot be transmitted between network devices, but may be transmitted within a network device.

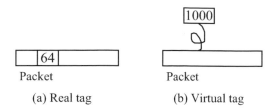

Packet   Packet

(a) Real tag   (b) Virtual tag

Fig. 1. Real and virtual tags

3. Types of Policy Combination

Policies change the behavior of a network in a consistent way. Thus, a set of policies that work together may be regarded as a distributed program. Each policy consists of if-then rules, so a set of policies is a rule-based program similar to expert system programs written in a language such as OPS5 [For 81].

In procedural programs, such as those written in C or C++, there are four relationships (control structures) between statements: concatenation (sequential application), parallel application, selection, and repetition. Despite the fact that a set of policies is a rule-based program, the application order and the *control dependence* [All 83] of policies must be specified. Thus, the relationships between policies can be classified into these four types.[2]

3.1 Concatenation

If two policies are sequentially applied, the relationship between these two policies can be called a concatenation. A concatenation can be represented by the following diagram.

For example, in a Diffserv network, a policy for MF (multi-field) classification and marking, and a policy for queuing may be concatenated and deployed to an edge router (see **Fig. 2**).[3] There are two possible policy rules in the classification and marking policy. They are as follows.

```
# Rule C1:
if (Source_IP is x.x.x.x) {
     DSCP = "EF";
}
```

---

[2] Kanada [Kan 00b] described a policy language in which the application order can be specified by using an unstructured method. However, the control should be structured as described in the present paper.

[3] A set of primitive building blocks (policies) for Diffserv was discussed by Kanada [Kan 00a] [Kan 00b].

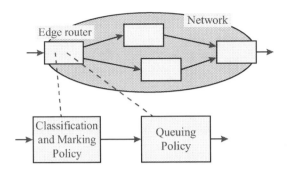

Fig. 2. Policy concatenation in a Diffserv network

# **Rule C2**:
else if (Source_IP is *y.y.y.y*) {
  DSCP = "DF";   # "DF" == 0
}

In these rules, "EF" refers to expedited forwarding [Jac 99], and "DF" refers to default forwarding or best-effort forwarding. Note that the two policies are ordered by the concatenation, and the two rules in these policies are connected by DSCP. The concatenation specifies a control dependence between the policies, and the DSCP specifies a data dependence (a flow dependence [Kuc 81]) between them.
Rules in the queuing policy in the concatenation may be as follows.

# **Rule Q1**:
if (DSCP is "EF") {
  Scheduling_Priority = 6; # Set an attribute for the scheduler.
  Enqueue;   # Put the packet into a queue until the scheduler pulls it off.
}

# **Rule Q2**:
else {
  Scheduling_Priority = 1;
  Enqueue;
}

DSCP is used as a real label in Rule Q1. DSCP "EF" connects Rules C1 and Q1, and DSCP "DF" connects Rules C2 and Q2.
Rules Q1 and Q2 assume priority scheduling. This means a priority scheduling rule is connected to the above rules. The EF traffic receives higher priority, and the DF traffic receives lower.

3.2 Parallel Application

Two policies may be applied in parallel if they do not conflict. Parallel application can be represented by the following diagram.

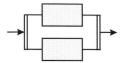

In a Diffserv network, a marking policy and a queuing policy may be applied in parallel. For example, the marking policy in the parallel application may contain the following rules.

# **Rule M1**:
if (VFL is "Policed-EF") {
  DSCP = "EF";
}

# **Rule M2**:
else {
  DSCP = "DF";
}

Here, the marking policy is separated from the classification policy. Rule M1 is applied to higher-priority packets, and Rule M2 is applied to other (lower priority) packets. The classification policy does not mark a DSCP, it just puts a VFL on the packets.

The queuing policy in the parallel application may contain the following rules.

# **Rule Q1'**:
if (VFL is "Policed-EF") {
  Scheduling_Priority = 6;
  Enqueue;
}

# **Rule Q2'**:
else {
  Scheduling_Priority = 1;
  Enqueue;
}

Rules M1 and Q1' refer to the same VFL value. VFL "Policed-EF" connects a rule in the classification policy to Rules M1 and Q1'.

3.3 Selection

If a policy outputs multiple types of application results depending on the conditions of the rules, and there are multiple policies each of which inputs each of the results, the relationship between these three policies can be called a selection. A two-way selection can be represented by the following diagram.

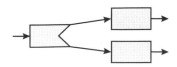

N-way selection, where *N* is larger than 2, is also possible.

For example, in a Diffserv network, a policy for policing may be combined with a policy for marking and a policy for absolute dropping, and these policies may be deployed to an edge router (see **Fig. 3**). Policy rules in the policing policy may be as follows.

```
# Rule P1:
if (DSCP is "EF" && Information_Rate <= 2 Mbps) {
  VFL = "Policed-EF";
}
```

```
# Rule P2:
else if (DSCP is "EF") {
  VFL = "Drop";
}
```

```
# Rule P3:
else {
  VFL = "Policed-DF";
}
```

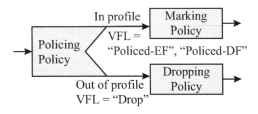

Fig. 3. Policy selection in a Diffserv network

Rules P1 and P2 are applied to packets whose DSCP is "EF". This means they are higher-priority packets. The packets are passed through an information-rate meter. Rule P1 is applied to in-profile packets, and Rule P2 is applied to out-of-profile packets. Rule P3 is applied to lower-priority packets whose DSCP is not "EF". Rules P1 and P3 attach a VFL that indicates that the packet must be forwarded with higher or lower priority, and Rule P2 attaches a VFL that indicates the packets must be dropped.

Rules in the marking policy may be the same as Rules M1 and M2 in Section 3.2. A rule in the dropping policy may be as follows.

```
# Rule D1:
if (VFL is "Drop") {
  Absolute_Drop;
}
```

This rule drops all the packets that have "Drop" as their VFL value.

3.4 Repetition

If a policy is repeatedly applied until a condition is met, the relationship of the policy to itself can be called a repetition. A repetition with only one policy can be represented by the following diagram.

A repetition may contain two or more policies as shown below.

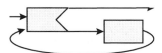

In a Diffserv network, for example, a hierarchical shaping function can be represented by a repetition. If the following three rules are included in a queuing policy, this policy represents a hierarchical shaping function, as shown in **Fig. 4**.

```
# Rule S1:
if (VFL is "Policed" && DSCP is "EF") {
  Scheduling_Priority = 6;
  Maximum_Rate = 700 kbps;        # shaping rate
  VFL = "Shape2";
  Enqueue;
}

# Rule S2:
else if (VFL is "Policed") {        # except EF
  Scheduling_Priority = 5;
  Maximum _Rate = 500 kbps;        # shaping rate
  VFL = "Shape2";
  Enqueue;
}

# Rule S3:
else if (VFL is "Shape2") {
  Scheduing_Algorithm = Priority_Queuing;
  Maximum_Rate = 1 Mbps;           # shaping rate
      # 200 kbps (700 k + 500 k – 1 M) or less traffic may be dropped here.
  VFL = "Outgoing";
  Enqueue;
}
```

A Queuing Policy

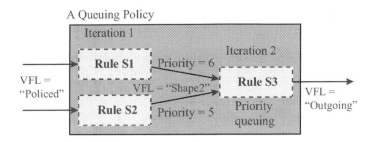

Fig. 4. Policy repetition for a Diffserv network

In this example, Rules S1 and S2 assign a virtual attribute called Scheduling_Priority to the packets and then the rules queue them. Each rule in the queuing policy has its own queue. Rule 3, which schedules packets by using a priority queuing algorithm, pulls off packets from the queues according to the Scheduling_Priority. VFLs are used for loop control. A different VFL value is used for each iteration. In this example, "Policed" is used for the first iteration, and "Shape2" is used for the second. When "Outgoing" is set as a VFL, there is no rule whose condition matches this VFL in this policy, so the loop terminates.

In this example, the number of repetitions is only two, but it may be an arbitrary value. This number, however, is usually assumed to be constant, and the rule to be applied in each iteration is usually different. Otherwise, mapping the combined policies to the network device functions is difficult, and infinite repetition might occur.

4. Methods of Policy Organization

In this section, two methods are defined for organizing combined policies. They are explained using examples, and compared.

4.1 Definitions

A set of combined policies can, in a wider sense, be regarded as a single "policy". Thus, a *compound policy* is defined as a set of combined policies collected for a specific organizational purpose.

There are two methods for organizing combined policies.

1. *Homogeneous organization*: If no compound policies are used, and the policies are organized such that all rules in a policy have the same type of conditions and the same type of actions, the policies are said to be organized homogeneously.

2. *Heterogeneous organization*: If the policies are not organized homogeneously, the policies are said to be organized heterogeneously.

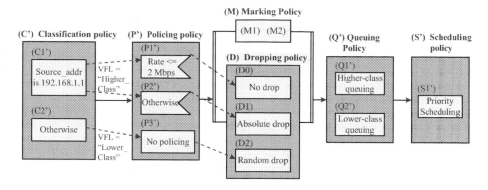

Fig. 5. A homogeneous policy set for Diffserv

In a typical homogeneously-organized policy, all the rules, except the default rule (the rule applied when the conditions of all other rule are not satisfied), test the same tag, and the actions of all the rules are the same type.

In heterogeneous organization, a compound policy may contain other compound policies and non-compound policies. Thus, compound policies are organized in a recursive way, and they may contain homogeneously organized policies.

In homogeneous organization, the same type of rules (instead of instructions) are applied to multiple data. In heterogeneous organization, different types of rules (instead of instructions) are applied to multiple data. Homogeneous organization is, therefore, analogous to single-instruction-stream multiple-data-stream (SIMD) [Fly 66] and heterogeneous organization is analogous to multiple-instruction-stream multiple-data-stream (MIMD) in parallel processing [Fly 66].

4.2 Examples

All the policies described in Section 3 are homogeneous. An example of homogeneously-organized set of policies for a Diffserv is shown in **Fig. 5**. An example of heterogeneously-organized set of policies for a Diffserv is shown in **Fig. 6**. The functions of both sets of policies are identical. These policies are only deployed to the outbound interface of an ingress edge router (**Fig. 7**). They classify and mark the packets, police the flow, and then queue and schedule the packets. There are two classes of service: premier and default. A customer whose IP address is 192.168.1.1 is a premier service customer here.

In Fig. 5, classification policy C' classifies the packets and attaches VFLs. Policing policy P' polices the classified traffics. P2' drops the excess higher-priority traffic, but P3' allows all the traffic to pass through (because the bandwidth for the lower-priority traffic do not need to be limited). P' contains rules similar to P1, P2, and P3 (described in Section 3.3), but the rules in P' test VFLs instead of DSCPs.

If a flow from the default service customer is detected (C2'), default service policy De is applied. A random dropping is applied to this flow (D2'), and the packets are

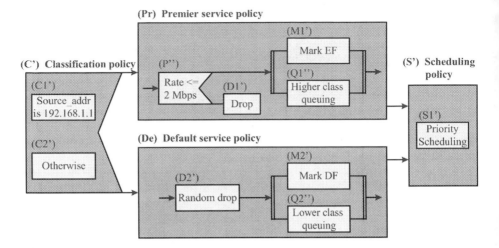

Fig. 6. Heterogeneous set of policies for Diffserv

marked 0 ("DF") on the DS field (M2') and queued. Finally, a Scheduling_Priority attribute is attached (Q2'').

The premier and default traffics are merged into priority scheduler S'. The premier traffic has a higher priority.

Marking policy M and dropping policy D are applied in parallel. M contains rules identical to M1 and M2 in Section 3.2. D drops all or part of the traffic if necessary. In the case of in-profile higher-priority traffic, the packets need not be dropped. So Rule D0, which explicitly passes through the traffic, is applied. Rule D1 is an absolute dropping rule, and is the same as that described in Section 3.3. Rule D1 drops the out-of-profile packets detected by Rule P2'. Rule D2 is a random dropping (WRED) rule applied to lower-priority packets.

Next, queuing policy Q' is applied and then scheduling policy S' is applied. Q' contains rules identical to Q1' and Q2' in Section 3.2. S' is different from the scheduling policy shown in Section 3.4. It is a simple priority scheduler.

In Fig. 6, if the premier service customer's flow is detected by Rule C1' in classification policy C', premier service policy Pr is applied. C' is identical to C'' in

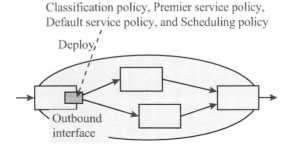

Fig. 7. Policy deployment

Fig. 5. Pr is a compound policy. The bandwidth is limited to 2 Mbps by the only rule in Policy P''. Out-of-profile packets are dropped by the only rule in Policy D1'. In-profile packets are marked "EF" on the DS field [Nic 98] and queued with the Scheduling_Priority attribute by rules in Policies M1' and Q1''. Policies M1' and Q1'' can be applied in parallel; i.e., packet marking can be done at anytime before the packet leaves the queue.

4.3 Comparisons

Homogeneous organization is more device-oriented because rules of the same type are collected and a policy type usually represents specific sets of device functions, such as those in Fig. 5. This structure may be directly mapped to pipelined or SIMD packet-processing hardware, such as the routing and QoS processors in Hitachi's GR2000 router [Aim 00] and network processors. Homogeneous organization, thus, seems better suited to device and performance management purposes, and to high-speed network. This is because pipeline processing offers better performance and translating a heterogeneous set of policies to a homogeneous set is not an easy task.

Heterogeneous organization is more service-oriented because compound policies usually represent abstract functions. In Fig. 6, Pr and De represent, respectively, services for premier and normal customer policies. We can see that heterogeneous organization seems better suited to service management.

Heterogeneous organizations are usually assumed to contain less rules than homogeneous ones, because two or more policies in a heterogeneous organization correspond to a single policy in a homogeneous one. Policy, such as P', D1', M1', and Q1'', often contain only one rule. Because this may increase the complexity of the set of policies, the policy editing interface must reduce the complexity.

5. Discussions

The advantages of explicitly specifying policy-combination types are discussed below.

5.1 Clarification of the Semantics

The semantics of a policy system can be clarified by explicitly specifying policy combination types. In commercial network policy systems, the relationships between policies are not explicitly specified. If the application order is inappropriate, policy applications may cause erroneous results. For example, the rule in the MF classification and marking policy described in Section 3.1 marks "EF" in the DS field. If a rule in a queuing policy contains the condition "DSCP is EF", and this rule is applied before the marking, the condition evaluation will cause a wrong action as a result. This problem can be avoided by specifying these policies as a concatenation. Introducing a parallel application causes a similar effect.

Introducing a selection also allows us to clarify the relationship between alternative policies.   For example, an alternative structure may be represented by using concatenations. The selection in Fig. 3 may be simulated by the following diagram.

This works correctly because the dropping policy works exactly on the packets to be dropped. However, if the order of the dropping and marking policies are altered and the marking policy rewrites the VFL, these policies generate a wrong result. The following rule is assumed to be used instead of M2 in marking policy M.

> # **Rule M2***:
> else {
>   DSCP = "DF";
>   VFL = "Policed-DF";
> }

Then, Rule M2 will be applied to the out-of-profile packet, the VFL will be rewritten, and the packet will not be dropped. This problem can be avoided if a selection is used instead of the concatenations.

5.2 Developing Policy Systems Suited to General Use

If the policy combination type is explicitly specified for each policy combination, the policy system becomes more suited to general use. If the relationships between policies are not explicitly specified by the user, the order of the applications must, at least be predefined in the policy system or inferred from the context. If the order is predefined, the usage of the policy system is restricted, and the system is less suited to general use. Inferring relationships from generic knowledge on policies is not easy. If the relationship is explicitly specified, the policies are context-free and, thus, more suited to general use.

In addition, introduction of a repetition makes repeated application of a policy possible. It cannot be specified in conventional policy systems.

5.3 Adaptation to a Variety of Devices

If the policy combination types are explicitly specified, the repertory of executable policies can be extended. If the application order is strictly sequential (i.e., each pair of contiguous policies are specified as a concatenation), the policies may be unmappable to device functions because the functions are limited and the application order is constrained. For example, in some router, packets must be marked before random dropping. If random dropping strictly precedes marking in the policy description, the policy translator, which resides in the device or in a proxy, may fail to convert the policy to an executable commands.

If parallel applications and selections are specified, however, the policies may be translated. For example, if random dropping and marking are specified as parallel application as shown in Fig. 5, the policies can be translated into router commands without a possibly complicated semantic analysis.

5.4 Optimization

Policies specified by an operator may be inefficient and may have to be optimized. If the types of policy combination are explicitly specified, the possibility of optimizing policies is improved by parallel application or reordering policies. If the function of the target router is flexible enough for a number of parallel applications to be specified, and the parallel applications of policies are translated into parallel commands, the performance will be better than that associated with sequential commands. However, if the parallel applications are specified and the performance is better for a specific command-execution order, performance can be optimized.

6. Summary and Conclusion

When two or more policies work together, four types of policy combination can be distinguished: concatenation, parallel application, selection, and repetition. If the policy-combination types are explicitly specified in a policy-based system:

1 . the system will be semantically clearer,
2 . the system will be better suited to general use,
3 . the range of functionality will be wider because the range of translatable policies widens, and
4 . the possibility of policy optimization will be improved.

We can add policy combination specification, which includes type specification, to existing policy-based systems. However, if a new policy language and system is designed, we can obtain a well-defined and more concise policy-based system.
If policy combinations are specified in a policy system, two types of policy organizations can be distinguished: homogeneous and heterogeneous organizations. Heterogeneous organization is more service-oriented, so it seems to be better suited to service management. Homogeneous organization, however, is likely better for device and performance management purposes. It is advantageous in high-speed networks.
Future work includes designing a new policy system in which policy combinations and organization can be explicitly specified. Future work also includes developing methods for translating a set of combined policies into a set of policies that can be implemented by network devices. The translation methods to be developed include policy fusion, which merges two or more policies into one, and policy division, which splits a policy into two or more policies.

Acknowledgments

The author would like to thank Brian O'Keefe from Hewlett-Packard for his contributions to the development of policy combination and organization concepts, especially on the repetition.

References

[Aim 00] Aimoto, T., and Miyake, S., "Overview of DiffServ Technology: Its Mechanism and Implementation", *IEICE Transaction on Information and Systems*, Vol. E83-D, No.5, pp. 957–964, http://search.ieice.or.jp/2000/pdf/e83-d_5_957.pdf, The Institute of Electronics, Information and Communication Engineers, 2000.

[All 83] Allen, J. R., Kennedy, K., Porterfield, C., and Warren, J., "Conversion of Control Dependence to Data Dependence", *10th ACM Symposium on Principles of Programming Languages*, (*POPL 83*), pp. 177symbol 150 \f "Times New Roman CE" \s 9–}189, 1983.

[Ber 99] Bernet, Y., et al, "A Framework for Differentiated Services", draft-ietf-diffserv-framework-02.txt, *Internet Draft*, February 1999.

[Fly 66] Flynn, M. J., "Very High-speed Computing Systems", *Proc. IEEE*, 54:12, pp. 1901symbol 150 \f "Times New Roman CE" \s 9–}1909, 1965.

[For 81] Forgy, C. L., "OPS5 User's Manual", *Technical Report* CMU-CS-81-135, Carnegie Mellon University, Dept. of Computer Science, 1981.

[Jac 99] Jacobson, V., Nichols, K., and Poduri, K., "An Expedited Forwarding PHB", RFC 2598, June 1999.

[Kan 99] Kanada, Y., Ikezawa, M., Miyake, S., and Atarashi, Y., "SNMP-based QoS Programming Interface MIB for Routers", draft-kanada-diffserv-qospifmib-00.txt, *Internet Draft*, http://www.kanadas.com/activenet/draft-kanada-diffserv-qospifmib-00.txt, October 1999.

[Kan 00a] Kanada, Y., "A Representation of Network Node QoS Control Policies Using Rule-based Building Blocks", *International Workshop on Quality of Service 2000* (*IWQoS 2000*), pp. 161–163, June 2000.

[Kan 00b] Kanada, Y., "Two Rule-based Building-block Architectures for Policy-based Network Control", *2nd International Working Conference on Active Networks* (*IWAN 2000*), Lecture Notes in Computer Science, No. 1942, pp. 195-210, Springer, October 2000.

[Kuc 81] Kuck, D. J., Kuhn, R. H., Padua, D. H., Leasure, B., and Wolfe, M., "Dependence Graphs and Compiler Optimizations", *8th ACM Symposium on Principles of Programming Languages* (*POPL 81*), pp. 207–218, 1981.

[Nic 98] Nichols, K., Blake, S., Baker, F., and Black, D., "Definition of the Differentiated Services Field (DS Field) in the IPv4 and IPv6 Headers", RFC 2474, December 1998.

Issues in Managing Soft QoS Requirements in Distributed Systems Using a Policy-Based Framework

Hanan Lutfiyya, Gary Molenkamp, Michael Katchabaw, and Michael Bauer

Department of Computer Science
The University of Western Ontario
London, Ontario, Canada N6A 5B7
hanan@csd.uwo.ca

Abstract. We address the problem of Quality of Service (QoS) requirements for multimedia applications (e.g., distance education, telemedicine, electronic commerce). These applications need to be able to co-exist with more traditional applications for transaction and data processing and have soft real-time requirements. Unlike most other work in QoS management, we provide a framework that does not require users or application developers to have detailed knowledge of the resources needed and resource scheduling and allocation techniques in use. These underlying details are effectively hidden. In this paper, we describe our strategy, an architecture of services to support the strategy and a prototype.
Keywords: QoS Requirements, Policies, Distributed Systems

1 Introduction

There is an increase in distributed applications requiring real-time services. This includes new multimedia applications such as video-on-demand, distance eduction, telemedicine, teleconferencing and electronic commerce. These applications will co-exist with more traditional applications for transaction processing, data processing, and software development.

Users of these applications expect a high level of quality of service (QoS). By quality of service, we are referring to non-functional requirements such as performance or availability requirements. An example of a QoS requirement for a multimedia application that receives a video stream is the following: "The number of video frames per second displayed to the user must be at least 25 plus or minus 2 frames". Most of the QoS requirements for multimedia applications are considered to be *soft* in that the applications are still considered functionally correct even if QoS requirements are not satisfied.

We refer to the allocation and scheduling of resources to meet QoS requirements as *QoS management*. Many QoS management techniques (e.g., [5]) provide a guarantee that resources will be available when needed by statically allocating resources based on worst-case needs. This is important in systems where applications must meet their timing constraints to avoid disastrous consequences, e.g.,

M. Sloman, J. Lobo, and E. Lupu (Eds.): POLICY 2001, LNCS 1995, pp. 185–201, 2001.

flight control systems, chemical process control systems, and patient-monitoring systems. However, most multimedia applications have *soft* real-time requirements. Some QoS management techniques support these types of applications by initially allocating resources based on optimistic estimates of resource needs and assuming that the resource will be available when needed. The application is informed if it is not possible to satisfy its resource needs. The application can then either renegotiate a new resource usage allocation with the operating system and/or adapt its behaviour.

Much of this work assumes that the user or developer is aware of resource needs in advance. For example, not only does there need to be a specification such as "The number of video frames per second displayed to the user must be at least 25", but also the number of CPU cycles needed to get the 25 frames per second. The derivation of this information needs in-depth knowledge of the hardware architecture, network and system software in the target environment. This places an additional burden on the developers of these applications and in most cases is not doable without having access to the environment in which the application is being deployed.

This paper defines a framework that is *policy-driven* to address the problem of QoS management for applications that have soft real-time requirements. This strategy does not require users or application developers to have detailed knowledge of either the resources needed nor the scheduling and allocation techniques used.

This paper is organised as follows. In section 2, we describe our strategy and in section 3 we outline the elements needed to implement the strategy. Section 4 describes how policies are used in the strategy. Sections 5 and 6 present details on an architecture. Section 7 presents some details of the related work. Sections 8 describes related work. Sections 9 and 10 describe our insights and future work.

2   Strategy

The following example illustrates the relationship between QoS requirements (or user expectations) and the resources allocated using our strategy. Assume that we have a QoS requirement that is informally stated as follows: "A given video application is to deliver video at a frame rate of 25 frames per second, plus or minus 2 frames". The process expecting the video is given an initial resource allocation, say this process is given a particular CPU priority among running processes. When a frame is received the metric representing the quality of service is measured (number of frames). If it exceeds the specified expectation, the resource allocation is reduced, i.e., the process's priority is reduced. This frees some of the CPU to be used for other processes. Otherwise, the process's priority is increased to gain more use of the CPU. Resource allocations are adjusted until a suitable one is found that satisfies expectations.

This strategy does not guarantee that a QoS requirement will be satisfied. It tries to dynamically adjust resources as needed by the application. This may not always be possible. For example, there may have been other multimedia processes with similar QoS requirements on the same host machine and it might not be possible to set CPU priorities to satisfy the processor needs of all.

There may also be additional constraints that dictate how the system should react in such situations. Such constraints might dictate that each of these processes should have equal access to resources and, hence, allow the performance of each of the processes to degrade. On the otherhand, it may be decided that some applications have priority over the others i.e., a differentiated resource allocation is allowed. Such constraints must also be realized within the overall management of the distributed system.

3   Realizing the Strategy

In order to realize this strategy, we must be able to a) enforce the QoS requirements and b) specify QoS requirements and any additional constraints as policies.

3.1   Enforcement

The services needed to make a system comply with QoS requirements are referred to as *enforcement* services. Enforcement consists of three logical phases: detecting the violation of a QoS policy, determining the cause of the violation and taking steps to take to adapt the system to bring it back into a state of compliance.

Violation detection occurs when the application behaviour is observed not to satisfy the specified QoS requirements. The violation (also called a *symptom*) is a manifestation of a fault in the system. The detection of a violation of a QoS requirement requires that we have the means of mapping the QoS requirement into mechanisms that collect data characterising run-time behaviour and evaluating it relative to the QoS requirements.

Violation location takes symptoms and identifies the cause and location of the fault in the system. In the earlier example, a violation would occur if the video application was not receiving frames at a frame rate of between 23 and 27 frames per second. This could be caused by several situations, e.g., the video application might not be getting enough local processor cycles, the server process might not be getting enough cycles, a process failed or there is an unexpected load on a network switch. Locating the cause is an important step in determining the appropriate resource allocation. For example, if the problem is that there is an unexpected load on a network switch, then there is no need to adjust resources on the video application process's host.

Adaptation refers to the actions taken to repair or otherwise recover from a fault, so that the system returns to compliance with the QoS requirements. Examples include providing more processor cycles, restarting a failed process or rerouting traffic around a congested network switch. The action(s) to be taken depend not only on the cause of the violation, but also depend on the constraints imposed on how to achieve the QoS requirement. For example, one possible corrective action is to adjust the CPU priority of the video application receiving the video stream. However, if there are several multimedia applications on the same host, then perhaps attaining the desired level of service for all is not possible and a different action is necessary, e.g. adjust the priority based on the user of the video application.

These constraints are a second category of requirements (hence referred to as administrative requirements). However, these are not user QoS requirements (hence referred to application QoS requirements) expected of an application, but rather they are administrative or organisational requirements. These requirements will vary between different administrative domains and will vary over time.

3.2   Requirement Specification and Distribution

Application QoS requirements for a particular application will change. For example, the requirements of an application depend on the user who has invoked the application. Thus different sessions of the same application will have different QoS requirements. Administrative requirements will also change since the constraints on the possible adaptations will also change during the lifetime of the system.

As described earlier, an application QoS requirement may be violated. It must be possible to specify an action which in many cases will be to send a notification to another entity that is doing the diagnostics and determining the adaptation to be taken.

The implication of these two observations is that it should be possible to store both application QoS and administrative requirements. The application QoS requirements should accessible by an application when that application is started up. It must also be possible to specify the action(s) to be taken if the application QoS requirement is not satisfied.

This suggests that we allow the requirements to be expressed as *policies*. A *policy* can be defined [20] as a rule that describe the action(s) to occur when specific conditions occur. A policy for an application QoS requirement has as its condition the negation of the QoS requirement which means that the specified action(s) is to take place when it has been detected that the QoS requirement has been violated. Policies can also be used for administrative requirements (which we will mostly refer to this as *rules*).

4   Specifying Application QoS Policies

There already exists formalisms for specifying policies. Our goal is not to invent a new formalism, but rather use (as much as possible) existing formalisms. We use a formalism defined in [6].

Example 1.
An example of an application QoS policy is the following.

```
oblig NotifyQoSViolation {
    subject (...)/VideoApplication/qosl_coordinator
    target fps_sensor,jitter_sensor,buffer_sensor,(...)QoSHostManager
    on not (frame_rate = 25(+2)(-2) AND jitter_rate < 1.25)
    do fps_sensor->read(out frame_rate);
        jitter_sensor->read(out jitter_rate);
        buffer_sensor->read(out buffer_size);
        (...)/QoSHostManager->notify(frame_rate, jitter_rate, buffer_size);
}
```

The subject is the actual application that the policy applies to, since it will have responsibility for the policy (this will be made clearer in the next section). Basically, VideoApplication refers to the name of an executable, qosl_coordinator refers to an instrumentation component that evaluates the conditions stated in policies at run-time (more on this in the next section) and (...) includes other identifying information such as hostname, the application that the executable belongs to, etc; (more on this in a later section).

In Example 1, frame_rate and jitter_rate are attributes of a video application. The constraint on the frame_rate attribute is that its value must be 25 give or take a couple of frames. The constraint on the jitter_rate attribute is that its value must be less than 1.25.

If the value of the frame_rate attribute is less than 23 or greater than 27 or the jitter_rate is less than 1.25 then the policy is considered to be violated. The do component of the policy specifies which actions are to be carried out when the policy has been violated. (...)/QoSHostManager refers to the process (discussed in the next section) that receives notification of the violation. The constructs fps_sensor $\rightarrow$ read(frame_rate), jitter_sensor $\rightarrow$ read(jitter_rate), and buffer_sensor $\rightarrow$ read(buffer_size) refer to operations on sensors (explained in the next section) that monitor the frame rate, jitter rate and communication buffer sizes, respectively. The (...) notation includes other identifying information such as hostname, etc; The actions to be taken are to read the frame rate, the jitter rate and the buffer size and send this information to the (...)/QoSHostManager.

5   Enforcement Architecture

The overall architecture for enforcing QoS requirements, specifying QoS requirements using policies and distributing them is described in this section and the next section. This section describes the specific architectural components to support services needed for enforcement. The description assumes that a running application knows its QoS requirements. How it knows its QoS requirements will be discussed in the next section which focusses on the part of the architecture that deals with policy management i.e., the specification of QoS requirements using policies and their distribution.

The approach used in this work requires the insertion of code into applications at strategic locations to facilitate the collection of quality of service metrics and exertion of control over the applications. While some measurements can be taken by observing external application behaviour and rudimentary control can be achieved through operating system interactions, work in this area has found that these approaches are limiting in both accuracy and the kinds of metrics and control available. The example policy used throughout this section is the one stated in Example 1.

We also assume that as part of the instrumentation each application will have a coordinator component. The role of the coordinator is to oversee the policies associated with the particular instantiation of the application and to communicate with a QoS Host Manager.

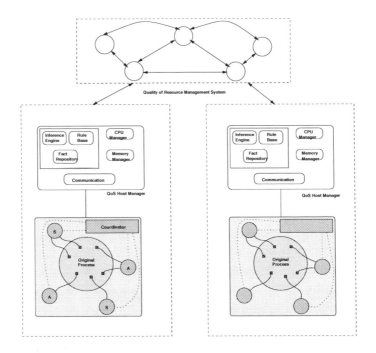

Fig. 1. Enforcement Architecture

5.1 Instrumented Process

An instrumented process is an application process with embedded instrumentation code. It is this instrumentation code that enables the management of the application process. The architecture components that comprise the instrumentation code are discussed in the following subsections.

Sensors. Sensors are used to collect, maintain, and (perhaps) process a wide variety of metric information within the instrumented processes. Sensors get their input data from probes inserted at strategic points in the application code or by reading other sensors. During run-time, sensors can be enabled or disabled, reporting intervals can be adjusted and thresholds can be modified.

Actuators. Actuators are used to encapsulate functions that can exert control over the instrumented process to change its operation or behaviour. In this current work, they are not used extensively, but can be used to support quality of service negotiation, adaptation, and other functions in the future.

Probes. Probes are embedded in process code to facilitate interactions with sensors and actuators. Probes allow sensors to collect metric information and allow actuators to exert control over process behaviour. Each probe is specific to a particular sensor or actuator. Probes are the only instrumentation component that must be injected into the original process source code—all other components need only reside in the same address space as the process, and do not require code modifications.

Sensors and actuators are classes. Probes can either be methods of the sensors and actuators or be functions that call these methods.

Example 2.
As an example, consider a video playback application that has the policy stated in Example 1. This QoS requirement is translated into initial thresholds for sensor s_1, capable of measuring the frame rate. The target, upper and lower thresholds are 25, 27 and 23 frames per second, respectively. This QoS requirement also translates into an initial threshold for another sensor, s_2, that measures jitter.

Sensor s_1 includes at least the following two probes which are also methods of s_1: (1) An initialisation probe that takes as a parameter the default threshold target value. This probe gives a value to the target, upper and lower thresholds. (2) A probe that does the following when triggered by the process after the application retrieves a video frame, decodes it and displays it: (i) Determines the elapsed time since the last frame delivered. (ii) Checks to see if this falls within a particular range defined by the lower and upper acceptable thresholds. Unusual spikes are filtered out. (iii) If the constraints on the values of the frame rate are not satisfied, it will inform the coordinator c. s_2 has similar probes. □

How does a sensor relate to policies that express application QoS requirements? A sensor collects values for an attribute of the process. This attribute is part of a policy (or policies) being applied to the application. Application policies specify constraints on process attributes. We assume that a sensor is responsible for monitoring a specific attribute. If the sensor finds that a constraint involving that attribute is violated, it reports this to the coordinator as an *alarm report*. For Example 1, it is assumed that two sensors are needed: one for the frame rate and one for the jitter. We also note that a sensor may provide values to be used in more than one policy. This means that there is a many to many relationship between policies and sensors. An application may also have more than one policy and it is possible that these policies share attributes. We note that not all sensors measure attributes that are directly used in the specification of a policy (see Example 5).

5.2   Coordinator

The coordinator is responsible for tracking adherence to the policies associated with the application process and maintains a list of policy objects. A coordinator receives the following information for each policy: (i) The policy identifier. (ii) A **condition list** in which a condition is represented by an attribute identifier, the identifier of a sensor that monitors that attribute, a comparison operator and value that the attribute is to be compared to using the comparison operator. (iii) An **action list** in which each element of the list is a pair which represents a target object and an action to be taken on that target object. A policy, then, is represented as a conjunction or disjunction of constraints on attributes.

The coordinator takes each policy from the set of policies received and creates a policy object. For each policy, the coordinator extracts the condition list, the action list and the boolean operator. For each condition in the condition list, a variable is generated to represent the condition that must hold between an attribute identifier and the value. This is added to a boolean expression based on the boolean operator to be used.

Example 3.
The policy in Example 1 has a condition list consisting of the following component parts: $frame\_rate > 23$, $frame\_rate < 27$ and $jitter\_rate < 1.25$. Boolean variables x_1, x_2 and x_3 are generated for each one. The boolean expression is x_1 AND x_2 AND x_3. □

For the sake of simplicity, we assume that each sensor is associated with one attribute and thus only needs one init method which can be given a value and a comparison operator. The init method can take a threshold value (represented as a character string) and convert it to the appropriate type. We also assume that each sensor has a read method that returns the value of the attribute in character form. The sensor is able to do the appropriate conversion. For each comparison retrieved from the comparison list, an internal identifier generated for that comparison which was passed to the sensor using init.

The algorithm for what the coordinator does when it receives an alarm from a sensor is described as follows. If the coordinator receives an alarm report from a sensor, it determines those policy objects that represent policies that use the attribute associated with the sensor. For each such policy object, the coordinator maps the alarm report (based on the internal identifier generated for the comparison) to a variable that is used in the boolean expression. This variable is set to false and the boolean expression is evaluated. If it is false, then a report is sent to the QoS Host Manager. All knowledge of the QoS Host Manager is confined to the coordinator, effectively hiding it from the remaining instrumentation components.

Example 4.
This example describes a coordinator that has the policy of Example 1. If an alarm report is received from s_1 then the coordinator checks the list of policy objects and evaluates the boolean expression associated with the policy specified

in Example 1. If the expression evaluates to false then the QoS Host Manager is notified. This expression evaluates to false if either s_1 and s_2 have sent alarm reports. If the evaluation is false, the coordinator reads the frame rate, jitter rate and buffer size, puts them into a message report and sends this off to the QoS Host Manager. □

Example 5 makes use of an additional sensor that is used to provide further monitored information that can be used by the QoS Host Manager. This sensor monitors the length of the communication buffer. The purpose of this will be illustrated later.

Example 5.
A socket provides for interprocess communication. In UNIX, a socket is a file descriptor. The kernel allocates an entry in a private table in the process area, called the user file descriptor table and notes the index of this entry. The index is the file descriptor that is returned to the process. The entry allocated is a pointer to the first inode. The operations *read()* and *write()* are done through the memory associated with the inodes of the process (which we will refer to as buffer). We can create a sensor s_3 that has a probe that given a file descriptor for a socket returns the length of the buffer. This length can be compared to a specified threshold. If the length is smaller then this threshold then this is taken to be an indication that the problem may not be local to the process. □

5.3   Quality of Service Host Manager and Domain Manager

The QoS Host Manager receives notifications from a process (through the process's coordinator) when a policy has been violated. The QoS Host Manager has a set of rules that are used to determine the corrective action(s). This involves determining the cause of the policy violation and then determining a corrective action(s). The process of determining the rules to be applied is called inferencing. Inferencing is used to formulate other facts or a hypothesis. Inferencing is performed by the Inference Engine component of the QoS Host Manager. The inferencer chooses which rules can be applied based on the fact repository. The inferencing that can take place can either be as complex as backward chaining (working backwards from a goal to start), forward chaining (vice-versa) or as relatively simple as a lookup. In this work we used forward chaining.

Consider the policy in Example 1. One rule for the QoS Host Manager is informally stated as follows: if the communication buffer size is above some threshold (implying that the process is not able to process frames fast enough), then the CPU manager component is invoked to adjust the CPU priority of the violated process. Additional rules are used to determine how much to increase CPU priority based on how close the policy is to being satisfied.

Another rule for the QoS Host Manager is informally stated as follows: if the communication buffer size is below some threshold then send a notification to the QoS Domain Manager, which can then locate the source of the problem, perhaps by interacting with the QoS Host Managers. The implication of a small buffer size is that the video client is able to process the received frames fast enough and that the problem is either a network problem or a server problem. The QoS Domain Manager also has a rule set which is used to drive the location process and guide the formulation of corrective actions. One such rule for the QoS Domain Manager is informally stated as follows: Upon receiving an alarm report from the client-side QoS Host Manager, ask the corresponding server-side QoS Host Manager for CPU load and memory usage. Another QoS Domain Manager rule states that if the CPU load exceeds some predefined threshold or the memory usage exceeds some threshold then an the alarm report is sent to the server-side QoS Host Manager.

This is a relatively simple set of rules[1]. A more complex set of rules would include rules that reflect administrative requirements.

6   Policy Specification and Distribution

Earlier we identified that we need to be able to accommodate changes in requirements; this included both policies and rules. This means that we need to support the addition and deletion of policies/rules and the distribution of polices/rules to the relevant management components. In this work, this means that policies about an application should be able to change each time the application runs and that the rules in the QoS Host Manager should also be able to change. These changes should not require recompilation (unless, of course, there is a change in the actual attributes needed). In this section, we describe the applications and services needed to support policy distribution. This is illustrated in Figure 6. The components (e.g., Policy Agent, Policy Repository, applications) in Figure 6 fit in the "Quality of Resource Management System" depicted in Figure 2. Our current implementation focusses on policies.

6.1   Information Model

We begin with a partial description of the information model used to represent the data needed to support policy distribution. We have identified the following different types of data needed. The data and the relationships between the data are described in this section.

An *executable* is instantiated on a host as a process. More information about the attributes of an executable class can be found in [14].

Sensors represent code that is instrumented into a program. A sensor collects values for an attribute of the process and is part of an executable. In the model, sensors are associated with the executable of the process. A sensor may be used for more than one executable and an executable may have more than one sensor (hence the many to many relationship). A sensor class includes a sensor identifier and a list of attribute identifiers.

An *application* ([14]) defines the application to be managed. An application is composed of at least one executable.

---

[1] Due to space considerations, we have not included the complete set of rules.

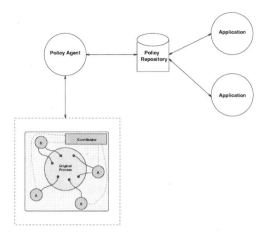

Fig. 2. Policy Distribution Architecture

A *policy* states that the application QoS requirement of an executable of an application and the actions to be taken if that QoS requirement is violated. We note that in one session an executable may have a different policy then one used in a second session simply because the application that is using that executable is different. Policies also differ depending on the user of the application. A policy is composed of policy conditions and policy actions. A *policy condition* can be reused in other policies as can a *policy action*. Hence, the reason for their separate class representation. One attribute of a policy represents how the policy conditions are to be evaluated e.g., conjunctively or disjunctively. Policies can also be subclassed e.g., QoS policies.

6.2 Description of Components

We will now describe the components needed for policy distribution.

Repository Service. The Repository Service allows for the storage and retrieval of the data specified in the previous section.

Management Applications. Authorized administrators must have a way to add and remove policies, define domains, browse policy information, etc; A policy administration application provides a user interface to facilitate this type of activity. Another management application can be used for checking information integrity e.g., an application can ensure that an application has sensors that collect the attributes specified in the policies (note that in Figure 6 the management application is just referred to as an application).

Policy Agent. This agent provides an interface that includes a method that is used by a process to register with an agent. When a process starts up, it registers with the policy agent. The process passes information about the process that is relevant in determining the policies that are applicable to that process. This includes a process identifier, an application identifier, an executable identifier and a role identifier. The Policy Agent uses this information and maps it to the appropriate policies. This is sent to the coordinator component that creates a list of policy objects.

7   Prototype

To explore and evaluate the architecture, we developed a prototype system based on the architecture presented in this paper. This prototype has been implemented for Solaris 2.8.

All of the sensors described in Section 5 were implemented. Instrumented processes communicate with the QoS Host Manager using message queues and socket calls at the initialisation of the processes. The QoS Host Manager has a simple set of rules that were described in Section 5. The QoS Host Manager adjusts allocations dynamically through a collection of resource managers that each manage a single system resource. To date, we have resource managers capable of adjusting CPU allocations (through manipulating time-sharing priorities, or by allocating units of real-time CPU cycles) as well as memory (through adjusting the number of resident pages each process has in physical memory). The inference engine, rule set and fact repository are implemented using CLIPs [18].

We have one management process in the Quality of Resource Management System that receives reports from QoS Host Managers. It has rules that can distinguish between a server machine problem and a network problem (this usually requires a query of other QoS Host Managers through a QoS Domain Manager) and can tell a QoS Host Manager on a server machine to increase the CPU priority of the server process (assuming the problem in that the server process is not getting enough CPU cycles).

Each of the classes defined in the information model were mapped to LDAP classes.

We have implemented a simple application that provides an interface that asks the user to input policy information based on the notation presented earlier. The possible values are retrieved from the repository server. Very simple information integrity checking is done which basically is making sure that that policy is being applied to an executable that has the sensors that can monitor the attributes specified in the policy. Another check is to make sure that the actions are either method invocations on sensors or a notification to the QoS Host Manager and that the notification is based on data returned by sensors (must be non-empty). This gets translated into an LDIF file which can be easily uploaded into LDAP.

Figure 3 compares the mean video playback throughput, in frames per second, for the MPEG video player [17] under normal Solaris scheduling and with our QoS Host Manager (with a CPU Resource Manager) in place. This assumes that the other processes are not multimedia applications. From this figure, we can see that video throughput dropped dramatically under an increasing CPU load when normal Solaris scheduling was used. With our resource manager in place, however, throughput remained reasonably consistent around 28 frames

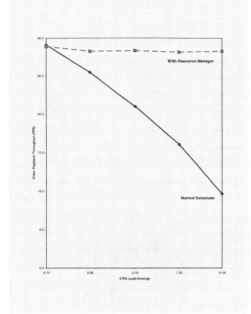

Fig. 3. Video Playback Throughput Comparison

per second – well within the acceptable limits set by the quality of service policy for the video player.

From measurements taken during experimentation, the overhead from our approach is minimal. An instrumented process on our UltraSparc system requires approximately 400 microseconds more time to initialise itself and report to QoS Host Manager. If the level of quality of service delivered meets expectations, one pass through the instrumentation code requires only 11 microseconds, on average. More detailed discussion can be found in [8, 15].

8   Related Work

There are three areas of related work: QoS management, policies and fault isolation.

8.1   Dynamic QoS Management

The work closes to ours is found in [1, 4] is very similar philosophically to our notion of QoS management without knowledge of detailed resource requirements. However, they have yet to address the issues related to developing an architecture that can deal with resource adjustments and fault location. There are also differences in the way CPU adjustments are done. Some work (e.g., [3]) allows for the adaptation of the application's operations (as opposed to resource adjustments) to accommodate violations of QoS requirements.

8.2   Policies

We divide our discussion into the following: Policy specification, architectures and vendor support.

Policy Specification.

IETF is currently developing a set of standards (current drafts found in [16, 19, 21]) that includes an information model to be used for specifying policies, a standard that extends the previous standard for specifying policies for specifying QoS policies and a standard for mapping the information model to LDAP schemas. Informally, speaking an IETF policy basically consists of a set of conditions and a set of actions. The standards focus on low-level details related to policy encoding, storage and retrieval. Our policy definition with its notion of reusable policy conditions and actions is very similar to that defined in the IETF standards. Our use of "userole" is similar to the intent of "role combination". One of our conclusions is that it is possible to use the draft standards for defining application QoS policies even though most of the work has been motivated by security or management of network bandwidth policies.

However, there are some problems with current policy specifications. For example, an alarm report from an instrumented process triggers one or more rules. The alarm report is an event that starts a collection of actions. Not all of these actions are necessarily taking place at one QoS Host Manager. Currently, none of the draft standard definitions nor higher level specifications of policies like [6] make it easy to represent this. We are intrigued by the suggestions made in [13] and we will be examining this work in more detail.

Architecture. The IETF has also defined a general architecture (a good description can be found in [20]) for a policy management system. The general architecture is very high-level and there is nothing to suggest that our more specific architecture does not fall within the proposed general architecture.

Vendors. Many network vendors such as 3Com, Cisco Systems, Lucent and Nortel are offering "primitive" versions of policy-based network management systems for control of their network devices.

8.3   Fault Isolation and Diagnosis

A literature survey (which includes [7, 2, 12, 11, 9, 10]) has shown that appropriate techniques exist for specific areas of fault management especially at the network layer. We use a combination of the approaches presented in the related work, but we focus on the application layer. In addition, most of the existing work focusses on availability issues and does not specifically deal with quality of service.

9   Discussion

Work to date has provided a number of insights several into QoS management. that we will discuss in this section.

Changing QoS Requirements. The separation of specifying QoS requirements using policy formalisms from applications allows for the following: (i) The use of the "UserRole" allows for different users to have different QoS requirements for the same application.(ii) Although not described, the sensors provide an interface that allows for a threshold to be changed. Thus, we are able to change QoS requirements while an application is executing.

Ease of Application Development. We have instrumented several third party applications (e.g., DOOM, Apache Web Server). The only knowledge needed was the name of the probes and knowing which libraries to link in. It was not necessary for the instrumentor to have any knowledge of what sort of QoS management was taking place.

In the applications that we have instrumented, the instrumentation took little time. However, we could see that as applications grow larger it will be more difficult for the developer to determine the probe points, especially if this is decided after the application has been written. This suggests that the instrumentation be partially automated.

Ease of Developing Policies and Rules. Policies expressing application QoS requirements seem relatively easy to specify. However, the administrative policies (or rules) are much more difficult. The learning curve for developing these types of policies is high. We found that learning how to put together a set of rules is difficult and time-consuming. These rules heavily interact with each other. This makes it difficult to debug a set of rules. This is similar to existing problems in developing rule sets for expert systems. We will be examining techniques for simplifying this development and evaluation. As discussed in the Related Work section, we also had a difficult time with the specification of rules. This is a subject for future work.

Dynamic Rule Distribution. The ability to change rules in a QoS Host Manager is very important, especially when taking into account the difficulty in debugging the set of rules. We believe that in a real-world environment that will be impossible to always know all the dependencies or correct resource allocations. Thus, it is very important to be able to dynamically add or delete rules and have this distributed to different management components at run-time.

Interconnecting QoS Domain Managers. A QoS Domain Manager is primarily responsible for locating sources of problems involving applications distributed across multiple hosts, as well as determining actions required for solving the problem. Each QoS Domain Manager is assigned to a collection of hosts (its *domain*); it interacts with QoS Host Managers on these hosts to enforce policies as necessary. At times, problems may span multiple domains, which introduces several interesting issues, as the relationship between these management entities is not clear. Should it be hierarchical or the will optimal relationship between the managers be more arbitrary, depending on organisational requirements and the relationship between different organisations.

10   Conclusions and Future Work

Our initial work has shown the feasibility of pursuing a policy-oriented approach to QoS management. Our work shows that (i) QoS management does not have to put an additional burden on application developers by forcing them to specify resource allocations in advance. (ii) Applications may be started with different QoS expectations.

We have identified a number of issues to examine in the previous section. Other future work includes the following: (i) Further developing fault diagnosis techniques and the configuration services needed to support these techniques (ii) We will work on supporting additional resources distributed across multiple hosts. (iii) We need to extend our work to handle overload conditions when there simply are not enough resources to meet demand. We will be looking at different application domain areas. (iv) The work we have done to date is reactive—when quality of service violations occur, we correct them. Another approach that we are investigating is proactive quality of service, where potential problems are detected and handled before they actually occur.

Acknowledgements

This work is supported by the National Sciences and Engineering Research Council (NSERC) of Canada, the IBM Centre of Advanced Studies in Toronto, Canada, Communications and Information Technology Ontario (CITO) and Canadian Institute of Telecommunications Research (CITR).

References

[1] G. Beaton. A Feedback-Based Quality of Service Management Scheme. In *HIP-PARCH Workshop, Uppsala*, June 1997.

[2] A. Bouloutas, S. Calo, A. Finkel, and I. Katzela. Distributed Fault Identification in Telecommunication Networks. *Journal of Network and Systems Management*, November 1995.

[3] S. Brandt, G. Nutt, T. Berk, and M. Humphrey. Soft Real-time Application Execution with Dynamic Quality of Service Assurance. In *Proceedings of the 6th IEEE/IFIP International Workshop on Quality of Service (IWQoS '98)*, pages 154–163, 1998.

[4] H. Cho and A. Seneviratne. Dynamic QoS Control without the Knowledge of Resource Requirements. *Submitted to IEEE Transactions on Computing*, 1999.

[5] H. Chu and K. Nahrstedt. A Soft Real Time Scheduling Server in UNIX Operating System. *European Workshop on Interactive Distributed MultimediaSystems and Telecommunication Services*, Darmstadt, Germany, September 1997.

[6] N. Damianou, N. Dalay, E. Lupu, and M. Sloman. Ponder: A language for specifying security and management policies for distributed systems: The language specification (version 2.1). Technical Report Imperial College Research Report DOC 2000/01, Imperial College of Science, Technology and Medicine, London, England, April 2000.

[7] K. Houck, S. Calo, and A. Finkel. Towards a practical alarm correlation system. In *Proceedings 4th IFIP/IEEE International Symposium on Integrated Nework Management*, pages 519–530, 1995.

[8] M. Katchabaw, H. Lutfiyya, and M. Bauer. Driving resource management with application-level quality of service specifications. *Journal of Decision Support Systems*, 28:71–87, 2000.

[9] S. Katker. A modelling framework for integrated distributed systems fault management. In *Proceedings IFIP/IEEE International Conference on Distributed Platforms*, pages 186–198, 1996.

[10] S. Katker and H Geihs. A Generic Model for Fault Isolation in Integrated Management Systems. *Journal of Network and Systems Management*, 1997.

[11] S. Katker and M. Paterok. Fault isolation and event correlation for integrated fault management. In *Proceedings of the 5th International Sypmposium on Integrated Network Management*, 1997.

[12] S. Kliger, S. Yemini, Y. Yemini, D. Ohsie, and S. Stolfo. A coding approach to event correlation. In *Proceedings of the 4th International Sypmposium on Integrated Network Management*, 1995.

[13] M. Kohli and J. Lobo. Policy based management of telecommunications systems. *1st Policy Workshop, HP Labs, Bristol*, November 1999.

[14] H. Lutfiyya, A. Marshall, M. Bauer, W. Powley, and P. Martin. Configuration maintenance for distributed application management. *Journal of Network and Systems Management*, 8(2):219–244, 2000.

[15] G. Molenkamp, M. Katchabaw, H. Lutfiyya, and M. Bauer. Managing soft qos requirements in distributed systems. *Accepted to Appear Multimedia Systems Workshop (ICPP)*, August, 2000.

[16] B. Moore, J. Strassmer, and E. Elleson. Policy core information model – version 1 specification. Technical report, IETF, May 2000.

[17] K. Patel, B. Smith, and L. Rowe. Performance of a Software MPEG Video Decoder. *Proceedings of the 1993 ACM Multimedia Conference*, Anaheim, California, August 1993.

[18] G. Riley. Clips: A tool for building expert systems. Technical report, http://www.ghg.net/clips/CLIPS.html, 1999.

[19] Y. Snir, Y. Ramberg, J. Strassner, and R. Cohen. Policy framework qos information model. Technical report, IETF, April 2000.

[20] Startdust.com. Introduction to qos policies. Technical report, Stardust.com, Inc., July 1999.

[21] J. Strassner, E. Ellesson, B. Moore, and Ryan Moats. Policy framework ldap core schema. Technical report, IETF, November 1999.

A Policy Based Management Architecture for Large Scale Active Communication Systems

Ian W. Marshall and Paul Mckee

BT Adastral Park, Martlesham Heath, Ipswich, IP5 3RE
ian.w.marshall@bt.com, paul.mckee@bt.com

Abstract. An initial design for a policy based management system combining conventional hierarchical control and significant local autonomy is described. A critical part of the design is a scheme of partial guarantees for policy distribution and execution. This scheme renders explicit the non-determinism that is implicit in policy based control schemes that include conflict resolution, and to some extent replaces the need for conflict resolution. Some preliminary implementations of the design are described, and implications for further work are discussed.

Keywords: Policy, Autonomy, Guarantees, Store, management requirements

1. Introduction

One of the key aims of next generation communication networks is to support the dynamic business relationships demanded in the new economy, for example by activities such as e-commerce. Aside from introducing obvious features such as mobility support it is crucial that operators create management and support systems that allow rapid response. Since human operators are the principal bottleneck in existing systems this means that network operations and business processes must become more distributed and more automated. Recently active services [1-4] have been proposed as a means of making the network more responsive to users demands. However this approach has so far not addressed management automation, and in addition creates new management challenges. The new challenges include that of supporting multiple, user based, management domains making independent decisions and using a wide range of technologies. Centralised control will not be possible and the response of the system will be the result of a collection of autonomous actions. There is however the need to exchange management information and policies between interacting systems. In order to achieve this we require common information models or at least a common information syntax. We are developing [5-11] an approach based on events (for monitoring the state of system components) and policies for expressing the desired behaviour of system components. The approach embeds a novel autonomous controller [12,13] that enables increased automation of some key low level management functions. To support heterogeneous systems it is essential that the information and policies are represented in a platform neutral way. We

M. Sloman, J. Lobo, and E. Lupu (Eds.): POLICY 2001, LNCS 1995, pp. 202-213, 2001.

propose the use of XML, a de facto standard for the representation and exchange of text based information, particularly where the information needs to be automatically processed. XML allows users to define representations specific to their own applications with a well defined formal syntax. In our approach we propose the definition of management data and concepts using XML DTD's or Schema. The use of DTD's or schemae gives a reference representation of information that has a consistent meaning in multiple systems. Ideally these representations would be standardised, but where this is not possible automated transformation may be used to transform policy and event formats to domain specific representations. XML based policies and events may be propagated between nodes in the system using commonly available Internet protocols ensuring the greatest possible reach of the proposed technology, but no single protocol is mandatory. Our current experiments have used XML to distribute policies that control the mobility of code in an active network application. Previous papers [5,6] have discussed the use of XML as a resource description approach and we are currently working on resource management monitoring using XML. One advantage of the use of XML and either DTD's or schema is the automatic checking for well formedness and validity that occurs when an XML document is parsed, allowing early rejection of erroneous input. The use of XML as an intermediate representation still allows policies to be developed using any existing management tools - they will just be transformed prior to transmission.

In this paper we present for the first time the details of the policy handling architecture required by our XML based management system. The architecture relies on a novel categorisation of policies, that enables us to support both dependable and best effort management activity. This is crucial since we cannot provide guarantees that all requests for management action emanating from users can be satisfied by the available resources. The paper also describes a preliminary implementation of key aspects of the architecture. In the next section we summarise ALAN, the infrastructure we are attempting to manage. This is followed (sections 3 and 4) by a high level description of the management architecture, and how policies are handled within it. In section 5 we motivate and describe the policy categorisation scheme, and give examples of its application. Section 6 presents our initial implementation and results.

2. ALAN

ALAN [1] is based on users supplying java based active code (proxylets) that runs on edge systems (dynamic proxy servers - DPS) provided by network operators. It is assumed that many proxylets will be multiuser, and most requests will be to "run" a proxylet that already exists in the network. Messaging uses HTML/XML and is normally carried over HTTP. There are likely to be many DPSs at a physical network node. It is not the intention that the DPS is able to act as an active router. ALAN is primarily an active service architecture, and the discussion in this paper refers to the management of active programming of intermediate servers. Figure 1 shows a schematic of a possible ALAN node.

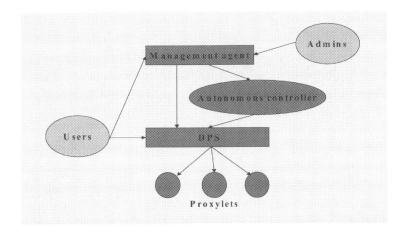

Figure 1. Schematic of proposed ALAN node design

We have designed and partially implemented an active management solution for multi-service networks based on role-driven policies [7,8] and Application Layer Active Networking (ALAN) [9]. The management system supports a conventional management agent interface that can respond to high level instructions from system operators [10,11]. This interface is also open to use by users (who can use it to run programs/active services by adding a policy pointing to the location of their program and providing an invocation trigger). Typically the management policies for the user programs are included in an XML metafile associated with the code using an XML container, but users can also separately add management policies associated with their programs using HTTP post commands. We refer to the metafiles as macropolicies since they may embed many statements concerning a range of entities. Individual IF-THEN-ELSE statements are referred to as atomic policies. For our purposes a policy must consist of one or more atomic policies referring to a single entity.

The agent can accept policies from other agents and export policies to other agents. Our system provides an extensible monitoring and configuration service that enables users to specify their configuration, monitoring and notification requirements to network devices using policies. Each policy specifies a subject (the policy interpreter), a target list (the objects to be changed if the policy is activated), an action list (the things to be done to each target) and the authorisation code, id and reply address of the originator. The policies can carry enclosures (e.g. the code required to execute an action, or a pointer to it), so we describe the management system as 'Active'. The enclosures can obviously be instances of active services. An event is simply a policy with a single action - "store the enclosed data", and an appropriate data enclosure. The policies are named using a universal policy name, which is also part of the policy. The names currently take the form *upn:originator id.subject.target_list.last_modified_time* and are likely to be globally unique. The policies are multicast to relevant hosts, where they are received by a management agent, and stored in a local policy store if the appropriate key is present (i.e. a key associated with a role authorised to supply policies to the target device). The management agent has an extensible table of authorisation policies to enable this decision. Roles are allocated using a public key infrastructure. A policy addressed to the management agent can also enclose a number of component policies, each of which specifies the subject (normally an object oriented program) intended to use it as part of their rule-base. The policy store has a table of policies for each registered subject and the local agent will store the component policies in the appropriate parts of the database.

Our approach avoids many information handling problems by using a lightweight scalable mechanism for policy transfer. The Information Management System [10] consists of a hierarchy of '*store and forward*' policy stores, with policies being classified by their propagation characteristics and storage duration. Two types of these information stores are used, their selection depending on the complexity of querying required against storage availability. While simple but fast stores offer a load balancing and traffic controlling function, more complex stores permit management information analysis.

The DPS also has an autonomous control system that performs management functions delegated to it via policies (scripts and pointers embedded in XML containers). This autonomous control system is intended to be adaptive, and is integrated with the conventional agent by sharing policy stores.

Not shown in the figure are some low level controls required to enforce sharing of resources between users, and minimise unwanted interactions between users. There is a set of kernel level routines [12] that enforce hard scheduling of the system resources used by a DPS and the associated virtual machine that supports user supplied code. In addition the DPS requires programs to offer payment tokens before they can run. In principle the tokens should be authenticated by a trusted third party. At present these low level management activities are carried out using a conventional hierarchical approach. We hope to address adaptive control of the o/s kernel supporting the DPS in future work.

3. Management Architecture

Previous publications have described our overall architecture for the management of multi-service networks [5] and a proposed architecture for active server management [11]. This paper describes the design and partial implementation of an event service element designed to use XML as both an event description format and as a policy and object metadata format [6]. This event service element is designed to run on a single physical platform, or to form part of a larger distributed system on multiple platforms. This system provides an extensible monitoring and configuration service that enables users and managers of the system to specify their requirements to system components using policies. The basic building blocks of our current implementation are shown in the following diagram.

The system is designed to be as flexible as possible and its operation is initiated when policies are provided. There are a number of different providers of policies that may interact with the system, every software component or user program installed on the system will have an associated metadata description that will be supplied to the event service element. This metadata description will contain a number of policies that pertain to the operation of that component or user program, it might be perhaps considered as a meta-policy. In a similar way the hardware upon which the system is running will have a metadata file containing policies that control for example access to hardware resources. End users and remote mangers may both supply single policies via the communications adapters and other event service elements may pass policies to any other element. At this stage we are assuming nothing about the structure of any policy except that it has a header in the XML description that describes it as a policy.

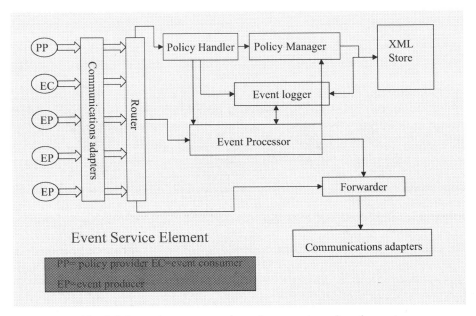

Fig.2 Schematic representation of an event service element

Once identified as a policy the incoming information is routed to the policy handler where the policy will be parsed and checked against the document type definition (DTD) that describes its structure. Again this imparts flexibility for the introduction of a range of new policy definitions to a live system. The policy handler also determines whether the policy is destined to manage the operation of the event service element or should be stored in order to be able to handle detected events. Management policies within the event service element are used as a means of traffic management, events may be aggregated and filtered in the event processor, and the time scales for any locally stored events may be modified.

In this initial prototype implementation the structure of the events is again left as flexible as possible. Events are received at the communications adapter and within the router the header will identify the XML as an event. It will then be passed to the event processor where it will be parsed and checked against a DTD, if no DTD is supplied the event is just checked for well formedness. This again accommodates future expansion in the types of events that may be specified and collected.

4. Autonomous Controller

The system described above will rapidly generate large numbers of policies and as it grows, the need for user intervention will tend to grow even faster. It is thus imperative to combine the policy based management approach with a significant improvement in management automation. Given the nature of the problem domain this can only be done using adaptive control as described earlier. We have recently developed a novel bacterial GA described elsewhere [13] that forms the basis of the adaptation performed by the autonomous controller in our architecture. In this paper we aim to identify the role of autonomous control in our policy driven management system and describe how the autonomous controller is integrated and provide only a brief sketch of the bacterial algorithm.

One of the most distinctive features of bacterial genetics is the process of plasmid interchange, in which one bacterium accepts copies of genes exported by another. This process is in effect a learning mechanism, and enables bacteria to acquire new capabilities (such as antibiotic resistance) extremely rapidly. In our controller we treat policies as though they were genes, and policy exchange between entities as plasmid interchange. If the controller is programmed (like a bacterium) to autonomously export policies that improve its performance, and de-activate policies that degrade performance, useful policies will spread and poor policies will cease to be executed (until conditions change).

In fact the controller monitors all the policies that it controls in the policy database, and autonomously deactivates those that are generating the least revenue (as recorded in the payment log). In order for a policy to be autonomously controlled it must therefore include an action such as 'Get_Payment'. The controller also exports the policies generating the most revenue when the node fitness function (revenue/cost) is high. Exported policies are addressed to the autonomous controller so the policy receiver simply stores them as de-activated policies. Whenever the autonomous controller deactivates a policy it will examine all the deactivated policies and activate a random selection, to compensate. The autonomous controller has two further capabilities: it will shut down the DPS if fitness has been low for some time, and copy the DPS to a nearby vacant site if fitness has been high for some time. Policies that are never useful will tend to disappear completely, since nodes that possess them will be more likely to shut down. Policies that are useful for some demand but not for others will persist but may not always be activated.

The autonomous controller is thus acting as a configuration manager, distributing policies/services to where they are needed and activating them on demand, without needing any knowledge of what the demand is or what the policies represent. It is also acting as a low-level account manager since all the policies it controls are generating payments (and will not execute without payment events being generated). This is very convenient since an active services network must respond rapidly to the introduction of new services, enabling them to spread to wherever there is demand, whilst providing a stable quality of service for existing services. When a user develops a new proxylet, or an improved version of an existing proxylet, he should not be required to identify all the locations where it should be stored and/or run. Typically the user lacks both the time and the knowledge to make such a decision for himself and in any case cannot predict demand from other users of his program. At the same time if a user introduces a new service he should not be able to access his service until he has paid the appropriate fee. Given that the number of DPSs will be large, and the number of proxylets unbounded, the correct configuration algorithm will be one that needs as little human/manual intervention as possible, as the manual optimisation of proxylet placement soon becomes untenable.

5. Policy Classification

Clearly, to support the hybrid management system we have designed we must be able to classify policies such that those that are appropriate for autonomous or adaptive handling are clearly identified. It is obvious that in order to enable the autonomous controller to take control of those policies sent to it, as identified above, the policies cannot be atomic. Policies addressed to the autonomous controller must encapsulate atomic policies for the entities it is controlling. However, it is also necessary for administrators to have a thorough grasp of which atomic policies can be allocated to autonomous control in this way. One reason is that the level of guarantee offered by the autonomous controller is weaker than that offered by a completely deterministic system. In addition if we are to retain the spirit of XML it must be possible to write policies behind tags that can be ignored by receiving entities that do not support the tag for local policy reasons. With this in mind we have attempted to devise a scheme allowing policy authors to specify the grade of service their policy requires. These specifications could be expressed as constraints in the existing policy notation of Sloman et. al. [7]. We would prefer to express them as a top level categorisation since this makes it more efficient to store the policies in a structure based on level of guarantee. Such a storage approach simplifies the task of conflict identification considerably by reducing the number of entries that must be considered. The basic classification is illustrated in table 1, and deserves some explanation.

The three rows represent different levels of guarantee concerning whether the action specified in a policy will be carried out. The highest class represents the case where the policy will always execute and corresponds to the grade of service assumed in most existing policy architectures. Clearly business critical actions specified by operators should normally be in this class. The second category assumes that policies are sent to many network elements and offers a guarantee that the policy will execute at some of the entities it is sent to. This is the level of guarantee offered by the autonomous controller, and is probably appropriate to many information gathering actions, particularly when multiple execution returns redundant information. In addition this class is ideal for the enhancement processes associated with intermediaries in an active network, since they typically are required once and once only on the path taken by the traffic being enhanced. The key benefit is that managers can specify actions without any need to decide where they should execute. In other words load balancing and conflict avoidance are automated. The third class emulates the level of service offered by the Internet and is intended mainly for end users (whose policies will also often get overridden by a conflict resolver in a more conventional system). It may also be of benefit to operators who can specify an experimental action without needing to worry about the impact on live traffic, since the action will only execute when load is light.

	Guaranteed correct (Account and Security)	Errors tracked (Configuration)	Best effort correctness (Fault and Performance)
Guaranteed execution wherever specified	Critical actions (e.g. authorisation changes)	Most configuration actions	Critical event logging and notification
Guaranteed to execute somewhere and/or sometime	Sample based billing	Some Proxylets	Most notifications and policy distributions
Best effort execution	Intrusion tracing proxylets	Active service composition, proxylets	Most event logging

Table 1. Examples of management activities to which the different grades of policy handling might apply

The three columns represent grades of service for a more complex concept. Correctness can refer to execution, distribution or persistence. It is envisaged that the notion of correctness will be context dependent, i.e. it will depend on the target, subject and action specified in the policy, together with any constraints. For the case where the action requires storage of information, such as an event, the three classes can be interpreted as follows. The first column represents the event being treated as a transaction and stored using a distributed transaction controller. This grade should only be used for requirements (e.g. charging?) where accuracy and consistency are paramount. Policies in the second column will trigger an exception message to the policy owner if the storage or execution fails, but will make no attempt to rollback system state. This grade is ideal for many configuration management records, since existing processes already tolerate inconsistency arising from unavoidable human errors at installation time. Policies in the third column will simply fail, or store incorrect data. This is ideal for most non critical management information collection, particularly where the information is only used for off-line analysis or data mining. In cases where storage of results are not required, correctness could apply to persistence of the policy being correctly maintained for the time specified in the constraints, or alternatively to distribution of follow on actions to the correct targets.

A policy in the second row of the second column will thus guarantee to execute once and tell at least one owner whether or not it succeeded. On the other hand a policy in the second row of the first column will distribute messages wherever specified whenever it executes.

Given this very flexible specification of the events and policies that may be used in our system the roles of some of the event service element components may be expanded.

- The router examines the header of any incoming XML fragment and sends the information to the appropriate subsystem. Policies to the policy handler, events to the event manager and any messages that are not intended for this system are passed to the forwarder for onward transmission via the output communications adapters.
- The policy handler examines any incoming policies and determines if they are intended to influence the operation of the event processor or event logger in which case they are routed accordingly. Or if they are intended to manage other installed software the policies are passed to the policy manager for eventual storage in the XML store.
- The policy manager interacts with the XML store loading policies, and formulating queries in response to detected events passed by the event processor.
- The event processor examines incoming events and checks if it has a policy defined to handle them. These policies will include actions such as pass to local store for a given period of time, discard as unimportant, aggregate if a large number arrive, query the policy manger for actions or in some cases pass on to another system.
- The event logger stores a local event history, this is another traffic management aid. In any system there will be a number of normal system events that only become of interest in the case of a system failure or other major problem. Rather than sending these events to a centralised store they are stored locally reducing network load. It is possible that the local store may be queried for patterns of events that might be indicative of failure conditions.
- The forwarder handles onward transmission of events, policies and any other messages received by the system.

6. Policy Store

The policy store is a key function in our system - it must be able to rapidly store and retrieve large numbers of XML fragments. In our initial prototype we will be storing a number of different types of document, events, policies and metapolicies so we require a fast and flexible XML store and search capability. In this system we are currently using XSet [14] a lightweight database for Internet applications developed at the University of California Berkeley. XSet is now in version 2 and can be described as a memory resident, hierarchically structured database with support for a partial set of ACID semantics. The version 2 release has extended the original memory resident database to include disc storage. During normal usage documents that are inserted are written immediately to disc. Insert and delete operations are logged both before and after the operation completes, the logs being buffered in memory, which is written to disc when full. XSet supports checkpoints, which may be carried out at regular intervals, this aids rapid recovery during restarts. At this time XSet doesn't support transactions, this allows it to use a coarse grain thread locking mechanism to minimise overhead and maintain high performance using a memory resident data structure allows us to gain a speed advantage during normal operation, important in a interactive environment. The number of documents stored at each element being unlike to exhaust the memory available. Currently queries in XSet are defined as

XML fragments so context based searching is possible, but correct formulation of queries is complex and will be the subject of further research. Currently queries will be built in the policy manger. As previously mentioned high performance is a pre requisite and given that we currently are flexible in our policy specification some tests were carried out on XSet using dummy files.

Number of files	Number of tags	Content	Search time on single tag msecs
2000	20	text	3.0
4000	20	text	11.0
6000	20	text	17.0

Table 2. Performance of XSet based implementation of Policy store

These results were obtained on a dual 300Mhz Pentium II PC running Windows NT version 4.0 service pack 4. This system had 256 megabytes of RAM, but use of memory was a limitation and it is highly likely that further optimisation will improve the memory usage, certainly the systems virus checking had to be disabled in order to obtain the above figures. These numbers of files seem adequate for a local store and search facility, and the performance is more than acceptable. Similar results were obtained on a single 450MHz Pentium II PC with 128mBytes of Ram running Windows 98.

Searching is only one of the performance components in XSet's operation, the other two are validation and indexing. Validation is the action of certifying the XML document against a DTD or XML Schema and indexing is the addition of a new XML document to the existing index. Indexing affects both insertions of new data into the index and recovery after a crash. Any queries requesting a document yet to be indexed will return null, so excessive indexing times may affect operation of the index. However for a production quality system with high reliability hardware the one off cost of validating and indexing a document will be far outweighed by the number of queries. Indeed in a well designed system validation and indexing may be performed in separate threads allowing uninterrupted query processing.

When used with the autonomous controller the policy store has to be able to deal with the three basic classifications of policy, guaranteed correct, errors tracked and best efforts correctness. Each of these three categories may be indicated by tags in the policy, an incoming policy will be routed to the policy manager via the policy handler. As it is inserted in the XSet store it is checked for well formedness, and validity against any supplied DTD or schema which confirms that it has an acceptable structure. This base level of operation is equivalent to the best effort correctness category of policy.

In order to achieve a higher of confidence in that the policy received is identical to the policy dispatched we must introduce further checks. At the simplest level this will just be a comparison of the structure of the document object model (DOM) tree at the originating node with the value at the receiver. This may be achieved with a digest or hash value of the XML object; the digest is a fixed length value, typically 128 or 160 bits that represents the tree [15]. Two trees are the same if their DomHash values are the same.

As the exchange of XML documents has such a key role in B2B e-commerce there are a number of available strategies for secure Internet B2B messaging to prevent information being stolen or modified during transmission. The XML security suite [16] recently made available by IBM provides security features such as digital signature, element wise encryption and access control. This secure communication can easily be accommodated in the communication adapter, and either of these approaches would satisfy the second class of policy, that of errors tracked.

The final most stringent class of policy that of guaranteed correct is a challenge for the current implementation. XSet was designed for speed and flexibility and does not in it's current form support transactions. For our purpose there is no reason why the policy manger should not take part in a distributed transaction that ensures that the guaranteed correct class of policy are successfully inserted in the local XSet store. Using the secure communication provided for the lower policy class already offers the guarantee of correctness. The Java technology used in our prototype includes support for distributed transactions through two specifications [17] the Java Transaction API (JTA) and the Java Transaction Service (JTS). JTA is a high level, implementation independent, protocol independent API that allows applications and application servers to access transactions. JTS specifies the implementation of a Transaction Manager, which supports JTA and implements the Java mapping of the OMG Object Transaction Service (OTS) 1.1 specification at the level below the API. JTS propagates transactions using the Internet Inter-ORB Protocol (IIOP). Further development of our prototype will include this additional functionality.

7. Discussion

As far as we are aware existing work on policies does not consider the impact of policies being best effort, and indeed does not often recognise that best effort response is the result of most approaches to conflict resolution. Although many of the details of our approach are debatable we feel strongly that explicit recognition of the non-deterministic nature of policy based management systems will aid designers and users. We therefore hope that our work will stimulate debate and creative effort elsewhere in the management and systems community.

In the future we intend to carefully evaluate the costs and benefits of a variety of approaches to managing a large scale active services network.

8. Conclusion

A novel management architecture for large scale distributed communication systems has been described. Conflict between system policies is largely handled by removing the assumption of guaranteed execution and encouraging users to explicitly mark those policies that are critical to them using a simple grade of service matrix. These policies can then be offered a higher grade of service than other less critical policies. Initial results suggest that it would be relatively straightforward to implement the proposed architecture. A full implementation could be used to evaluate the number of policies required in each class of service. The required system resources could then be compared with those of more conventional systems. We are confident that the proposals made in this paper offer significant advantages in terms of scalability, required resource and user satisfaction.

References

[1] M. Fry and A. Ghosh "Application Layer Active Networking" Computer Networks, 31, 7, pp. 655-667, 1999.

[2] E. Amir, S. McCanne, R. Katz, "An active service framework and its application to real time multimedia transcoding" Computer Communications review 28, 4, pp178-189, Oct 1998.

[3] P. Cao, J. Zhang and K. Beach, "Active Cache: Caching Dynamic Contents (Objects) on the Web", Proc middleware 1998 (Ambleside).

[4] G.Parulkar *et.al* "Active Network Node Project", Washington University

[5] I.W.Marshall, C.Mallia, J.Bates, M.Spiteri, L.Velasco "Active management of multiservice networks" Proc IEE colloquium 99/147

[6] P.Mckee and I.W.Marshall "Behavioural specification using XML" Proc IEEE FTDCS '99 (Capetown), pp53-59

[7] Sloman M., "Policy Driven Management for Distributed Systems", Plenum press Journal of Network and Systems Management, Plenum Press

[8] Lupu E., Sloman M., " A Policy-based Role Object Model", Proceedings of the 1st IEEE Enterprise Distributed Object Computing Workshop (EDOC '97).

[9] I.W. Marshall et. al. "Application Layer Programmable Internetwork Environment", British Telecom. Technol. J., 17, 2, pp 82-94, April 1999.

[10] Bates J., Bacon J., Moody K., and. Spiteri M., "Using Events for the Scalable Federation of Heterogeneous Components", *Proceedings of 8th ACM SIGOPS European Workshop*, Sintra, Portugal. September 1998.

[11] I.W.Marshall, H.Gharib, J.Hardwicke and C.M.Roadknight, "A novel architecture for active service management" DSOM2000

[12] D.G. Waddington and D. Hutchison, "Resource Partitioning in General Purpose Operating Systems, Experimental Results in Windows NT", Operating Systems Review, 33, 4, 52-74, Oct 1999.

[13] C.M.Roadknight and I.W.Marshall, " Future Network Management - A Bacterium Inspired Solution", British Telecom Technol J. Oct 2000

[14] "XSet: A Lightweight XML Search Engine for Internet Applications", Ben Y Zhao, Anthony Joseph http://www.cs.berkeley.edu/~ravenben/xset/

[15] Digest Values for DOM (DOMHASH) Proposal, http://www.trl.ibm.co.jp/projects/xml/domhash.html

[16] XML Security Suite, http://www.alphaworks.ibm.com/tech/xmlsecuritysuite

[17] TRANSACTIONS AND JAVA™ TECHNOLOGY, http://java.sun.com/j2ee/transactions.html

Policy-Driven Management of Agent Systems

Antonio Corradi[1], Naranker Dulay[2], Rebecca Montanari[1], Cesare Stefanelli[3]

[1]Dipartimento di Elettronica, Informatica e Sistemistica
Università di Bologna
Viale Risorgimento, 2 - 40136 Bologna - Italy
{acorradi, rmontanari}@deis.unibo.it
[2]Department of Computing
Imperial College
180 Queen's Gate – London SW7 2BZ – United Kingdom
nd@doc.ic.ac.uk
[3]Dipartimento di Ingegneria
Università di Ferrara
Via Saragat, 1 - 44100 Ferrara - Italy
cstefanelli@ing.unife.it

Abstract. The agent paradigm has the potential to help in the development of applications for the open and heterogeneous Internet environment. Agents acting on the behalf of users can autonomously fulfil assigned goals, thus relieving users from complex and time-consuming tasks. Agent-based applications typically involve multiple agents, and each agent has to play a specific role that defines what the agent can and must do in order to achieve its application goal, and how it interacts with other agents and with the environment. This paper describes the integration of a policy language (Ponder) within an agent infrastructure (SOMA) in order to flexibly model agent roles and agent behaviour according to application specific requirements. The Ponder language is used to specify both agent permissions and duties and to model agent behaviour in terms of roles and relationships. SOMA is a rich infrastructure to support agent execution and provides a set of facilities that can help to build Ponder policy enforcement services. The integration of the two provides a flexible framework to the development and management of agent applications.

1 Introduction

Agent-based computing represents a promising programming paradigm for engineering complex distributed applications [1]. Software agents acting on behalf of end-users can reduce the effort required to perform elaborate and time-consuming tasks. Agents can autonomously fulfil specific goals, can execute in dynamic and uncertain environments, and can operate within changing organisational structures by responding in a timely fashion to environment changes [2]. Several agent-based solutions have already been developed and exploited for different application domains [3].

M. Sloman, J. Lobo, and E. Lupu (Eds.): POLICY 2001, LNCS 1995, pp. 214-229, 2001.
© Springer-Verlag Berlin Heidelberg 2001

Adding mobility to agents can further increase their potential uses. Mobile agents can execute locally to information servers providing better network utilisation and a more suitable approach to nomadic users that can disconnect from a network while their agents roam and compute on their behalf [4].

However, the research on agent systems still has to address a number of issues. For instance, in agent-based applications each agent performs a specific task, but it also interacts with local and remote resources and with other agents. This requires appropriate support to specify *access control policies* for agent-to-resource and agent-to-agent interactions. Modelling access control in terms of roles can improve the manageability of applications that have a diverse community of agents. Furthermore, the ability to define *event-triggered policies* is essential for expressing agent duties. Event-triggered policies can specify which agents must respond to triggered events and how they must behave accordingly. There is a need for policy languages that can suitably model and express all of these policies and that can be integrated within an agent infrastructure. A number of solutions have already been proposed in the field of policy-driven management and role-based access control models that can be exploited to support the specification of agent roles and role relationships [5] [6].

The paper presents the integration of a policy-based framework within an agent infrastructure to support policy-driven agent management. We adopt the Ponder policy language to model agent roles and relationships, and to specify agent roles in terms of both access control policies (*authorisations*) and event-triggered policies (*obligations*) [7]. For the agent infrastructure, we use the SOMA programming framework that supports agent execution and provides the needed services for the development of mobile agent-based distributed applications [8].

This paper focuses on the services needed to map Ponder authorisation and obligation policy specifications into enforcement services in the SOMA infrastructure. The service for supporting authorisation policies is designed to perform flexible and fine-grained access controls that depend on both static and dynamic attributes. Static attributes include, for instance, the identity/role of the user responsible for agent execution and the host from where the agent code was loaded (in the case of mobile agents). Dynamic attributes relate to the current context in which the agent operates such as, for instance, the current time, the current application state, and the state of the resources that the agent is accessing.

Similar considerations apply to the service for obligation policy enforcement: it supports the triggering of obligation actions based on events and action execution based on static and dynamic attributes. The obligation enforcement service requires a monitoring service for detecting events and a delivery service for notifying events to the agents interested in their occurrence.

The above enforcement services are integrated in the Java-based SOMA infrastructure. In particular, the mapping of authorisation policies has required extension of the Java security architecture to enforce both static and dynamic access controls. The enforcement of obligation policies exploits SOMA facilities for event monitoring and for the delivery of events to interested agents.

The next section outlines our policy requirements for agent-based systems. Section 3 introduces the Ponder language and shows how it can be used to specify policies for agent applications. Section 4 presents the SOMA policy enforcement architecture while Section 5 provides a case study from systems management. Section 6 presents our conclusions.

2   Policy Requirements for Agent Systems

The development of complex and distributed agent-based applications needs to take into account many design requirements [9]. This paper does not address all these issues, but focuses only on the requirements for developing policy-driven agent systems. The research in the field of agent computing has not extensively addressed the problem of modelling agent permissions and duties, although, in our opinion, agent systems can greatly take advantage of contributions stemming from the policy research area [5] [6]. We claim that the integration of a policy-based framework that supports policy specification and enforcement can significantly enhance any agent-based system. This integration can permit to define the policies for agent systems separately from agent implementation and can allow the dynamic change of policies and hence to vary the behaviour of a running agent system without having to re-implement agents themselves.

Some general properties have to be considered during the development of policy-driven agent systems. We consider the following as basic requirements:

- the ability to group policies that apply to agents into roles to simplify the management of agent permissions and duties (*roles*). For instance, agents could be assigned to or removed from roles dynamically without changing the policies contained in the role;

- the ability to define what actions an agent is permitted or forbidden to do on available resources and with other agents (*authorisations*). For instance, in the case of mobile agents authorisation policies could specify the resources to be made available to incoming agents on the basis of mobile agent attributes, such as the identity/role of the agent responsible user or the host from where the agent code was loaded;

- the ability to define the actions agents are obliged to perform either periodically or in response to triggered events or simply on the basis of dynamic factors such as the current state of the application (*obligations*). Obligation policies could define when and how agents should exploit mobility and how mobile agents should adapt their behaviour with respect to changing execution environment.

Other requirements can include the ability to define mutual policies between roles (*relationships*) and to define how agent roles interact with each other (*interaction protocols*). In large-scale agent systems the possibility of structuring roles and relationships could be also required to facilitate policy manageability.

A final but fundamental consideration for the implementation of policy-driven agent systems is to provide policy enforcement mechanisms transparent to the application level and suitable to multiple and possibly heterogeneous host and network environments.

3   The Ponder Language for Agent Systems

The specification of policies in agent-based applications can be complex due to the wide range of factors that need to be considered. For instance, agent authorisations can vary based on static and dynamic agent attributes, while agent obligations can depend on time or dynamic attributes and can be triggered on elaborate event specifications. The need for highly flexible and fine-grained policies calls for expressive policy languages that can accommodate the elaborate policy requirements of agent-based applications by cleanly separating policy from implementation.

We have chosen the Ponder language for policy specification in agent systems because it provides: *expressiveness* to handle the wide range of policy requirements for agent systems, *simplicity* to ease the policy definition tasks to systems administrators with different degrees of expertise, *enforceability* to ensure a mapping of policy specifications into implementable policies for various security aware platforms and *analysability* to allow reasoning about policies [7]. We limit our description of Ponder only to those concepts necessary for understanding the paper. For further details, refer to [7] [10].

The main objective of Ponder is to be able to separately specify the access control and management policies that apply to the objects of a distributed system. The policies can easily be modified in order to change system behaviour without modifying objects at all. This avoids embedding policy definitions in the application and relieves systems administrators from the effort of mastering multiple enforcement mechanisms.

Ponder is a declarative, object-oriented language that supports the specification of several types of basic policy, and the composition of basic policies into roles, relationships and management structures. A basic policy is considered a rule governing the choices in system behaviour and is specified by a declaration between a set of *subjects* and a set of *targets*. These sets are used to define the managed objects that the policy operates over. Policies can be typed and multiple instances of the policy created. Policy types can also be parameterised and the instances created with context-specific parameters, for example, the subject sets and target sets for a policy can be passed as actual parameters.

The fundamental policy types in Ponder are obligations and authorisations. **Obligations** specify what activities a subject (or a set of subjects) must perform on a set of target resources in response to events. The subject of an obligation policy is typically a specialised policy management agent but can be a normal managed object that implements the obligation policy enforcement interface.

The following example illustrates obligation policies in Ponder. The policies state that the system administrator agent is obliged to update web-browsing software in all administered nodes. This action takes place either when a new node enters the administrative domain (policies p1 and p2) or a new version of a browser is to be deployed (policy p3). In particular, this agent should update the browsing software depending on the operating system of the node.

```
type oblig newNodeP (OS, browser) {
  subject /agents/sysadmin;
  on newNode (Node);
  target /nodes ^ {Node};
  do install (browser);
  when Node.ostype = OS
}

inst oblig p1 = newNodeP (linux, netscape);
inst oblig p2 = newNodeP (windows, explorer);

inst oblig p3 {
  subject /agents/sysadmin;
  on newVersion (OS);
  target /nodes -> select (x | x.OS = OS);
  do update (OS.browser);
}
```

Note: the use of an OCL expression (Object Constraint Language) [11] to `select` the subset of nodes for updating a particular browser based on operating system.

Authorisations specify what actions a subject is either permitted to perform (positive authorisation policies) or forbidden from performing (negative authorisation policies) on a set of target objects.

For example, the following policy specifies that backup agents have read access to all files of managed machines nodes at backup hours, i.e. from 9 p.m. to 6 a.m. every day:

```
type auth+ backupP
  (subject bkagents, target files) {
    action   read;
    when     time.between (2100, 2359) or
             time.between (0000, 0600);
}
inst auth+ b = backupP (backup/agents,
            nodes/files);
```

Note the use of the constraint clause `when` to limit read access to the files of managed machines and in particular, of the `time` object that the standard Ponder runtime library provides to consider timing constraints.

Ponder does not currently support the specification of default rules for policies. For example, if an authorisation policy is not specified for an action, it is implementation dependent if the action is permitted or forbidden.

It is worth noticing that both obligation and authorisation policies can include constraints clauses. Constraints can be used to limit the applicability of policies on the basis of dynamic factors that can be system and/or application-dependent. In particular, in MA applications constraints can be used to take into account attributes specific to mobility features, such as the names and the number of visited nodes. For instance, if the agent itinerary contains untrusted nodes, the current hosting node could decide to deny access to resources – in this case the authorisation policy constrains MA access on the basis of the history of agent itinerary.

Positive authorisation policies can define *filters* to modify the ingoing and outgoing parameters of an authorisation action and hence to change the behaviour of the system externally to the implementation of the actual subject and target objects.

Ponder supports the definition of roles and relationships. Ponder *roles* are defined to group policies with a common subject and specify the rights and duties associated with positions within an organisation. Note that a single subject may be assigned more than one role. The following example shows an accounting role that defines the behaviour of accounting agents in charge of controlling the allocation of CPU time to processes. In particular, an accounting agent is required to monitor the CPU usage every 10 minutes and can kill processes that exceed a specific threshold of CPU usage (70% in this example).

```
type role accountingRole () {

    inst oblig {
        on timer.every (10*60);
        target t = /processes/running;
        do kill ();
        when t.usage > 70;
    }
    // other policies for role. }
```

Although Ponder permits the specification of role-based access control, it is based on a different model from the one in [6]. Ponder uses inheritance between role types rather than between role instances and permits multiple subjects to be assigned to a role to indicate that they have the same permissions, although a common convention in Ponder policies is to ensure that only one object in the subject set of a role performs obligation actions [12].

Ponder *relationships* are used for specifying policies between roles whilst Ponder *management structures* are used to group roles and relationships in order to form hierarchies of management structures. Although both these compositional abstractions are useful when performing policy management in large systems and provide added flexibility, we will restrict our architecture to the enforcement of authorisation policies, obligation policies and roles, since these provide the underlying support for handling higher-level abstractions.

4   The SOMA Policy Enforcement Architecture

In this section we outline the design of a general architecture for supporting transparent policy enforcement in agent systems. The aim is to provide an automatic mapping of Ponder policy specifications into platform-dependent implementable policies. We propose an architecture organised in terms of the following services (see Figure 1):

- a *Policy Specification Service* (PSS) that supports the editing, updating and removal of policies and which can compile high-level policy specifications into low-level platform-dependent policies;
- a *Policy Repository Service* (PRS) that stores all currently active policies and which can be queried to retrieve policies;
- a *Policy Coordinator Service* (PCS) that is responsible for distributing policies to runtime entities at policy instantiation and at any successive change;

- an *Authorisation Enforcement Service* (AES) that is responsible for applying run-time access controls;
- an *Obligation Enforcement Service* (OES) that is responsible for the correct enforcement of obligation policies.

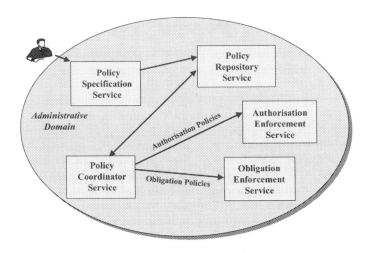

Figure 1: Policy Architecture Services

We integrate these 5 services into the SOMA programming framework, to make possible the development of mobile agent applications where agent behaviour is controlled by high-level policies. The SOMA infrastructure provides a wide range of support facilities for agent applications organised according to a layered architecture [8]. SOMA basic facilities support agent naming, communication, migration, and resource monitoring, while advanced SOMA facilities offer a collection of tools to achieve proper levels of agent security and interoperability.

SOMA exploits the Java technology to achieve platform independence and integration with the Web and the Internet. We have started the implementation of the Policy Enforcement Architecture on top of the SOMA facilities. It is worth stating that the integration of the Ponder framework within SOMA has required a mapping between Ponder policies and Java ones. We believe that all results shown in this paper could be easily ported to different Java-based agent systems.

4.1   The Policy Specification Service

The Policy Specification Service (PSS) provides administrators with the necessary support for specifying and compiling Ponder policies. Figure 2 depicts the PSS internal organisation, which currently consists of a Policy Editor and a Policy Compiler. The editor handles the editing, browsing, and structuring of policies. The compiler provides tools for parsing policy specifications, for semantic analysis, and for the automatic generation of policies to be interpreted in the Java 1.2 environment

[13]. We envisage that the PSS will also include tool support for policy analysis and reasoning.

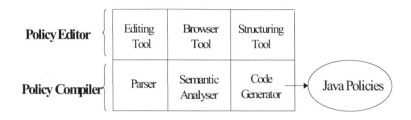

Figure 2: The internal layered structure of the PSS

In the following, we outline the implementation of the Code Generator that translates Ponder policy specifications into Java classes and corresponding Ponder policy instances into suitable Java enforceable policies. The Code Generator is in charge of transforming policy specifications into Java code that the AES and the OES can directly interpret and enforce without further modifications.

Ponder authorisation policy instances are mapped into Java policy grant entries (in the java.policy file) that have been extended to include constraints (necessary to perform an access control that can also depend on dynamic attributes) and filters (needed to perform transformation on action results). The following is an example of the authorisation policy specified in section 3 transformed into a Java grant policy entry (note that the authorisation policy refers to the policy subject BackupAgent):

```
grant Principal PolicySubject "BackupAgent" {
    permission PonderFilePermission "c:\-", "read"
    constraint backupHours "2100" "0600"
}
```

The generated Java grant entries are published along with their corresponding Ponder authorisation policy instances in the PRS.

The Code Generator parses obligation policy instances and creates appropriate Java stubs for each obligation policy field (*on*, *do*, *when*). In particular, the Java stub for the *on* field is distributed to the Obligation Enforcement Service that uses it to register the relevant event with the monitoring system in charge of its detection. The Java stubs related to the *do* and the *when* clauses are loaded into the agents that represent the policy subjects and exploited at event occurrence to support action execution and constraint checking accordingly to policy specification. Agents can also receive an additional Java stub that can help them to handle any exception occurring during policy action execution. The Ponder obligation policy instance with all the generated Java stubs is published in the PRS.

With regard to the Ponder role policy type, the Code Generator derives the authorisation and obligation policies relating to the role instance from all inherited role types. It performs the ad-hoc transformations for each derived policy and publishes the results along with the corresponding Ponder policy instances in the PRS. Similar considerations apply to the Ponder relationship policy type.

4.2   The Policy Repository Service

The Policy Repository Service (PRS) is in charge of storing information on enabled policies. We organise the PRS as a distributed directory service. The Directory Information Tree (DIT) related to policies is designed to store policy data in a hierarchy of policy entries that reflects the policy classification given in the Ponder framework. Ponder policies are divided into basic and composite policies. Basic policies include both authorisation and obligation policies, composite policies include roles, relationships and management structures. Every policy entry is associated with a unique identifier, i.e. a distinguished name, and a set of attributes characterising the policy. For instance, authorisation policy templates have a distinguished name, i.e. the template name, followed by the Java class representing it. Authorisation policy instances are stored below their corresponding policy templates with their name as well as the target name they refer to, and with the corresponding Java policy grant entries as pertinent attributes.

The DIT for enabled policies is currently implemented in an LDAP directory service provided by the SOMA infrastructure, and uses the SOMA naming system (also LDAP-compliant) to obtain the names and locations of agents and resources.

4.3   The Policy Coordinator Service

The Policy Coordinator Service (PCS) is in charge of monitoring changes in the PRS. Whenever a change of either a policy or membership of the directory information tree occurs, it causes the distribution of policies to the interested entities. For instance, when a new policy is enabled, the PCS distributes it to the targets of the policy in the case of authorisation policies, or to the subjects of the policy in the case of obligation policies. The targets/subjects of a policy are determined by querying the PRS.

We have chosen to implement the PCS in terms of coordinated agents that interact in a master/slave mode to improve distribution efficiency. Slave agents are in charge of monitoring changes in the PRS and of communicating modifications to the master agent along with all policy related information (e.g. target location, Java policy files for access controls). Based on the information yielded back from the slaves, the master agent can decide the distribution modality of policies.

In the case of authorisation policies, the master agent can delegate other mobile agents to distribute and install policies to the target environment. Mobile agents can be programmed to ensure correct policy installation even in presence of errors. For instance, when a policy target is temporarily unreachable and cannot receive the new or modified authorisation policies, a mobile agent can autonomously react to the situation, it can either wait until the failure is recovered or decide to report the error back to the master agent.

For the distribution and installation of obligation policies, the PCS coordinates with the obligation enforcement service that is responsible for the task as detailed in section 4.5.

4.4 The Authorisation Enforcement Service

The target nodes of authorisation policies perform access control decisions based on the authorisation policies received from the PCS. For this purpose we provide each target node with an Authorisation Enforcement Service composed of the following components:

- a *Permission Checking Component* (PCC) that receives access requests from agents and evaluates its active policy set to see whether the access can be granted. If the permission check fails, it denies access to the agent;

- a *Filtering Executor Component* (FEC) that is in charge of applying any filter specified in the policy if the permission check succeeds.

The PCC can grant permissions to agents on the basis of both static and dynamic attributes. Static attributes refer to the agent identity/roles. Dynamic attributes are expressed in the form of constraints that are checked at run-time when one agent requests resource access. The PCC is designed to enforce authorisation policies in the Java environment and executes an access control algorithm that extends the default Java access control steps [13], [14] to include run-time constraint checking. Essentially we check that all callers in the current execution context have the requested permission and that they satisfy the specified constraint. If any caller fails the check, an access control exception is thrown.

From the implementation point of view, we have augmented the Java access control architecture to enable the Java run-time environment to:

- interpret Java policy grant entries with constraints and filters (the PCC receives the authorisation policies in the form of Java grant policy entries from the PCS);

- perform run-time constraint checking and parameter filtering.

We have extended the Java default access control model along two directions. Firstly, a specialised Policy class has been implemented to suitably parse the Java policy grant entries generated by the Code Generator to map Ponder authorisation policy specifications into Java. The policy class supports the interpretation of constrained and filtered policy grant entries and the loading of agent permissions in proper Java protection domains with the target, action, constraints and filters set to the values specified in the corresponding policy grant entry. Secondly, a specialised hierarchy of Ponder permission classes has been defined to replace the default Java hierarchy where each Ponder permission class in the hierarchy is designed to maintain the internal representation of constraint and filter parameters in addition to the typical information on permission targets and actions. Each Ponder permission class is implemented to support not only run-time permission comparison, but also constraints checking.

We encapsulate the PCC and the FEC within a proxy. Agents do not have direct references to resources, but can instead access proxies that encapsulate resources and offer the same resource interface. When one agent attempts to access a resource, the proper resource proxy intercepts the requests and it coordinates with the PCC to determine whether to allow the access depending on the current access control policies. If the PCC permits agents to access the requested resources, the FEC is delegated to apply resource filtering according to the filtering policies. The filtering results are then passed to the proxy that is in charge of returning them back to the agent.

4.5   The Obligation Enforcement Service

The Obligation Enforcement Service (OES) is in charge of installing and enforcing obligation policies in order to carry out management tasks. The OES includes:

- an *Obligation Coordinator* (OC) that is responsible for registering events with the monitoring system and for delivering events to relevant agents as they occur;
- a *Monitoring Service* (MS) that is responsible for collecting events and for delivering them to the OC when they occur.

The OC maintains for every registered event, the list of all enabled obligation policies that use it, along with the corresponding policy subjects. At any event occurrence, the OC selects the correct obligation policies and delivers the event to all interested policy subjects.

The OC also receives updates from the PCS when a new obligation policy is enabled or a change occurs on an existing policy, e.g. a new subject is added to the subject set of the policy.

An obligation policy can refer to either one or multiple policy subjects. The latter case occurs, for instance, when the obligation policy defines the duties of a Ponder role: multiple policy subjects can be assigned to the same role and consequently share the same obligations. In this case, the OC can use different delivery strategies. It can deliver the event either to all the policy subjects or to only one (for instance the first available). We have chosen to apply the second delivery strategy in conformity with the Ponder role model [12]. At any event occurrence, the OC delivers the event to the first interested policy subject in the list. If the subject fails in performing the obligation actions, the OC can delegate the second policy subject in the list, and so forth until one subject can successfully fulfil the triggered duties.

From the implementation point of view, we have decided to rely on a distributed enforcement solution to ensure more scalable and effective obligation policy deployment in large administrative domains. At each physical node there is one MS component that locally monitors all the policy-relevant events, while we have decided to provide only one OC for each network locality (a LAN for instance). However, an alternative more distributed OC implementation is currently under investigation. Each OC knows and manages all the MS's in its network locality. The OC registers policy events with the appropriate MS's, receives the notification of all events that occur in its locality and delivers them to the interested policy subjects.

In our prototype, all policy subjects, MS's and OC's are implemented in terms of SOMA agents (see Figure 3).

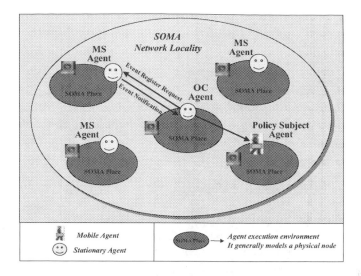

Figure 3: OES implementation in terms of Agents

The MS agent exploits the underlying SOMA monitoring facility [15] for the monitoring and dissemination of events that occur both inside and outside the Java Virtual Machine. For instance, the monitoring service can be configured to visualise the usage of the local processor, the quantity of used memory and the generated network traffic, for any Java thread and any other process outside the Java Virtual Machine.

The OC agent is designed to autonomously perform and coordinate management tasks whose goal is to ensure correct obligation enforcement. In particular, when an event occurs, the OC agent directly delivers the event to the interested agents that embody the policy subjects inside the OC agent network locality. Otherwise, it coordinates with other OC agents to achieve the correct delivery. OC agents in different network localities coordinate and interact with each other by exploiting all available communication models. In addition, the OC agent has the management goal to provide all policy agents with the stubs to enable them to react at event reception, to perform appropriate obligation actions and to handle exceptions in case of encountered problems. Notice that the underlying assumption is that agents, once notified of events, will perform obligation actions because of the existence of a trust relationship between agents and their responsible users. Agents are expected to behave accordingly to obligation policy specifications because their users define agent behaviour in response to triggered events. The OC support simply distributes new/updated policy specifications to interested agents and notifies events.

Finally, we are aware of the difficulties of respecting hard deadlines for obligation enforcement in large-scale distributed agent environments, but we are not currently focusing on the development of a real-time obligation enforcement service.

5   Case Study

This section discusses a case study in the field of systems management in order to demonstrate the successful integration of the Ponder policy framework in the SOMA agent infrastructure.

In recent years, the increased complexity of systems management has motivated the research of automated approaches. Management by Delegation (MbD), for instance, represents an effort toward decentralisation and increased flexibility of management functionality [16]. MbD dynamically distributes management components to extensible remote managers that can learn new modes to handle resources. While MbD is shaped after the Remote Evaluation programming paradigm [17], the mobile agent paradigm has broader capability in handling mobility and subsumes MbD [4]. The flexibility of mobile agent technology for network management has already been demonstrated in [18] where automated agents can move to administered nodes to carry out their management tasks in a more reliable or efficient manner.

We have worked in the development of an environment for the management of applications and systems, based on the SOMA agent technology [19]. The idea is to exploit such an environment to provide system administrators with policy-driven agents that can perform management tasks on their behalf. Some agents simply execute their tasks on a specified node, others by moving across nodes of the network. There are also agents that can perform periodic actions scheduled at fixed intervals and agents that perform event-triggered actions. Let us consider, for instance, some management tasks:

- the upgrade of a software program on all managed nodes when a new program release is available. In particular, such an upgrade should proceed only if the managed machines do not have already the new version and if they have enough memory and adequate CPU capacity; the installation steps could require a copy of the old version to be made, installation of the new version, a successful test of its operation and finally deletion of the old version;
- the control of CPU usage in order to avoid some specific processes exceeding their assigned execution time. In the case of excessive resource consumption, administrators may wish to suspend or kill the responsible process or move it to a less loaded node.

These are two simple examples that can be effectively delegated to SOMA mobile agents. In the first case one agent can be created to periodically initiate the visit of all managed nodes in order to perform the automatic software upgrading. In the second example, it is possible to send one agent to each of the controlled nodes, in order to locally control the CPU usage (by exploiting the SOMA monitoring component) and to promptly react in the case one process/agent exceeds its allowed CPU usage.

It is important to consider that these management tasks require us to clearly specify and identify which actions agents are permitted/forbidden/obliged to do, because of the sensitivity of management actions. An agent should be authorised to perform only its specific management task to ensure correct system behaviour, and should be granted the least privileges needed to perform it.

These considerations should motivate the importance of the integration of the Ponder policy framework in the SOMA infrastructure. The Ponder policy language allows administrators to define several different administrative roles, each devoted to a specific management task, and to specify composite management policies that are then carried out by SOMA agents. Administrators can also dynamically change management policies with the assurance that these policy changes are correctly propagated to SOMA agents. The agents can then accordingly adjust their behaviour to accommodate and to enforce in the system the evolving administrative requirements.

To be more precise, administrators can use the Policy Editor included in the PSS to specify management policies. The specified authorisation and obligation policies are then transformed by the Ponder Code Generator into Java policy grant entries and Java stubs respectively and published in the PRS. The different services of the SOMA Policy Enforcement Architecture coordinate to transparently force one agent to behave according to the specified policies.

When a SOMA agent is created, the SOMA naming system is updated to store the agent name and its current location, and the PCS queries the PRS to retrieve all agent relevant policies. The authorisation policies are distributed to the relevant policy target nodes, while the obligation policies are sent to the OC agents in charge of their enforcement. In particular, OC agents receive all the relevant Java stubs created by the Code Generator: they execute the Java stub related to the *on* obligation policy field to handle the specified policy events, and forward the Java stubs for the *do* and *when* clauses to the interested subject agents. At event occurrence, subject agents use the loaded stubs to execute the specified management actions.

Similar considerations apply in the case of policy updates. The PCS detects all policy changes and triggers their distribution to the interested entities to replace the old policies. The AES at each target node simply installs the updated policies in order to perform its access control decisions accordingly. The OC agents force subject agents to load new Java stubs. It is worth noting that any subject agent can be dynamically extended with the new management functionalities embedded within the received Java stubs without requiring agent designers to a priori embed in the agent code all management actions. The use of SOMA agents written in Java helps to update agent behaviour without agent execution suspension: the new stubs are dynamically loaded and executed when the agent is required to react to policy event occurrence.

6   Conclusions

In the agent community there is an increasing interest on role modelling as a mean to simplify the analysis and design of agent systems. Some proposals in the research field of multi-agent systems outline the usefulness of roles to model the social behaviour of agents in the context of complex organisational structures [1], [20]. An agent can be defined in terms of set of roles where a role is characterised by a collection of duties, permissions, and interaction protocols ruling how roles interact with each other.

Role modelling and in general policy modelling can be also very effective to facilitate the security management of agent systems. To this purpose, we propose the integration of the Ponder policy framework within the SOMA agent infrastructure and present an architecture that is composed of a set of services for developing, enforcing and updating policies for controlling agents.

The architecture advocates the separation of policy specification from agent implementation as well as the application-transparent enforcement of policies. Ponder authorisation policies are compiled into Java grant entries extended with constraints and filters and enforced by the Authorisation Enforcement Service, Ponder obligation policies are mapped into Java objects and stubs that are loaded into agents and invoked by the Obligation Enforcement Service. Further work is still required on mapping Ponder relationships and management structures as well as supporting policies about policies (meta policies). Techniques and tools are also needed that allow us to reason about policies, as well as to detect and resolve the conflicts at runtime that inevitably arise in any large agent system.

Acknowledgments

This research was supported by the Italian "Consiglio Nazionale delle Ricerche" in the framework of the Project "Global Applications in the Internet Area: Models and Programming Environments" and by the University of Bologna Funds for Selected Research Topics: "An Integrated Infrastructure to Support Secure Services". We also thank Emil Lupu and Morris Sloman for valuable discussions on policy-based distributed systems management.

References

1. N. R. Jennings: On Agent-Based Software Engineering. Artificial Intelligence, Elsevier, 117(2), 2000.
2. M. Wooldridge, et al.: A Methodology for Agent-Oriented Analysis and Design. Proc. 3rd Int. Conference on Autonomous Agents (Agents-99), Seattle, 1999.
3. R. Guttman, et al.: Agent-mediated Electronic Commerce: A Survey. Knowledge Engineering Review, 1998.
4. A. Fuggetta, et al.: Understanding Code Mobility. IEEE Transactions on Software Engineering, 24(5), 1998.
5. M. Sloman: Policy Driven Management For Distributed Systems. Plenum Press Journal of Network and Systems Management, 2 (4), 1994.
6. R. Sandhu, et al.: Role-Based Access Control Models. IEEE Computer, 29 (2), 1996.
7. N. Damianou, et al.: Ponder: A Language for Specifying Security and Management Policies for Distributed Systems. V 2.0", Imperial College Research Report DoC 2000/1, 2000.
8. P. Bellavista, et al.: Protection and Interoperability for Mobile Agents: A Secure and Open Programming Environment. IEICE Transactions on Communications 2000, IEICE/IEEE Special Issue on Autonomous Decentralized Systems, E83-B(5), 2000.
9. N. R. Jennings: Agent-based Computing: Promise and Perils. Proc. 16th Int. Joint Conf. on Artificial Intelligence (IJCAI-99), Stockholm, 1999.
10. E. Lupu: A Role-Based Framework for Distributed Systems Management. Ph.D. Dissertation, Imperial College, Dept. of Computing, London, 1998.
11. Rational Software Corporation. Object Constraint Language Specification. Version 1.1, http://rational.com/uml/, 1997.

12. E. Lupu, and M. Sloman: Reconciling Role Based Management and Role Based Access Control. 2nd ACM Role Based Access Control Workshop, Fairfax, 1997.
13. L. Gong: Inside Java 2 Platform Security. Addison Wesley, 1999.
14. C. Lai, et al.: User Authentication and Authorization in the Java Platform. 15th Annual Computer Security Applications Conference (ACSAC'99), IEEE Computer Society Phoenix, 1999.
15. P. Bellavista, et al.: Java-based On-line Monitoring of Heterogeneous Resources and Systems. Proc. of the 7th Workshop of the HP OpenView University Association (HP OVUA '00), Santorini, 2000.
16. G. Goldszmidt, and Y. Yemini: Distributed Management by Delegation. Proc.15th Int. Conference on Distributed Computing Systems, IEEE Computer Society, Vancouver, 1995.
17. J.W. Stamos, and D.K. Gifford: Remote Evaluation. ACM Transaction on Programming Languages and Systems, 12(4), 1990.
18. A. Bieszczad, et al.: Infrastructure for Advanced Network Management Based on Mobile Code. IEEE/IFIP Network Operations and Management Symposium (NOMS'98), IEEE Press, New Orleans, 1998.
19. P. Bellavista, et al.: An Open Secure Mobile Agent Framework for Systems Management. Journal of Network and Systems Management, Special Issue on Mobile Agent-based Network and Service Management, 7(3), 1999.
20. E. Kendall: Role Modeling for Agent System Analysis, Design and Implementation. IEEE Concurrency, 8(2), 2000.

On Policy-Based Extensible Hierarchical Network Management in QoS-Enabled IP Networks

Paris Flegkas, Panos Trimintzios, George Pavlou, Ilias Adrikopoulos, and Carlos F. Calvacanti

Centre for Communication Systems Research,
School of Electronic Engineering and Information Technology,
University of Surrey, Guildford, Surrey, GU2 7XH, U.K.
{P.Flegkas, P.Trimintzios, G.Pavlou, I.Andrikopoulos,
F.Calvacanti}@eim.surrey.ac.uk
http://www.ee.surrey.ac.uk/CCSR/Networks/

Abstract. Policy-based Management has been the subject of extensive research over the last decade. More recently, the IETF has been investigating Policy-based Networking as a means for managing IP-based multi-service networks with quality of service guarantees. Policies are seen as a way to guide the behaviour of a network or distributed system through high-level, declarative directives. We mainly view policies as a means of extending the logic of a management system at runtime, so that it can be adaptive to changing or newly emerging requirements. We are interested in particular in the coexistence of *hard-wired* hierarchical management systems with policy logic in a fashion that the overall system becomes programmable and extensible. In this paper we consider generic issues behind hierarchical policy-based management systems and we present initial work on such a system for dimensioning and dynamic resource management in IP Differentiated Services networks.

Keywords: Policy-based Networking, Hierarchical Management, IP Differentiated Services

1 Introduction

Policy-based Management has been the subject of extensive research over the last decade [1], [2]. More recently, the IETF has been investigating Policy-based Networking as a means for managing IP-based multi-service networks with quality of service guarantees [3]. Policies are seen as a way to guide the behaviour of a network or distributed system through high- level, declarative directives. Although the declarative high-level aspect of policies is very important, particularly for human managers, we mainly view policies as a means of extending the logic of a management system at runtime, so that it can be adaptive to changing or newly emerging requirements. We are interested in particular in the coexistence of hierarchical management systems realised through *hard-wired*

M. Sloman, J. Lobo, and E. Lupu (Eds.): POLICY 2001, LNCS 1995, pp. 230–246, 2001.

management logic with interpreted policy logic, targeting a programmable and extensible overall system. In this paper we consider generic issues behind hierarchical policy-based management systems and we present initial work on such a system for dimensioning and dynamic resource management of IP Differentiated Services networks.

The rest of the paper has the following structure. In section 2, we present an overview of the current state-of-the-art in policy-based research. This presentation is twofold, covering work in the research community, which includes policy classification, policy refinement and policy languages, and also work in the IETF, which includes recent work of the Resource Allocation and Policy Framework working groups. In section 3, we first discuss aspects of policy-based management and compare and contrast the approach to traditional, *hard-wired* management approaches. We then examine key aspects of hierarchical management systems and present a preliminary framework for the coexistence of such systems with management policies. In section 4, we present our preliminary work on hierarchical policy-based management for IP Differentiated Services, including an overview of the functional architecture for a relevant system and paying particular attention to policy aspects. We finally present a summary and point to our future research work in this area, in section 5.

2 Policy Management and Policy-Based Networking State-of-the-Art

2.1 Policy-Based Management in the Research Community

A lot of research has been carried out in the area of policies for the management of distributed systems, with most of the concepts pioneered by Imperial College London. [2] presents the concepts of domains and policies in the context of a generic management architecture, see Figure 1. Assuming a distributed management system that reflects the distribution of the system being managed, policies are specified as objects which define a relationship between *subjects* (managers) and *targets* (managed objects). Policies are separated from the automated managers, facilitating the dynamic change of the behaviour and the adaptivity to new requirements without re-implementing the management applications. Domains provide the framework for partitioning management responsibilities by grouping objects in order to specify a management policy that applies to a domain. Domains are defined as objects, which maintain a list of references to their member managed objects [4]. Figure 1 depicts a generic management architecture for distributed management systems consisting of: **a)** *communication services* for communication between applications as well as between applications and managed objects, **b)** *object services* for class and instance administration - the architecture assumes a distributed objects framework such as e.g. OMG CORBA, **c)** *distributed processing services* supporting interaction between distributed components, **d)** *common management services* which support the fundamental concepts of domains, policies and monitoring and **e)** the *management applications* which are capable of interpreting and applying policies.

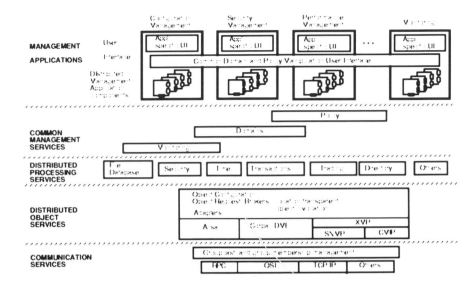

Fig. 1. Policy-based Distributed Management System Architecture [2].

The following types of policies are identified in [5], while [6] specifies also a list of criteria for the classification of policies:

- **Authorisation Policies** (positive and negative), which specify what a subject is authorised/forbidden to do with respect to a set of managed objects. These are essentially access control policies.
- **Obligation Policies**, which specify what operations the subject must perform on a set of target objects. Positive obligation policies are triggered by events.
- **Refrain Policies**, which define the actions that subjects must not perform on target objects.
- **Delegation Policies** (positive and negative), which specify which actions subjects are allowed to delegate to others.

[1] discusses the issue of the refinement of a high level policy into a number of more specific lower level policies to form a policy hierarchy. Several different relationships can be identified between policies in a hierarchy:

- **Partitioned Targets**: the target set of a lower level policy may be a subset of the target set of the higher-level policy.
- **Refinement**: the goal of a higher-level policy may be refined into one or more lower level goals, referring to the same target.
- **Arbitrary Refinement of Objectives**: in this form of refinement of objectives, the goal and target are quite different from the higher-level objectives.
- **Procedures**: where a policy may be refined by an unordered set of lower ones.

– **Delegation of Responsibility**: in this type of relationship, one subject delegates responsibility for the objective to another subject.

Related work in the area of policy hierarchies has been presented by [6], specifying a four level hierarchy: Corporate or High-level Policies, Task-oriented Policies, Functional Policies and Low-level Policies.

A declarative, object-oriented language has also been developed for specifying policies for the management of distributed systems, including constructs for specifying the basic types of policies described before [7].

2.2   IETF Policy-Based Networking

Two working groups in the IETF have considered policy management or *policy-based networking*: the Resource Allocation Protocol (RAP) Working Group (WG) and the Policy Framework WG.[1] The purpose of the RAP WG is to establish a scalable policy control model for RSVP and specify a protocol for use among RSVP-capable network nodes and policy servers. The Policy WG has provided several drafts describing a general framework for representing, managing, sharing and reusing policies in a vendor independent, interoperable and scalable manner as well as defining an extensible information model for representing policies and an extension to this model to address the need for QoS management.

The RAP WG has described a framework for policy-based admission control specifying the two main architectural elements [8]: the Policy Enforcement Point (PEP) and the Policy Decision Point (PDP). PEP represents the component that always runs on the policy-aware node and it is the point where the policy decisions are actually enforced. The PDP is the point where the policy decisions are made. When a PEP receives a notification or a message that requires a policy decision, it creates a request that includes information which describes the admission control request. Then, the PEP may consult a local configuration database to identify which policy elements can be evaluated locally, passes the request with this set to the Local Policy Decision Point (LPDP) and receives the result. The PEP then passes all the policy elements and the partial result to the PDP which combines its result with the partial result from the LPDP and returns the final policy decision to the PEP.

The Policy Framework WG defines policy as an aggregation of *Policy Rules*. Each policy rule comprises a set of conditions and a corresponding set of actions that are intended to be device- and vendor-independent. Policy Rules are of the form: if <condition> then <action>. The <condition> expression may be a compound expression and it may be related to entities such as hosts, applications, protocols, users, etc. The <action> expression may be a set of actions that specify services to grant or deny or other parameters to be input to the provision of one or more services.

The four major functional elements of the Policy Framework described by this group are:

---

[1] See: www.ietf.org/html.charters/{rap, policy}-charter.html

Fig. 2. a) RAP WG Policy Framework for Admission Control, b) Policy WG Framework.

- A **Policy Management Tool** to enable an entity to define, update and optionally monitor the deployment of Policy Rules.
- A **Policy Repository** to store and retrieve Policy Rules.
- A **Policy Consumer** which is a convenient grouping of functions, responsible for acquiring,deploying and optionally translating Policy Rules into a form useable for Policy Targets.
- A **Policy Target** which is an element whose behaviour is dictated by Policy Rules carrying out the action indicated by the Policy Rule.

A detailed description of the functionality of each element can be found in [3].

3   Considerations on Policy-Based Network Management

3.1   Policies as Means for Programmable, Extensible Management Systems

One of the key motivations behind policy-based management is flexibility and graceful evolution of the management system so that it can adapt to changing requirements over a long period of time. This is achieved by disabling/modifying old policies and by introducing new ones in order to meet changing requirements. A key aspect of a policy-based management system is that changes to *targets* should be performed in a consistent fashion, avoiding policy conflicts that may leave the managed system in an inconsistent state. Conflicting actions do not occur only in policy-based management systems but are potentially possible in any control system which performs intrusive management actions by *modifying* targets rather than simply *observing* them. Below we consider aspects of policies, intrusive management and conflicts in different management frameworks.

Enterprise networks are typically managed with SNMP, using a relatively simple management architecture consisting of a single, centralised *network management centre (NMC)* . The latter supervises network elements located typically in a cluster of local/metropolitan area networks. In this architecture, the elements are typically configured one-by-one, in an isolated fashion, through the supervision of a human network manager and according to an overall network operation policy, which is worked out beforehand. This means that (re-) configuration is infrequent and takes place manually. In an evolution of this scheme, configuration parameters for every device are stored in a repository e.g. a directory, which is contacted by the devices upon cold or warm starts so that a device picks up necessary parameters and configures itself; this makes the system more scalable.

The NMC supervises, i.e. monitors, the managed devices, provides a view of the current network state, alerts the human manager in case of abnormal changes but does not attempt to reconfigure the network using automated logic. Reconfiguration is typically left to human managers who may modify first the network operation policy using their intelligence in order to overcome the problem. There are no conflicts in this architecture, they might only occur because of a wrong human-derived configuration policy but, with the right precautions, this should not happen. While this simple, centralised architecture with emphasis in monitoring rather than control, works adequately for best- effort IP networks, it cannot meet the needs of emerging multiservice networks with QoS guarantees. The latter require frequent, automated configuration changes according to a network-wide view, as presented in section 4.

Telecommunication networks are managed according to the hierarchically distributed Telecommunications Management Network (TMN) model. Initial and subsequent (re-)configuration of network elements occurs through element managers, which are orchestrated by a logically centralised but physically distributed, network manager. The latter has a view of the network-wide policy and implements it through automated logic by supervising the network elements and reconfiguring them in order to introduce new services or to recover from performance, fault and other problems. This management logic can be altered to a limited extent by modifying managed objects that model its operation. An example of TMN-influenced proactive and reactive management systems for ATM management can be found in [9].

All configuration changes occur through a configuration manager, which holds the physical and logical network topology and partitioning. Requests coming from service, performance, fault and other managers are carefully validated, in order to maintain network consistence and integrity. Despite this validation, it is possible that different managers have conflicting configuration requirements. This can lead to inconsistent network state which satisfies only one of them, or to race conditions, in which the managers keep requesting changes to their preferred configuration state when they sense it has been changed back. Such conflicts can be avoided by careful modelling, design and testing of the management system, but conflicts may still occur at run-time when the system is stressed by real-world conditions not previously anticipated. This is rare though and also points to system integrity issues which are outside the scope of the paper.

Policy-based may be applied to both enterprise and telecommunication networks. The view taken by IETF seems to be compatible with the centralised model used in managing enterprise networks, though policy work in the research community has previously pointed to distributed models. In this discussion we will consider the centralised model to demonstrate the points and we will examine policies in distributed hierarchical systems in the next section.

The key aspect of a policy-based system is that management logic is expressed through declarative policies, evaluated in policy consumers. In the IETF model, the policy consumer can be thought as a centralised manager, with the execution of provisioning policies resulting in configuration operations on managed objects within network elements. In [10], the policy consumer is seen as a hybrid manager-agent where the policies express the manager intelligence and access the co-located managed objects of the agent part; we consider and extend this model in the next section. The essence though is that management intelligence can be modified, added and removed by manipulating policies as requirements change. In policy-based systems, management intelligence does not follow the rigid analysis, design, implementation, testing and deployment cycle, and as such, conflicts may be the norm rather than the exception. Conflict analysis and detection is required both statically, at policy introduction and deployment time, and also dynamically, at run time. Policies are often associated with interpreted logic but we believe their salient characteristic to be the composition of a system from building blocks which can be introduced, modified and withdrawn at any time, without having rigorously tested the resulting system in every such modification.

Taking the policy approach to the extreme, all management intelligence could be policy-based, starting with a system which comprises only manageable network elements and policy consumer capabilities in the role of an *empty* centralised manager. This is the complete opposite of the rigid, hierarchical TMN approach, but results in a pretty undefined and fluid system, which will be very difficult to protect against conflicts, or to even realise it with declarative policies in the first place. We see policies mostly as a means to *late bind* functionality to an existing management system, which is hierarchically distributed in order to meet the management needs of multiservice networks. In this case, policies can be seen as a means to achieve *programmability* of the system with new functionality and lead to a flexible system that can cope with evolving requirements. We feel this is a much more realistic proposition than a purely policy-based approach for complex management systems. Until now it is not clear how policies can be used in the context of a hierarchical system. In the next section we consider policies that follow and mirror the hierarchical system decomposition.

3.2 Hierarchical Policies

In hierarchical management systems, hybrid agent-manager applications exist at different levels of the hierarchy, managing ultimately network elements at the lowest level. Manager-agent or managing- managed interactions occur top-down and possibly peer-to-peer but never bottom-up. A hierarchy may be *strict*, in which case the management layer $N + 1$ builds on the functionality and services of layer N, or *relaxed*, in which case layers may be bypassed. In the following discussion we will assume a strict hierarchy for simplicity.

At layer N of the hierarchy, an agent-manager application comprises:

- Managed objects presenting the management capabilities of the application to the layer $N + 1$ (or to the same layer N for peer-to-peer interactions).

– Management logic accessing managed objects of the layer $N - 1$ (or of the same layer N for peer-to-peer interactions).

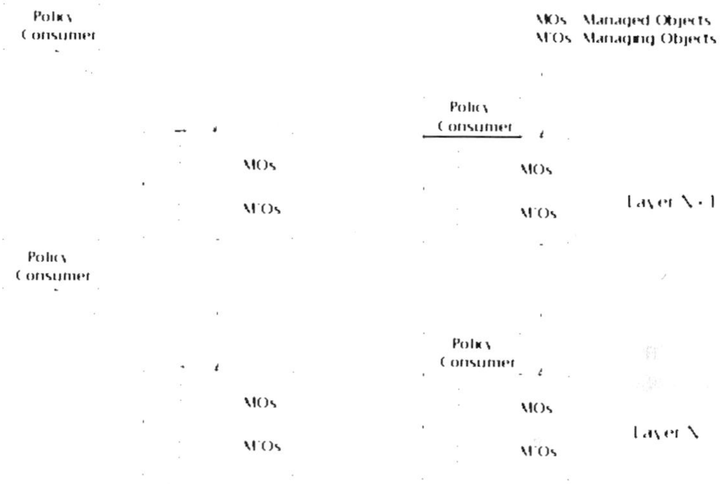

Fig. 3. Hierarchical management with loosely (left) and tightly-coupled (right) policy consumers.

The managed objects constitute the top, i.e. agent, part of the application (see Figure 3), which is why we prefer the term agent-manager as opposed to manager-agent used in the literature. The managed objects and associated managing logic or managing objects represent *static* management intelligence, following a rigorous analysis, design, implementation, testing and deployment cycle. Parametrisation of the functionality of such an agent-manager application is possible to a limited extent by configuring managed object values. The deployment of such a hierarchy takes place bottom- up but the decomposition and design of the whole system takes place top-down, according to the management services to be provided.

The simplest form of introducing policies in such a system is through a separate policy consumer point where policies execute and access managed object at various different layers of the management hierarchy. In other words, the policies manipulate targets, i.e. managed objects, at all the layers of the hierarchy. The problem with this approach is that the policies are monolithic, logically and physically centralised, operating on a hierarchical distributed system. A better approach would be to structure the policies hierarchically, mirroring the system hierarchy, as explored next.

In a hierarchical policy system, policies at layer $N + 1$ operate on managed objects of layer N. This implies in fact that these policies may be considered as part of the managing intelligence of layer $N + 1$, in addition to the static intelligence of agent-manager applications. This approach is shown in the left of Figure 3. If these policies access managed objects in more than one layer N agent-managers, they could execute at a layer $N+1$ consumer point which complements the managing intelligence in this layer. If though they access managed objects in a single subordinate agent-manager, they could execute _at_ that agent-manager, having local access to managed objects. In this case, the manager-agent at layer N is programmed with policy logic that belongs conceptually to the layer $N+1$ but since it relates to a particular agent-manager of the layer below, it has actually _migrated_ there. This is shown in the right part of Figure 3 where the two policy consumers have migrated and now form an integral part of the agent-manager they relate to. In this paradigm, every agent-manager may potentially become a policy consumer, including of course ultimately the agents within network elements.

We view policies as complementing the static management system intelligence. One key aspect when designing a policy-capable hierarchical system is how much intelligence should be realised in a static fashion. Static intelligence should offer enough functionality to allow relatively easy extension of the system through policy logic but not too much so that there is still flexibility in terms of changing requirements. In principle, higher amount of static intelligence leads to a more rigid, less extensible but potentially more stable system while less amount of static intelligence leaves the system fluid, easily extensible but may result in instability as more and more functionality is realised through policies (more frequent conflicts etc.)

A key aspect in such a hierarchical system is policy refinement and this should naturally follow the hierarchical composition of the system. Policies may be introduced at any level but higher-level policies may possibly result in the introduction of related policies at lower levels. In a similar fashion to the bottom-up deployment of a static hierarchical system, policy hierarchies should be introduced in a bottom-up fashion, maintaining the completeness and integrity of the policy space. Policy refinement and transformation is a process analogous to software system analysis and design but in the context of a hierarchical system of a specific nature, e.g. IP Differentiated Services (DiffServ) network management, guidelines may be devised and followed.

We are thinking in particular of policy classification specific to a problem domain, going further than the general-purpose classification encountered in the literature. For specific classes of policies, we are thinking of policy refinement guidelines and rules that will assist and possibly automate refinement of policy instances. We are in fact envisaging situations in which changing parameters of a high level policy will result in changes throughout the policy hierarchy.

In the next section we present first the functional architecture of a distributed hierarchical system for IP DiffServ; this is designed from the beginning with policy extensibility in mind. In this system we are thinking of network dimensioning, resource management and admission control policies. We then explore further the hierarchical nature of dimensioning and resource management aspects, presenting an elementary example of hierarchical policy decomposition.

4   Hierarchical Policy-Enabled IP Network Management

4.1   The TEQUILA Functional Architecture

The objective of the TEQUILA project (Traffic Engineering for QUality of Service in the Internet, at LArge Scale) is to study, specify, implement and validate a set of service definition and traffic engineering tools in order to obtain quantitative end-to-end Quality of Service guarantees through careful dimensioning, admission control and dynamic resource management in Differentiated Services [11] IP networks. The technical areas addressed by the project are: (a) the specification of static and dynamic, intra- and inter-domain Service Level Specifications (SLSs), (b) protocols and mechanisms for managing (negotiating, monitoring and enforcing) SLSs, and (c) intra- and inter- domain traffic engineering schemes to ensure that the network can cope with the contracted SLSs both within domains, and in the Internet at large. The rest of this paper assumes a basic understanding of the DiffServ architectural framework and terminology.

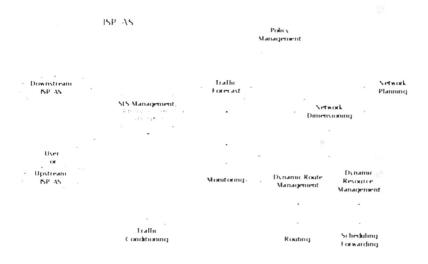

Fig. 4. The TEQUILA functional architecture.

In order to achieve its technical goals the project has defined a functional architecture shown in Figure 4 [12]. There are two main parts in this architecture, the SLS-related part and the Resource Management part. The first includes the SLS Management Functional Block (FB), which can be further decomposed to the Subscription, Admission Control and Interdomain SLS Request blocks. It also includes the SLS-related part of Monitoring and the Traffic Conditioning block. This part of the overall functional model is responsible for subscribing and negotiating long-term SLSs with users or other peer Autonomous Systems (ASs) and it performs admission control of dynamic SLSs. The Traffic Conditioning

FB classifies and marks packets according to negotiated SLS, as well as performs metering policing and shaping.

The other major part of the architecture concerns resource management. The Planning FB is responsible for long-term (order of months or years) planning of physical resources. Network Dimensioning works in order of days or weeks. This functional block is responsible for mapping the traffic onto the physical network resources and it configures the network in order to accommodate the forecasted traffic demands. The Network Dimensioning FB defines Multi-Protocol Label Switching (MPLS) paths at layer 2 and uses pure layer 3 capabilities in order to accommodate the expected traffic. The Traffic Forecast FB gets information from the current SLS subscriptions, traffic projections and historical data provided by the Monitoring FB, and uses traffic and economic models in order to provide the appropriate forecasted traffic matrices to the Dimensioning and Planning FBs. Based on constraints/rules provided by Network Dimensioning, the Dynamic Route Management FB modifies (in a timescale of minutes or hours) routing parameters in routers. If MPLS is used it dynamically adds/merges/splits/reroutes paths while there is an equivalent behaviour in the case of pure layer 3 routing. This functional block adjusts routing parameters (weights, load distribution on equal multi-paths) or modifies MPLS paths. The Dynamic Resource Management FB sets buffer and scheduling parameters on links according to network dimensioning directives and constraints. It also allocates capacity to existing/newly created paths. The Routing FB is Constraint-based, DiffServ class-aware and uses constraints to reduce algorithm complexity and hence reduce the convergence time. The Scheduling and Forwarding FB implements Per-Hop-Behaviours (PHBs), e.g. Expedited/Assured/Default Forwarding (EF/AF/DE), using buffer management and scheduling mechanisms. The Monitoring FB performs monitoring and measurements in various levels of abstraction. This FB has both network-wide and detailed per node view of the network, and operates as an agent to other FBs of the architecture, providing the necessary monitoring information they request.

The Policy Management FB is an essential part of the TEQUILA system and is described in more detail in the following section.

4.2 Hierarchical Policy Management in the TEQUILA System

The policy functional block in the functional architecture includes (see Figure 5) the Policy Management Tool, the Policy Storing Service and the Policy Consumers which correspond to their associated functional blocks (note "A TEQUILA Functional Block" in Figure 5), e.g. SLS related admission policies for the SLS Management block, dimensioning policies for the Dimensioning block, dynamic resource/route management policies for the Dynamic Resource Management block, etc.

In this model there exist many Policy Consumers, associated with particular functional blocks of the hierarchical management structure. Targets can be the managed objects of the associated functional block or of lower-level functional blocks (but never of higher-level blocks). Policy Consumers need also to have direct communication with the Monitoring functional block in order to get information about traffic-based policy-triggering events. Note that triggering events may be also other than traffic- related, in which case it is typically generated by the specific functional block with which the Policy Consumer is associated.

Policies are defined in the Policy Management Tool, which provides a *policy creation environment*. Policies are defined in a high-level language, are translated to object-oriented policy representation (information objects) and stored in the policy repository (Policy Storing Service). New policies are checked for conflicts with existing policies, although some conflicts may only be detected during execution time. After the policies are stored, activation information may be passed to the associated Policy Consumer.

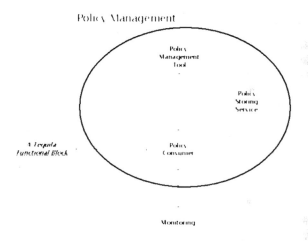

Fig. 5. Decomposition of the Policy Management Functional Block.

Every time the operator enters a high level policy, this should be refined into policies for each layer of the TEQUILA functional architecture forming a policy hierarchy that reflects the management hierarchy. As mentioned in the literature [1], it is very difficult to support an automated decomposition of a policy without human intervention. The administrator should define generic classes of policies and provide some refinement logic/rules for the policy classes that will help the automated decomposition of instances of these classes into policies for each level of the hierarchical management system shown in Figure 4. These generated policies can be interpreted and enforced by the Policy Consumer associated with the responsible functional block (agent-manager). The Policy Consumers will retrieve the policies from the Policy Storing Service in a format so that all the necessary information can be mapped to the specific set of functions of the FB (agent-manager). This is done by setting the appropriate parameters to influence or modify the agent-manager's behaviour and by registering the appropriate events in order to be notified about when this Policy must be enforced. This refinement logic can be stored in the Policy Management Tool and all the policies of the hierarchy will be generated at the tool, stored in the repository and then retrieved by the responsible policy consumers. Another possibility could be to distribute the refinement rules in the appropriate consumers so that each one will be responsible for generating and sending the next lower-level policies to the consumers that reside in the next lower layer of the management system.

4.3   An Example of Hierarchical Policy Decomposition

Let's assume that the administrator of an AS wants to ensure availability of a specific traffic class for a time period, for example s/he wants to enforce the following policy:

$$\text{"}\underline{\text{At least}}\ \underline{10\%}\ \text{of Network Resources should }\underline{\text{always}}\text{ be available for }\underline{\text{EF}}\text{ traffic"} \tag{1}$$

In order for this policy to be enforced, it must be refined into policies that apply to each layer of the management architecture. Before specifying this policy the operator must go through the following three steps so that automated refinement can be supported:

1. Define the template of the generic policy class.
2. Define the range of parameters/attributes of the policy class.
3. Provide the guidelines and rules for the refinement.

Policy (1) is an instance of a generic policy class. This resource management policy class has four parameters and has the following generic form:

$$\texttt{<bound> <percentage>}\text{ of Network Resources }\texttt{<period>}\text{ available for }\texttt{<traffic type>} \tag{2}$$

As described above, the human operator should first define the template of the generic class (2) and then the range of the parameters/attributes that can be specified for a valid instance of this policy class (see Table 1). In order to create an instance of this class, such as (1), the operator has to edit the above template and set the required parameters to specific values (e.g. `<bound>` = "≥", `<percentage>` = "10%", `<period>` = "from 9am to 2pm", `<traffic type>` = "EF"). If the parameters specified are in the previously defined range of values then the procedure for enforcing this policy will normally proceed, otherwise the validation function of the Policy Management Tool will return an error. Table 1 shows the valid range of values of the parameters in the above resource management policy class:

    The final step is to provide some refinement rules and logic that will assist the automated decomposition of *every* instance of the resource management policy class (2) to policies for each level of the hierarchical management system as shown in Figure 6.

    The functional blocks that are responsible for enforcing any instance of policy class (2), are Dimensioning and Dynamic Resource Management. Assuming a

Table 1. Range of values for parameters of the resource management policy class.

Parameter	Attribute
<bound>	$\leq, \geq$
<percentage>	$0 - 100$
<period>	*any time period expression*
<traffic type>	EF, AFxy, BE, CS1-8

strict management hierarchy in the TEQUILA functional architecture, any function of the Dimensioning functional block will operate on managed objects of the Dynamic Resource Management functional block. Consequently, high-level resource management policies will be decomposed into dimensioning and dynamic resource management policies. In this architecture, the policy consumers will be eventually tightly coupled with their respective functional blocks (or agent-managers), in a similar fashion to the model depicted in the right part of Figure 3.

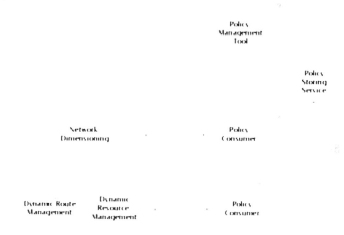

Fig. 6. Enforcement of the Resource management policy at each level of the TEQUILA Functional Architecture.

More specifically, in the Dimensioning functional block, every instance of the resource management policy class (2) is enforced as follows: when the generated policy for this layer of the management architecture is downloaded to the Policy Consumer, at the time <period> when this policy is active, it must first check the current configuration, i.e. how the network is already dimensioned. This is done by passing the appropriate parameters taken from the policy instance regarding the <bound>, <percentage> and <traffic type> to a check_current_configuration() method that will trigger a re-dimensioning of the network if it is needed. Then, when re-dimensioning is required, i.e. when network/traffic conditions are such that Dynamic Route and Resource Management algorithms are no longer able to operate effectively, at the time `<period>` the policy instance is enforced by passing the parameters to the `check_forecast()` method that will check the traffic matrices retrieved from the traffic forecast functional block, and are input to the dimensioning algorithm. If the `<percentage>` allocated to the traffic type specified in the policy instance does not violate the policy, then there is no need to influence the dimensioning algorithm. Otherwise, if the traffic matrices are not compatible with the policy then the dimensioning algorithm function must be executed with a different/modified traffic matrix. For the specific policy instance (1), the `check_current_configuration()` method will trigger a re-dimensioning only if the current configuration is such that less than 10% of resources are allocated to the EF traffic class. Moreover, at re-dimensioning, the `check_forecast()` method will modify the traffic matrices so that at least 10% of resources are allocated to EF.

After the network is configured according to the dimensioning output, Dynamic Resource Management is responsible for adjusting the resources according to the dynamic changes in traffic demand. The dynamic adjustment of resources might result into situations where the policy is no longer enforced; therefore we need to make this functional block policy aware.

The generated policy for this layer of the functional management architecture is enforced in the Dynamic Resource Management block as follows: at the time `<period>` that the policy is active, the Policy Consumer should pass the needed parameters (`<bound>`, `<traffic type>`) to the `check_set_operation()` method and this will indicate whether the operation performed by the Dynamic Resource Management block is allowed or not. Actually, this will check through the `set_resources()` method if the addition or removal of resources allocated to the `<traffic type>` violates the specified policy. For example, assuming the policy instance (1) of the resource management class (2), additional resources allocated to the EF traffic will always be allowed and deletion of resources will only be performed if the overall allocation of resources for EF is greater than 10%.

In the previous example we have assumed that the Dynamic Resource Management Block is logically and physically centralised. If the functionality of the block is physically distributed to reflect the distribution of the network being managed, agent-managers will contain replicas of functions. This makes the enforcement of the above policy instance more complex since an overall knowledge of the modifications of the allocated resources to the traffic type is needed. This can be done either by adding some cooperation ability to the distributed agent managers or by enforcing the policy in a non-optimal way, restricting each agent-manager to cause a less than 10% allocation of resources to EF traffic in the local managed area of the network.

From the above example one may observe that if the functional architecture was not designed to be policy aware, some methods of the functional blocks such as `check_current_configuration()` and `check_forecast()` in Dimensioning and `check_set_operation()` in Dynamic Resource Management would be redundant. Though obvious, it should be mentioned that these methods are part of the computational interface of the respective block or may be derived from other methods, which are part of that interface. It is for further investigation whether this logic could be automatically generated and downloaded to the appropriate blocks or it should be hardwired beforehand in the agent-managers. The whole area of hierarchical *policy-aware* system specification/design and the subsequent population of that system through hierarchical policies with (some) automated support in policy-refinement constitute the core of our future research in this area.

5 Summary and Future Work

While most research work on policies has concentrated in necessary fundamental aspects such as classification, policy language, conflict detection and most recently in policy representation and storage, little work has been done in the area of the harmonic coexistence of policies and traditional, possibly hierarchical, management systems. Policies, apart from their high-level declarative nature, can be also seen as a vehicle for *late binding* functionality to management systems, allowing for their graceful evolution as requirements change. It is this aspect of policies we find most interesting and we have been exploring the potentiality of designing *policy-aware* management systems, in which a line has to be carefully drawn between *hard-wired* functionality and policy logic.

In this paper we first described the salient characteristics of policy-based management and we explored their coexistence with hierarchical management systems, presenting first an initial version of a generic framework and showing then how a system for IP Differentiated Services management can be designed and built using such a framework. There are many issues that are still unresolved but the fundamental target is to be able to come up with a system that will be able to sustain requirement changes and evolve gracefully through policies without any changes to its carefully thought-out, *hard-wired* initial logic. We are interested in deriving generic guidelines on how this can be done and also guidelines on hierarchical policy decomposition and refinement. We are not sure if such guidelines can be problem domain independent but we hope at least to produce such guidelines in the context of IP Differentiated Services management.

As a continuation of the work presented in this paper, we will be concentrating in the definition of an object-oriented information model representing the capabilities of each layer of the hierarchical functional architecture that was described in Section 4.1. This information model will assist us in the definition of QoS policies. Realisation of this model will be done by parametrising the management functions of the hierarchical management system, following, initially in a bottom-up approach to capture each layer's functionality and then in a top-down analysis to record the policy-management requirements. Moreover, we will be focusing on the specification of dimensioning, resource and route management policies, by defining generic policy classes for specific resource management cases. We will further explore the concept of the automated decomposition and transformation of instances of these policy classes by providing specific guidelines. Finally a realisation of the above concepts will be demonstrated by using a prototype implementation. We will report our findings in the future.

Acknowledgments

Part of this work was undertaken in the context of the IST TEQUILA project, which is partially funded by the Commission of the European Union. The authors would also like to thank David Griffin of University College London for his participation in the initial discussions towards the formulation of some of the ideas mentioned in this paper.

References

[1] J. Moffett and M. Sloman, "Policy Hierarchies for Distributed Systems Management," *IEEE Journal on Selected Areas in Communications*, vol. 11, pp. 1404–1414, December 1993.

[2] M. Sloman, "Policy Driven Management for Distributed Systems," *Journal of Network and Systems Management*, vol. 2, pp. 333–360, December 1994. Plenum Publishing.

[3] M. Stevens et al., *Policy Framework*. Internet draft, <draft-ietf-policy-framework-00.txt>, work in progress, September 1999.

[4] M. Sloman and J. Moffett, "Domain Management for Distributed Systems," in *Integrated Network Management I* (B. Meandzija and J. Westcott, eds.), pp. 505–516, North Holland, 1989.

[5] Imperial College London, "Policies for network and distributed systems." see: http://www-dse.doc.ic.ac.uk/policies/.

[6] R. Wies, "Policy Definition and Classification: Aspects, Crieteria, Examples," in *Proc. of the 5th IEEE Workshop on Distributed Systems Operations and Management*, (DSOM), (Toulouse, France), October 1994.

[7] N. Damianou and N. Dulay and E. Lupu and M. Sloman, "Ponder: A Language for Specifying Security and Management Policies," tech. rep., Imperial College Report DoC-2001, January 2000.

[8] R. Yavatkar, D. Pendarakis, and R. Guérin, *A Framework for Policy-Based Admission Control*. RFC-2753, Informational, January 2000.

[9] P. Georgatsos et al., "Technology Inter-Operation in ATM Networks: the REFORM System," *IEEE Communications Magazine*, vol. 37, pp. 112–118, May 1999.

[10] M. Sloman and E. Lupu, "Policy Specification for Programmable Networks," in *Proc. of the 1st Int'l Conference on Active Networks* (S. Covaci, ed.), LNCS, (Berlin, Germany), Spinger-Verlag, June 1999.

[11] S. Blake et al., *An Architecture for Differentated Services*. RFC-2475, Informational, December 1998.

[12] D. Goderis et al., *Functional Architecture and Top Level Design*. TEQUILA Consortium - Deliverable D1.1, September 2000.   available at: www.ist-tequila.org/deliverables.html.

Towards Extensible Policy Enforcement Points[*]

Raouf Boutaba[1], Andreas Polyrakis[2]

[1] Dept. of Computer Science, University of Waterloo,
200 University Avenue West, Ontario, N2L 3G1, Canada
rboutaba@bbcr.uwaterloo.ca

[2] Dept. of Computer Science, University of Toronto
10 King's College Road, Toronto, Ontario, M5S 3G4, Canada
apolyr@cs.toronto.edu

Abstract. For several years, Configuration Management has been conducted mainly through command line or SNMP. However, while computer networks started growing bigger in size and complexity, it became apparent that these approaches suffer from significant scalability and efficiency limitations. Policy-Based Networking (PBN) seems to be a promising alternative for Configuration Management, and has already received significant attention. This approach involves the processing of the network policies by special servers (PDPs) that send the appropriate configuration data to the Policy Enforcement Points (PEPs) that reside on the managed entities. COPS and its extension for policy provisioning, COPS-PR, are currently being developed by IETF to implement PBN. In COPS-PR, the PDP installs to the PEP policies that the latter should enforce. However, the types of policies that the PEP can understand are limited and hardwired to it by the manufacturer. In this paper, we propose an architecture that attempts to raise such limitations and push the decision taking from the policy servers to the managed devices.

1. Introduction

Configuring network devices, such as routers and switches, has always been a hard task. In most cases, the administrator was required to configure each of the devices independently, even when these were configured to operate similarly. Initially, the configuration was done through the Command Line Interfaces of the devices; later, other technologies attempted to automate this process. The most widely used one was SNMP, which, although designed for monitoring purposes, gave a satisfactory solution to the problem. However, as the networks start growing considerably both in size (number of managed nodes) and in complexity (different types of devices, number of configuration parameters), significant scalability and efficiency problems appeared in the existing configuration methods. IETF attempts now to address such issues through the next version of SNMP (SNMP v.3). However, there are serious doubts whether SNMP will eventually manage to overcome its limitations and

---

[*] This research work is supported by research grants from Nortel Networks and the Natural Sciences and Engineering Research Council of Canada.

M. Sloman, J. Lobo, and E. Lupu (Eds.): POLICY 2001, LNCS 1995, pp. 247-261, 2001.

become the dominant protocol for Configuration Management again. On the other hand, an alternative to SNMP that has already received considerable attention is Policy-Based Networking (PBN) [1], [2], [3].

The basic concepts in PBN are the control/management policies [4], i.e. the rules that govern the network behavior. The administrator edits the policies in a management tool that performs syntax, semantics and basic conflict checking. These policies are then distributed, either directly or through the use of a directory, to special policy servers, called Policy Decision Points (PDPs) [5], [6]. The PDPs process these policies, along with other data such as network state information, and take policy decisions regarding what policies should be enforced and how this will happen. These policies are sent as configuration data to the appropriate Policy Enforcement Points (PEPs), which reside on the managed devices and are responsible for installing and enforcing them. Typically, PDPs run on dedicated servers and PEPs on the managed entities. Usually each device is controlled by one PEP, and a single PDP may control several PEPs. However, different configuration schemata may exist [7]. PBN is demonstrated in Figure 1 [3].

PBN is based on a client-server model of interaction between PEPs and PDPs. It distinguishes two modes of operation: the outsourcing and the provisioning [6]. In the outsourcing model, when the PEP receives a network event that it does not know how to treat, it issues a request to the (appropriate) PDP, notifying it for the event occurrence. The PDP replies to the PEP by sending configuration data that must be installed in order to respond to the event. On the other hand, in the provisioning model, as soon as the PEP connects to the PDP, the latter sends to the former the policies that must be enforced. Of course, these policies are in a format that the PEP can understand. The policies are stored in the PEP, and all incoming events are served according to them. In both cases, the PDP is aware of the policies enforced by the PEP, and if it may decide to update them by installing, deleting or replacing them, whenever it decides that they no longer reflect the desired behavior.

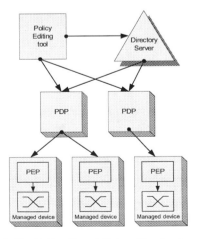

Figure 1. The Policy-Based Networking basic schema

2. COPS and COPS-PR

IETF has proposed the Common Open Policy Service (COPS) [8] as a protocol to implement the described architecture. COPS has recently received considerable attention, and applications based on it have already emerged [8], [9], [10].

The COPS protocol relies on a TCP connection for the exchange of data between PEPs and PDPs. Each PEP may support a number of client-types for the different policy areas (security, QoS, admission control, accounting, etc); those client-types are the actual enforcers of the policies. The clients connect to the appropriate PDP (they are redirected there by the default PDP) and register information about themselves and the device that they serve. Note that a PEP may have clients that each connects to a different PDP. In the outsourcing mode, the clients report to the PDP the events that they do not know how to handle, and the PDP sends them configuration data that define how to handle those events. The PDP may decide to update this data at any time, in a provisioning style. In the provisioning model, the clients register their capabilities to the PDP, and the PDP sends the appropriate policies (in a pre-agreed format) that the PEPs should enforce. COPS also describes synchronization procedures between the PDP and the PEP, and it defines how the PEP should react if the connection to the PDP is lost. Furthermore, COPS defines mechanisms that secure and ensure the integrity of the exchanged messages. However, COPS does not define the content of the messages; this has to be defined for each client-type separately.

COPS-PR [11] describes the use of COPS for support of policy provisioning. COPS-PR clients have a well-defined Policy Information Base (PIB) ([11], [12]), a structure similar to a MIB, where they store all the policies that are sent by the PDP. Each client reports the capabilities of its PIB to the PDP when it connects to it. The PDP has to maintain the PIB of the PEP updated, according to the current network state and policies. The PEP has to enforce the policies that exist in its PIB. Whenever there is a change to the policies or the state of the network, the PDP has to check whether the PIBs of its PEPs need to be updated with new policies. COPS-PR assumes that the various clients of a PEP serve non-overlapping policing areas. Finally, COPS-PR does not define details for any PIB; this has to be done in separate documents for each management area.

Further description of COPS and COPS-PR is out of the scope of this paper; however the reader may refer to [8], [11] for more details.

3. The Motivation

In COPS-PR, the PDP installs policies in the PIBs of its clients in an attempt to make the network behave in accordance with the policies that the administrator has defined. These policies can be represented in the form:

$$If\ [(c_1)\ o_1\ (c_2)\ o_2\ (c_3)\ ...]\ then\ \{(a_1)\ and\ (a_2)\ and\ ...\}$$

Where c_i are conditions, o_i are logical operators, a_i, b_i are actions.

Each network element that needs to enforce policies has a PEP. The PEP may have more than one client of different client-types, since each client-type is designated for different policing areas. Each client connects to a PDP, which controls the information of its PIB and, consequently, the device. Throughout this paper, we examine the interaction between a PDP and a single client. Thus, in many cases when we refer to a PEP, we may actually mean the client of the PEP. However, this should be obvious from the context.

Given a specific client of a PEP of a network element, only some of the defined policies may apply to it. However, even if a policy applies to a client, some of its actions may refer to other devices, and some others may be too generic, since they determine the behavior of several devices. Hence, for that specific client, the policy may be considered equivalent to a policy p, translated for the client:

$$If\ [(c_1)\ o_1\ (c_2)\ o_2\ (c_3)\ ...]\ then\ \{(a_1')\ and\ (a_2')\ and\ ...\}$$

This policy has to be sent by the PDP to the PEP and be enforced to the device. However, the policies that the PEP can store and understand are bound both by the definition of the PIB that allows only predefined types of conditions and actions to be stored, and by the capability of the enforcing mechanism to interpret them (i.e., even if the PIB was able to store any kind of policy, the PEP might not be able to interpret, evaluate and enforce it). Therefore, the PDP needs to transform the policies, from the general form, to a form that the PEP can understand. In order to do so, it must evaluate all the conditions c_i that cannot be stored in the PIB (and, hence, be evaluated by the PEP), as well as any possible parameters in the actions of the policy.

In other words, the PEP can store specific and limited types of policies p_i in its PIB. The PDP has to convert the set of policies to match one of the supported policy types, p_i. Since some policies do not directly fold into any of those types, the PDP has to evaluate the conditions and action parameters that cannot be fitted in the PIB, and according to their values, transform and send the policy according to one of the supported policy formats.

The following example demonstrates the previous. Suppose that the PIB of a router supports only policies (filters) of the form:

> "if (packet IP matches X) then allow packet"
> "if (packet IP matches Y) then deny packet"

However, the administrator has set a policy

> "Do not allow access from network A between 5pm and 8am",

or equivalently,

> "if ((packet IP matches A) and (time between 8am and 5pm)) then allow"
> "if ((packet IP matches A) and (time between 5pm and 8am)) then deny"

In this case, the PDP has to monitor the time, and depending on its value, send either the policy p_1:"if (packet IP matches with A) then allow" or the policy p_2:"if (packet IP matches with A) then deny". In the general case, the initial policy may also be parametric; in this case, specific values must be given to the parameters, prior to being send to the PEP.

We observe that the role of the PDP is to monitor the conditions that the PEP cannot understand and send the appropriate policies to the PEP according to the values of these conditions. Besides, the PDP may have to embed to the policies that it sends the values of some parameters of the original policy. Nevertheless, if the PEP (i) could store the initial policy p and (ii) could be aware of the values of all relevant conditions and parameters (hereinafter, both will be called "parameters"), it would be able to take the same policing decisions by itself. Moreover, some of these parameters might be possible and efficient to be evaluated by the PEP, supposing that it could be directed how to do so. For example, if the PEP resides on the central router of a network, it may evaluate the condition "general congestion to the network", as long as it is directed to look to the MIB of the router for the appropriate values.

The proposed architecture attempts to extend COPS-PR PEPs so as to become able to (i) store policies of non-predefined types (ii) be notified for the value of all the parameters that they cannot evaluate and (iii) be programmed to self-evaluate some of those parameters, whenever this is considered efficient.

4. The Architecture

The proposed architecture, demonstrated in Figure 2, attempts to address the goals described previously. Three basic decisions drove the design:
- For interoperability reasons, the PDP and PEP should adhere to COPS (COPS-PR may not be sufficient). New client-type(s) might need to be defined.
- The internal PEP (iPEP), for the same reason, should be functionally similar to a COPS-PR PEP. In this way, existing implementations and work on COPS-PR client-types could be reused.
- The internal PDP (iPDP) should be a generic module that can cooperate with any client-type of any iPEP. The iPDP should be able to store policies independently of their contents and the iPEP that those policies are directed to.

4.1. General Overview

In our architecture, the PEP comprises two components: An internal PEP (iPEP) and an internal PDP (iPDP). The iPEP is functionally similar to a COPS-PR PEP: it may contain one or more clients, each having a PIB that controls the device. The iPDP controls the contents of the PIB(s) of the iPEP. For simplicity reasons, we shall consider the case of an iPEP with a single client. As in COPS, the communication flow is:

$$PDP \leftrightarrow PEP,$$

which is equivalent in our architecture to:

$$PDP \leftrightarrow iPDP \leftrightarrow iPEP.$$

The iPDP intervenes between the PDP and the iPEP. It controls the iPEP in a way similar to COPS-PR, i.e., by controlling the contents of its PIB. The PDP controls the behavior of the iPDP by controlling the contents of its Policy Base and by supplying it with values for the relevant policy parameters that the iPDP cannot evaluate. In this way, the PDP can indirectly control the contents of the PIB in the iPEPs, and consequently, the managed device. In more detail, when the PEP connects to the PDP, the latter sends to the former all the initial, relevant configuration data and parameters. This data is actually handled by the iPDP, which stores them in its Policy Base (PB) and process them. The Policy Base is a structure for storing policies (do not confuse it with a PIB, which is a standard, well-defined Policy structure, for specific types of policies. PBs are discussed later in this paper). At any time, the policies in the PB and the parameters maintained by the iPDP (either evaluated by

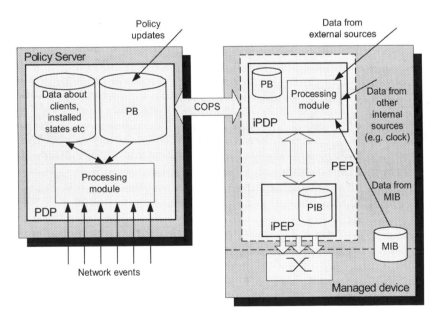

Figure 2. The architecture

itself or sent by the PDP) can be considered as a projection of the current global policies and network status on the specific PEP. Whenever a change in the global policies or the network status is detected by the PDP, it must decide whether their projection on the PEP is affected, and if it is, it should update the data of the iPDP (PB and/or parameters). The iPDP, always having a consistent view of the network policies and status, may send the appropriate commands to the iPEP and manipulate its PIB so as to achieve the desired behavior. Of course, the PDP must be aware of the capabilities of the PEPs that it controls, i.e., their iPDP and iPEP capabilities and type.

In this architecture, the PDP controls the PEP mainly by updating its policy parameters, rather that the policies themselves (policies are sent initially and seldom change). In this way, less data is exchanged through the network. However, the greatest advantage is that the PEP can be programmed to evaluate any parameter by itself. This is not efficient in all cases for scalability reasons (for example, it would be inefficient to program all PEPs to poll the entire network in order to evaluate the condition: "global congestion"). However, there are several cases that such an evaluation is efficient and desired. For example, in some cases, the evaluation of certain conditions may derive from the MIB of the managed device. By letting the iPDP evaluate those parameters, the PEP can take more decisions independently of the PDP. This is a very important property for fault-tolerant and self-configurable networks.

More details on the functions of each of the proposed entities follow, after a simple example.

4.2. A Simple Example

In order to demonstrate a simple example, we consider a router that connects four networks (Figure 3). The router has a very simple, imaginary PIB (a real one would unnecessarily complicate the example). This PIB has a table with five columns: The id of the policy, the router interface to which the policy applies, the IP address of the incoming packets, the action (1=allow, 0=deny) and the priority of the rule. In order to enforce the policies, the IP address of each incoming packet is compared with the IP addresses in the PIB. If the IP matches, then the device takes the decision that the policy specifies (allow/deny). The policies are examined according to their priority. Packets that do not match any authorized IP address are denied.

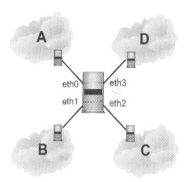

Figure 3. Topology of the network

The policies that govern the router's behavior are:
1. *During maintenance in a network, no access to it is allowed.*
2. *Subnets can exchange data only between office hours (8am to 5pm).*
3. *If the link to A is more that 80% utilized, traffic from A to B and C and vice versa is not allowed.*

(In case of conflicts between policies, the order determines the priority)

Suppose that the following events take place:

> **3.50:** The router boots. Its interface to A is less than 80% utilized.
> **4.00:** The interface to A becomes more than 80% utilized.
> **4.15:** Maintenance starts at network B.
> **4.20:** The interface to A becomes less than 80% utilized.
> **4.45:** Maintenance ends at network B.
> **5:00:** End of working hours.

Figure 4.(a) demonstrates the interaction that would take place in COPS-PR. The arrows indicate exchange of data. We observe that in all cases, the PDP updates the policies in the PIB of the device. Each time, the number of the removed/installed policies equals to the missing/added PIB rows (columns in the figure), respectively.

Let us now examine the same example in our architecture, demonstrated in Figure 4.(b). Suppose that the device is equipped with a clock. Also, suppose that the iPDP can be programmed to check the utilization of its interface eth0 through the MIB of the device. Hence, the PDP can assume that it does not need to monitor and evaluate those two parameters. The PDP translates the set of the original policies to the form shown in Figure 4.(b), and only checks if any network is under maintenance (the way that this happens is not relevant), The values that are necessary for the evaluation of the policies of the iPDP ($M, $S, $E1, $E2, $E3) are send from the PDP to the PEP, whenever necessary. The arrows again indicate data exchange. Notice that apart from the initialization cost of the PB of the iPDP, the amount of data exchanged between the PDP and the PEP was significantly reduced. Also, notice that in several cases, the iPDP is able to take policing decisions without interaction with the PDP.

4.3. The Entities

This section discusses in more detail the functionality of the proposed architectural entities. Implementation issues are discussed in section 5.

The Policy Decision Point (PDP): Although some new client-type(s) may need to be defined, the PDP is a COPS PDP. Hence, it has to provide the PEP with the appropriate configuration data that ensures that it operates as desired. This data is the set of the applicable policies and the value of parameters that the PEP cannot evaluate.

As defined in COPS, the PEP has to send information about its capabilities and the device that it serves as soon as it first connects. In this way, the PDP can send policies and parameters in a format that the PEP can understand. Moreover, the PDP is aware of which of the conditions and parameters cannot be evaluated by the PEP (neither by the iPDP nor by the iPEP). Hence, when the PEP connects, the PDP has to perform the following tasks: (i) Find all the relevant policies (ii) determine which parameters need to be monitored and evaluated on behalf of the PEP (iii) register these parameters for monitoring (iv) transform the policies in the appropriate form that the PEP can understand and (v) send the policies and the initial values of the parameters.

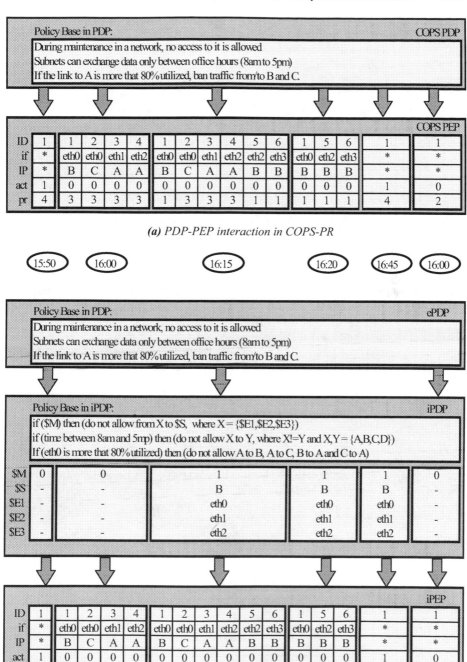

(a) *PDP-PEP interaction in COPS-PR*

(b) *ePDP-iPDP and iPDP-iPEP interaction in the proposed architecture, for the same example*

Figure 4. A simple example

After the initialization, the PDP has to monitor the parameters registered in step (iii) of the initialization, and notify the PEP for changes in their values (As described later, in certain cases the PDP may decide not to monitor and/or update the value of a parameter, if it knows that this will not affect the decisions taken by the iPDP.) Finally, whenever there is a change to the (global) policy repository, the PDP may need to inform the PEP by deleting, updating or installing new policies into it.

The Policy Enforcement Point (PEP): The PEP is a COPS PEP. As described in the previous paragraph, the PEP reports its capabilities to the PDP when it connects to it, and enforces the decisions sent to it. It is comprised of two modules, the iPDP and the iPEP. The iPDP-iPEP relation in the PEP is similar to the client-hardware relation in a COPS PEP: The iPDP has some configuration data (policies and parameters) sent to it by the PDP, and this configuration data is used to control the iPEP.

The internal Policy Decision Point (iPDP): The internal Policy Decision point acts similarly to a COPS-PR PDP for the iPEP that it controls. Although this architecture describes a 1:1:1 relation between iPDPs, iPEP and clients (i.e., each iPEP has one client, and it connects to one iPDP that serves only this client), we believe that it can easily be extended to support a scheme where iPEPs with multiple clients connect to the same iPDP.

The iPDP communicates with the iPEP in a way similar to COPS-PR: the iPDP maintains information about the contents of the PIB of the iPEP, and it decides which policies should be installed or updated into it.

The iPDP maintains information that reflects the view of the network state and policies projected on the specific PEP, at the given time. The policies in this PB may be parametric, i.e., the conditions and actions may be associated with some parameters. For each parameter, information is registered on whether its value is obtained by the PDP or calculated locally. In the second case, the way that this value is computed should also be registered (e.g., MIB variable, clock, SNMP command, other process, etc.).

Finally, the iPDP should check the policies for conflicts prior to installing them to the iPEP, since there may be valid policies that conflict to each other under certain circumstances.

The internal Policy Enforcement Point (iPEP): The internal Policy Enforcement Point (iPEP) has similar functionality to a COPS-PR PEP. The main difference is that the iPEP is controlled by the iPDP, instead of by an (external) PDP, hence it does not need to implement the full COPS-PR protocol. However, the commands that it receives, and its reaction to them are similar to COPS-PR.

5.   Implementation Issues

In the previous section we presented the design of our architecture, mainly in the form of requirements in the functionality of the entities. Although we are still in the process of designing the architecture, several implementation issues have been taken into consideration. These are discussed in this part.

5.1. iPEP Implementation

The iPEP is similar to a COPS-PR PEP. The basic difference is that they do not need to implement the communication details of the COPS-PR protocol (TCP connection, encryption, integrity, time-outs, redirection to other PDPs, etc.). However, the cores of an iPEP and a COPS-PR PEP (client) are exactly the same. They implement the same PIB and they are controlled with similar commands; also they produce similar errors and warnings. Hence, similar client-types are expected to exist.

5.2. Parameter Optimization

The following are some ideas that may reduce the number of exchanged messages and resource consumption, both in the PDPs and the PEPs.

1. Obviously, when more than two policies in the PB of the iPDP depend on the same condition or parameter, the PDP only needs to send the value of this parameter once, and this value is shared by all the policies that depend on it.

2. Suppose that there is a policy in the PDP

$$If\ [(c_1)\ and\ (c_2)\ and\ (c_3)\ and\ (c_4)\ and\ (c_5)]\ then\ \{(a_1)\ and\ (a_2)\ and\ ...\}$$

and the PDP knows that the PEP can evaluate c_3, c_4 and c_5. Also suppose that no other policy depends on c_1 and c_2. In this case, the PEP can replace these two conditions with $c= (c_1$ and $c_2)$ and send one parameter instead of two.

3. Suppose that the PDP has a policy

$$p_1:\ If\ [(c_1)\ and\ (c_2)]\ then\ ...$$

Where c_1 and c_2 are conditions evaluated by the PDP. Also, suppose that c_2 is not used by any other policy of the iPDP. While c_1 has value "false", the PDP may decide not to send (or even monitor) the value of c_2, because this would not affect the decision of the iPDP. However, the PDP should send the values of c_2 while c1 is "true". In this way, unnecessary exchange of data in the network is prevented.

4. Suppose that the PDP has a policy

If [(c$_1$) and (c$_2$)] then ...

Where c_1 can be evaluated by the iPEP but c_2 cannot. In most policies, the conditions that cannot be evaluated locally, represent global, slow-changing conditions, while the ones that are evaluated locally, usually change frequently. However, there may be cases in which this rule does not apply. If c_2 changes frequently but c_1 does not, the PDP must frequently inform the PEP of the value of c_2, even when c_1 is false (the PDP is not aware of the value of c_1). For such policies, the PDP may decide to monitor c_1 as well. In this way, when c_1 is false, the PDP will not send values for c_2, and unnecessary communication between the PDP and the PEP will be avoided.

5.3. Representation of Policies in the iPDP

Suppose that a policy in the PDP

If [(c$_1$) o$_1$ (c$_2$) o$_2$ (c$_3$) ...] then {(a$_1$') and (a$_2$') and ...}

is equivalent to

If [(c$_1$) o$_1$ (c$_2$) o$_2$ (c$_3$) ...] then p$_1$

where p_1 is a policy that can be understood by the iPEP (i.e., they can be stored in its PIB). PIBs are structures similar to MIBs. Each PIB is a tree of Policy Rule Classes (PRC's) [11], [12]. The leaves of the tree are instances of those classes, and they are called Policy Rule Instances (PRIs). PRCs (and PRIs) can be described by (standardized) identifiers, similar to MIB identifiers. Policies in the PIB are represented as a set of PRIs. Hence, a policy p_1 could be described as a set of PRIs (identifiers and values) that have to be installed or removed.

The PDP has to maintain three tables: The first table stores the policy id and the policy itself, in the form of a table of PRIs that have to be installed or removed. In this way, p_1 can be stored in this table. The PRIs may be parametric. The second table stores the values of all parameters of all policies in the PIB (either these send by the PDP or evaluated by the iPDP). The third table has a column that stores a list of the conditions that the iPDP should evaluate, and a column with a list of the policy ids that should be installed if the conditions evaluate "true". Of course, the iPDP has to perform other actions as well, such as maintaining information for the status of its iPEPs, like the PDPs keep similar information for their PEPs.

For the example presented in section 4, the policies would be stored as shown in Figure 5.:

ID	policy
1	ID=N/A If=$E1 IP=$S act=0 PRI=1
2	ID=N/A If=$E2 IP=$S act=0 PRI=1
3	ID=N/A If=$E3 IP=$S act=0 PRI=1
4	ID=N/A If=* IP=* act=0 PRI=2
5	ID=N/A If=eth0 IP=B act=0 PRI=3
6	ID=N/A If=eth0 IP=C act=0 PRI=3
7	ID=N/A If=eth1 IP=A act=0 PRI=3
8	ID=N/A If=eth2 IP=A act=0 PRI=3

Par.	Value
$C	16:23:58.03
$U	83%
$M	TRUE
$S	B
$E1	eth0
$E2	eth2
$E3	eth3

if	then
($M=true)	1,2,3
(8:00<$C<17:00)	4
($U>80%)	5,6,7,8

Figure 5. An instance of the tables of the iPDP

In this way, the policies are represented in a unified way, independent of the PIB of the served iPEP. This allows standardizing the way that policies are sent by the PDP. Also, due to this property, the iPDP can be an entity independent of the vendor and the iPEP client that it serves. However, before sending the policies to the iPEP, a client-dependent (but not vendor dependent) module should perform conflict checking, since the policies in the PB may be conflicting under certain circumstances.

5.4. Communication between PDP and PEP

Since the policies and the parameters are rows of two well-defined tables in the iPDP, the communication between the PDP and the PEP could be COPS. Of course, a new client-type would need to be defined, which would standardize the exchange of those objects. Notice, also, that the exchange of information is performed in a provisioning mode, similar to COPS-PR. We are examining whether an extension of COPS-PR would be suitable for such exchange of data.

In COPS, when a client connects to a PDP, it sends information about the capabilities of its clients and the managed device. This information is used by the PDP in order to map the network state and policies to the specific device. In our architecture, the PEP must send the capabilities of both its iPDP and iPEPs. Hence, when it connects to the PDP, it has to declare that it contains an "internal PDP" and report its capabilities, and then, send to the PDP the capabilities of its (client-types of its) iPEPs, in a COPS-PR style.

6. Conclusions and Future Work

This paper presented an architecture that attempts to extend COPS-PR PEPs in order to be able to take more policy decisions locally. For this purpose, those PEPs are slightly modified and wrapped into an extended PEP, which contains those PEPs (as iPEPs), as well as an internal PDP (iPDP). The iPDP is used in order to push some of the intelligence of the external PDP down to the device.

We claim that this architecture has several advantages, compared to COPS-PR. The most obvious one is that the network utilization is reduced. However, the most important property is that more decisions can be taken by the managed device itself. This property is an important feature that contributes significantly towards fault-tolerant and self-configurable networks. Furthermore, since the device is the converging point of the decisions of different PDPs, by moving the intelligence into the managed device, conflicts can be detected and resolved more efficiently.

As a future work, our first objective is to implement the proposed architecture and evaluate its efficiency in comparison to COPS-PR. Some longer-term objectives have also been set. One of them is to examine the case of multiple clients in each iPEP, which may need to connect (through the iPDP) to different PDPs. Besides, we want to examine how the iPDP can be optimized, especially in terms of storage of policies. Obviously the table representation is not the optimal solution since a significant amount of information may be redundant. Finally, an interesting issue is to examine how mobile agents can be used for the evaluation of (non-local) parameters by the iPDP.

References

1. Shepard, S.J.; "Policy-based networks: hype and hope"; IT Professional, Volume: 2 1, Jan.-Feb. 2000, Page(s): 12 –16
2. "Introduction to Policy-based Networking and Quality of Service"; IPHIGHWAY, White paper, January 2000
3. Hugh Mahon; Yoram Bernet; Shai Herzog; "Requirements for a Policy Managed System"; IETF; Internet draft draft-ietf-policy-req-01.txt, October 1999
4. M. Sloman, "Policy Driven Management For Distributed Systems", Plenum Press Journal of Network and Systems Management, vol 2, no. 4, Dec. 1994, pp. 333-360
5. A. Westerinen; J. Schnizlein; J. Strassner; Mark Scherling; Bob Quinn; Jay Perry; Shai Herzog; An-Ni Huynh; Mark Carlson; "Policy Terminology"; IETF, Internet Draft draft-ietf-policy-terminology-00.txt, July 2000
6. "Policy Standards and IETF Terminology"; IPHighway, White paper, January 2000.
7. R. Yavatkar; D. Pendarakis; R. Guerin; "A Framework for Policy-based Admission Control", IETF, RFC 2753, January 2000
8. D. Durham, Ed.; J. Boyle; R. Cohen; S. Herzog; R. Rajan; A. Sastry; "The COPS (Common Open Policy Service) Protocol"; IETF, RFC 2748, January 2000
9. "Policy-based Networking Products, Design and Architecture"; IPHighway, White paper, January 2000.
10. "Policy-Powered Networking and the Role of Directories"; 3COM, White paper, July 1998.

11. Kwok Ho Chan; David Durham; Silvano Gai; Shai Herzog; Keith McCloghrie; Francis Reichmeyer; John Seligson; Andrew Smith; Raj Yavatkar; "COPS Usage for Policy Provisioning"; IETF, Internet Draft draft-ietf-rap-pr-03.txt, July 2000

12. M. Fine; K. McCloghrie; J. Seligson; K. Chan; S. Hahn; R. Sahita; A. Smith; Francis Reichmeyer; "Framework Policy Information Base", IETF, Internet Draft draft-ietf-rap-frameworkpib-01.txt, July 2000

URLs:
- IETF home page:
  http://www.ietf.org
- Resource Allocation Protocol (rap) Charter:
  http://www.ietf.org/html.charters/rap-charter.html
- Policy Framework (policy) Charter:
  http://www.ietf.org/html.charters/policy-charter.html
- IETF Rap Working group mailing list:
  http://majordomo.iphighway.com/

Author Index

Lecture Notes in Computer Science

For information about Vols. 1–1905
please contact your bookseller or Springer-Verlag

Vol. 1935: S.L. Delp, A.M. DiGioia, B. Jaramaz (Eds.), Medical Image Computing and Computer-Assisted Intervention – MICCAI 2000. Proceedings, 2000. XXV, 1250 pages. 2000.

Vol. 1937: R. Dieng, O. Corby (Eds.), Knowledge Engineering and Knowledge Management. Proceedings, 2000. XIII, 457 pages. 2000. (Subseries LNAI).

Vol. 1938: S. Rao, K.I. Sletta (Eds.), Next Generation Networks. Proceedings, 2000. XI, 392 pages. 2000.

Vol. 1939: A. Evans, S. Kent, B. Selic (Eds.), «UML» – The Unified Modeling Language. Proceedings, 2000. XIV, 572 pages. 2000.

Vol. 1940: M. Valero, K. Joe, M. Kitsuregawa, H. Tanaka (Eds.), High Performance Computing. Proceedings, 2000. XV, 595 pages. 2000.

Vol. 1941: A.K. Chhabra, D. Dori (Eds.), Graphics Recognition. Proceedings, 1999. XI, 346 pages. 2000.

Vol. 1942: H. Yasuda (Ed.), Active Networks. Proceedings, 2000. XI, 424 pages. 2000.

Vol. 1943: F. Koornneef, M. van der Meulen (Eds.), Computer Safety, Reliability and Security. Proceedings, 2000. X, 432 pages. 2000.

Vol. 1945: W. Grieskamp, T. Santen, B. Stoddart (Eds.), Integrated Formal Methods. Proceedings, 2000. X, 441 pages. 2000.

Vol. 1948: T. Tan, Y. Shi, W. Gao (Eds.), Advances in Multimodal Interfaces – ICMI 2000. Proceedings, 2000. XVI, 678 pages. 2000.

Vol. 1949: R. Connor, A. Mendelzon (Eds.), Research Issues in Structured and Semistructured Database Programming. Proceedings, 1999. XII, 325 pages. 2000.

Vol. 1950: D. van Melkebeek, Randomness and Completeness in Computational Complexity. XV, 196 pages. 2000.

Vol. 1951: F. van der Linden (Ed.), Software Architectures for Product Families. Proceedings, 2000. VIII, 255 pages. 2000.

Vol. 1952: M.C. Monard, J. Simão Sichman (Eds.), Advances in Artificial Intelligence. Proceedings, 2000. XV, 498 pages. 2000. (Subseries LNAI).

Vol. 1953: G. Borgefors, I. Nyström, G. Sanniti di Baja (Eds.), Discrete Geometry for Computer Imagery. Proceedings, 2000. XI, 544 pages. 2000.

Vol. 1954: W.A. Hunt, Jr., S.D. Johnson (Eds.), Formal Methods in Computer-Aided Design. Proceedings, 2000. XI, 539 pages. 2000.

Vol. 1955: M. Parigot, A. Voronkov (Eds.), Logic for Programming and Automated Reasoning. Proceedings, 2000. XIII, 487 pages. 2000. (Subseries LNAI).

Vol. 1956: T. Coquand, P. Dybjer, B. Nordström, J. Smith (Eds.), Types for Proofs and Programs. Proceedings, 1999. VII, 195 pages. 2000.

Vol. 1960: A. Ambler, S.B. Calo, G. Kar (Eds.), Services Management in Intelligent Networks. Proceedings, 2000. X, 259 pages. 2000.

Vol. 1961: J. He, M. Sato (Eds.), Advances in Computing Science – ASIAN 2000. Proceedings, 2000. X, 299 pages. 2000.

Vol. 1963: V. Hlaváč, K.G. Jeffery, J. Wiedermann (Eds.), SOFSEM 2000: Theory and Practice of Informatics. Proceedings, 2000. XI, 460 pages. 2000.

Vol. 1964: J. Malenfant, S. Moisan, A. Moreira (Eds.), Object-Oriented Technology. Proceedings, 2000. XI, 309 pages. 2000.

Vol. 1965: Ç. K. Koç, C. Paar (Eds.), Cryptographic Hardware and Embedded Systems – CHES 2000. Proceedings, 2000. XI, 355 pages. 2000.

Vol. 1966: S. Bhalla (Ed.), Databases in Networked Information Systems. Proceedings, 2000. VIII, 247 pages. 2000.

Vol. 1967: S. Arikawa, S. Morishita (Eds.), Discovery Science. Proceedings, 2000. XII, 332 pages. 2000. (Subseries LNAI).

Vol. 1968: H. Arimura, S. Jain, A. Sharma (Eds.), Algorithmic Learning Theory. Proceedings, 2000. XI, 335 pages. 2000. (Subseries LNAI).

Vol. 1969: D.T. Lee, S.-H. Teng (Eds.), Algorithms and Computation. Proceedings, 2000. XIV, 578 pages. 2000.

Vol. 1970: M. Valero, V.K. Prasanna, S. Vajapeyam (Eds.), High Performance Computing – HiPC 2000. Proceedings, 2000. XVIII, 568 pages. 2000.

Vol. 1971: R. Buyya, M. Baker (Eds.), Grid Computing – GRID 2000. Proceedings, 2000. XIV, 229 pages. 2000.

Vol. 1972: A. Omicini, R. Tolksdorf, F. Zambonelli (Eds.), Engineering Societies in the Agents World. Proceedings, 2000. IX, 143 pages. 2000. (Subseries LNAI).

Vol. 1973: J. Van den Bussche, V. Vianu (Eds.), Database Theory – ICDT 2001. Proceedings, 2001. X, 451 pages. 2001.

Vol. 1974: S. Kapoor, S. Prasad (Eds.), FST TCS 2000: Foundations of Software Technology and Theoretical Computer Science. Proceedings, 2000. XIII, 532 pages. 2000.

Vol. 1975: J. Pieprzyk, E. Okamoto, J. Seberry (Eds.), Information Security. Proceedings, 2000. X, 323 pages. 2000.

Vol. 1976: T. Okamoto (Ed.), Advances in Cryptology – ASIACRYPT 2000. Proceedings, 2000. XII, 630 pages. 2000.

Vol. 1977: B. Roy, E. Okamoto (Eds.), Progress in Cryptology – INDOCRYPT 2000. Proceedings, 2000. X, 295 pages. 2000.

Vol. 1979: S. Moss, P. Davidsson (Eds.), Multi-Agent-Based Simulation. Proceedings, 2000. VIII, 267 pages. 2001. (Subseries LNAI).

Vol. 1983: K.S. Leung, L.-W. Chan, H. Meng (Eds.), Intelligent Data Engineering and Automated Learning – IDEAL 2000. Proceedings, 2000. XVI, 573 pages. 2000.

Vol. 1984: J. Marks (Ed.), Graph Drawing. Proceedings, 2001. XII, 419 pages. 2001.

Vol. 1987: K.-L. Tan, M.J. Franklin, J. C.-S. Lui (Eds.), Mobile Data Management. Proceedings, 2001. XIII, 289 pages. 2001.

Vol. 1989: M. Ajmone Marsan, A. Bianco (Eds.), Quality of Service in Multiservice IP Networks. Proceedings, 2001. XII, 440 pages. 2001.

Vol. 1995: M. Sloman, J. Lobo, E.C. Lupu (Eds.), Policies for Distributed Systems and Networks. Proceedings, 2001. X, 263 pages. 2001.